Becoming a researcher

A companion to the research process

Máiréad Dunne, John Pryor and Paul Yates

Open University Press

Open University Press
McGraw-Hill Education
McGraw-Hill House
Shoppenhangers Road
Maidenhead
Berkshire
England
SL6 2QL

email: enquiries@openup.co.uk
world wide web: www.openup.co.uk

and Two Penn Plaza, New York, NY 10121-2289, USA

First published 2005

Copyright © Máiréad Dunne, John Pryor and Paul Yates 2005

A catalogue record of this book is available from the British Library

ISBN-13   978 0335 21394 8 (pb)   978 0335 21395 5 (hb)
ISBN-10   0 335 21394 4 (pb)   0 335 21395 2 (hb)

Library of Congress Cataloging-in-Publication Data
CIP data has been applied for

Typeset by RefineCatch Ltd, Bungay, Suffolk
Printed in Poland by OzGraf. S.A.
www.polskabook.pl

Contents

Introduction

What sort of book?

In the bookshop at the University of Sussex where we work there is a large shelf of books on doing research aimed mostly at postgraduate students. Almost all the books in this section are what might be termed manuals or handbooks, which take the reader through the practicalities of undertaking social and educational research. As teachers and supervisors of research students we recommend our students at the start of their studies to go out and buy at least one of these books on research methods. If nothing else, the how-to-do-it approach can help in giving a bit of confidence when faced with the daunting task of embarking on a new degree. However, while they fulfil a valuable service, these books can also be seen as rather dangerous. If they are not read carefully and critically they can lead to a view of empirical research as a series of functional challenges to be faced and overcome. Although they might touch on wider issues, their purpose is essentially that of 'tips for researchers', where complexity is essentially introduced as a procedural or practical issue.

However, most people who consult these methods books soon realize that the process of doing research and of becoming a researcher is much deeper and more complicated than it seems at first. Even those who aim to keep it simple for as long as possible are finally confronted with the idea that they must write about their methodology and that this means more than 'what I did'. At this stage they may then look for books and articles on methodology, which present theoretical perspectives to problematize the research process. The danger here to the inexperienced researcher, is that these texts often seem difficult and their relevance to their own particular project, at the early stages of their research, may be rather hard to detect. These texts usually seem much more relevant in the later stages but by then many opportunities to profit from the understandings they afford have already been missed.

Our aim in writing this book is to bridge the gap between the research methods manual and the methodological essay. At first sight, we seem to be following a standard design with chapters dealing with the usual research methods. However, behind the titles of these chapters, you will not find a comprehensive guide on how to go about getting data. Indeed you are more likely to find a warning against the whole notion of 'best practice'. Rather than being a substitute for the research manual this book is seen as a parallel text. What we aim to do is to get behind the different methods at the wider methodological issues that are raised by doing the methods or in the different stages of the research. The book is dealing with the complex yet fundamental issues that confront the researcher but rather than being a guide it offers itself as a companion in exploring these. Like a human companion it will sometimes be opinionated and we do not expect that you will always agree. However, being in full agreement is not necessarily companionable.

Because the book approaches methodology via a consideration of methods, abstract notions are therefore encountered through reflection on the practical, and we often refer to our own experiences as researchers. In the text you will therefore find reference to the research manuals such as Bell (1999), Cohen et al. (2000) and Flick (2002). However, you will also see citations of researchers who have had a profound effect on methodology such as Foucault, Giddens, Barthes, and even Aristotle. We hope that it will both mediate between these two sorts of texts and lead our readers to explore them and others with a critical eye. Thus, far from seeking to resolve issues, the book aims to help you to let them stand as problematic – to open them out rather than close them down. This book combines what many other books separate, namely research as a practical activity, and intellectual engagement in the way the research project is accomplished. By treating research as the construction, deconstruction and reconstruction of text, it locates the researcher at the centre of the process and the outcomes of the research.

Writers' voices

Much of the content and orientation of the book derives directly from our experience of teaching research methods both collaboratively and individually. The ideas have therefore evolved over a number of years and have been applied by our students and collaborators from a variety of backgrounds to contemporary ideas in social and educational research. However, the book does not just derive from our teaching, it is also research-based; that is, we are also writing from our positions as researchers ourselves. This means that we draw above all on our own personal field experience. By calling the book *Becoming a researcher* we do not mean that it is only *you*, the reader who is becoming one, but also *us*, the writers. Although we may be rooted in a past that seems more tangible than the present, our identity is always shifting, hybrid and multi-dimensional. Moreover, new research always brings with it new problematics.

Given this standpoint, we have seen no merit in trying to present the book as a seamless text, the work of a totally consistent authorial team. Instead we have sought to preserve our different voices. We have seen the writing of the whole text as a sort of discussion between us, where the reading of each other's work has influenced what we have each written. We hope that the different voices give a dialogic quality to the writing, which will enhance rather than detract from the quality of the reading. Although we have each taken main responsibility for a chapter, we have chosen not to give a byline to them but simply to stick to the alphabetical listing on the title page. Also, when we write in the first person we use both 'I' and 'we' depending on the context. (Interestingly, I found that as I got further into the writing I tended to use 'we' more often! – so did I, . . . me too!) The authorial voice in this book therefore does not have a homogenizing influence on text: the assumption of evenness is absent and with it the impression of faux-objectivity is to a certain extent disrupted.

This does not mean, however, that the book is an anthology like, for example, Denzin and Lincoln's (1998a, b, c) *Handbook of Qualitative Research*, where different chapters present a variety of different perspectives. Our discussions and collaboration have aimed at achieving a coherence of approach to research, where we are mainly in agreement about the assumptions about the nature of the research. This approach may keep you guessing about who has done which bits. However, we each remain what the Germans would call a *Verantwortliche(r) Redakteur(in)*, a responsible editor, and so stand by what the others have written. (We all – Paul and John especially – also ask that you do not reduce us to '*et al.*' in citing the book!) Further traces of the social interaction that gave rise to the text can be seen in the tabloid titles of the chapters and parts which were originally a way of teasing each other, but which we grew rather attached to over the course of writing and editing and decided to keep.

Making a reading

If we have not reduced ourselves to a singular authorial voice we have also tried to avoid reducing you to a singular idealized reader. Nevertheless we have had in mind the needs, concerns and reactions of the sort of people we encounter in our professional lives and, as well as arising from our interaction with each other, the text is derived from many encounters

with our colleagues and students. As social researchers located in an education department of a British university we therefore expect to be talking
frequently to those who are entering the research field as mid-career and
senior professionals in education, health, social work and other public
services. We hope the text makes sense for practitioner researchers as well
as those who are researching aspects of the social where their professional
identity is not so salient. Many of you will come from a background where
practice is seen as unproblematic and expectations of research are directed
towards positivist assumptions about generating evidence. However, if
you are working towards a higher degree or publishing your research in
academic journals it will be judged against the criteria involving the questioning of common-sense notions of research practice, knowledge and
social reality. The tensions inherent in this will be explored in the book.

The idea behind *Becoming a researcher* is that you will be someone who is
'trying on' research. When you start reading, you may have already done
quite a bit of research, have become dissatisfied with the way you have
been approaching the enterprise or you may just be starting out and have
not decided what sort of research you will be doing. Any way, we hope
that the book may alert you to different possibilities and open up new
ways of thinking and working. One way in which we have tried to avoid a
closing down is that we have included the chapters dealing with some of
our central concepts, methodology and identity, not at the start but at the
end of the book. We have thus tried to make the book open to different
readings. The chapters are given a specific order as befits the genre and
that is a conventional one; it is also likely to appeal to those who are
anxious to get started. However, we rarely read books in the order that
they are printed and see no reason why you should. You may even sub-
vert our intention and read the identity chapter first! Although you will
see cross-references to different chapters we see these as an aid to a non-
linear reading rather than as a hindrance. Each of the chapters may be
read separately, but we think the more you read, the richer the experience will be. As indicated above we have thought of the book as something to be read at the start of a project. However, as a companion to the
research process, it would also make sense to consult it at any time as an
aid to developing reflexivity.

Themes

Becoming a researcher is not neutral or objective, but although it is about
methodology, neither does it advocate a particular systematic methodology. We are not trying to say that the world is like this and so you have
to do that – though we do say sometimes what it is not like. Rather it
contains statements of our own positions, which we try to follow through

by looking at their methodological implications. We intend that this should challenge our readers to do the same.

The underlying perspective of the book is that research derives from the social interaction of the researcher with the researched. The nature of the social world and of power relations is therefore unavoidably implicated. Reflexivity involves, then, a consciousness of the centrality of the researcher and of their position in social research. This is not a doctrinaire position, but a device to make clearer and more explicit the methodological issues that underlie the journey from initial ideas to the finished report and beyond. *Becoming a researcher* presents the research process as an engagement with text. It is a process in which, as researchers, we are both readers and writers. Indeed the idea of texts and textualization in research runs through the book as what we call a vertical theme. In the first place, the researcher collaborates with participants to construct text in the form of data. Analysis of this data set when accompanied by reflection on context involves a process of deconstruction. The choice of data to present and interpret and the movement towards the final report is then seen as a reconstruction of a final text. Within the three sections of the book each chapter takes a practical concern or group of methods and interrogates the methodological concerns associated with it.

The other vertical theme which runs through all the chapters, is that of researcher identity. Here we suggest that as well as the identity of the researcher being an important issue for other participants, it also becomes a focus for the interest and investigation of the researcher. This involves the development of a critical awareness of oneself as a social and professional practitioner and is especially useful to those researching in insider situations or settings, which are similar to those where they normally function. Beyond this, the book stresses the process whereby one also comes to think of oneself as a researcher, rather than someone who is just doing research. However, in line with the idea of becoming a researcher we see identity as connected with narrative and that it is 'fabricated, constructed, in process . . . fragmented, full of contradictions and ambiguities' (Sarup, 1996: 14). Becoming a researcher is therefore not analogous to learning a role in a play but engaging in an open-ended enquiry into the social being of ourselves and others. Although we recognize the importance of a repertoire of technical and intellectual skills in research, at the heart of the enterprise is the dynamic and unending flux of the social.

Structure

Becoming a researcher is divided into three parts, though as we said before, the partitions are to be seen rather more as a navigational aid than as a strict agenda. In line with the idea of research as text, the first part,

'Distinguishing data – constructing text', deals with the idea of building a data set or constructing a working text. After an initial chapter addressing issues of design, three chapters work around the most common research methods for 'collecting' data.

Chapter 2, 'The logic of enquiry', explores the nature and possibility of social research. It suggests that different methodological perspectives embody differing social realities. Choosing a research strategy therefore is not simply a matter of looking in the toolbox for the best instrument for the job. We argue that it is more than a technical matter and that it depends upon the logic of enquiry. This critical initial phase in the research process brings us immediately to a point of making decisions. The initial conceptual issue is that of problematizing the mundane. This is prior to finding a focus and then moving from focus to research questions. Converting our research interest into research practice and data collection forces us to engage with a range of methodological issues.

The third chapter, 'Talking with people – interviewing', is the first of two chapters about the explicit use of questions for respondents in research. A review of a variety of interview forms considers the social relations of the interview, their influence on the data gathered and its relation to the research questions. The tension between the researcher's focus and their responsiveness to interpretations and views of the interviewee(s) will be explored as a dynamic within the research process. In particular, this will be related to the vertical themes of researcher identity, the text constructed through the interview and the possibilities of analysis. The interplay of the practical and the epistemological are discussed as part of the research process, together with a consideration of how the texts generated through interviews may influence the research design.

The fourth chapter, 'Knowing with numbers – questionnaires', investigates the nature of quantification through the example of questionnaires. It suggests that construction and format of the 'instruments' shape both the substantive field and the respondent group. Issues of identity and text are explored in relation to the type of questions, anticipated responses and field contexts; issues of interpretation are raised as critical in the research process. The taken-for-granted nature of questionnaires is problematized and we attempt to 're-methodologize' them. We explore the possibilities of different readings and writings and consider the blurred boundary between quantitative and qualitative approaches to research and ways in which they can be mutually supportive.

Chapter 5 is called 'Being there – observation'. This chapter uses the concept of triple mimesis to show how being in the field, constructing a data set and reporting of research are all mutually implicated. They are all bound by our identity as a researcher and the narratives that we produce and that produce these identities. It continues the central argument of the book that, even when the researcher's presence is vicarious, data can be seen as text generated by the interaction of the researcher with the researched. Observation is then seen as an essential part of field research, but the 'naturalness' of the method is shown as problematic and illusory.

Part 2 is called 'Dicing with data – deconstructing text' and deals with what is usually called analysis and interpretation. Chapter 6, 'Breaking down data – routes to interpretation', initiates this section by focusing on the way in which researchers' interpretations are fundamental to the research process. The reflection outwards to the substantive field and context as well as inwards to researcher identity and position are signalled as pivotal in research. Although there are generic processes of interpretation, different methodological genres rule in or rule out different kinds of engagement with a data set and so produce different texts. The epistemological implications of differing forms of interpretation and the coding of research texts are problematized. The constant interplay and tensions between the researcher stance and emergent themes from the data are explored as discursively productive in the research process.

'Worrying at words – discourse analysis', the seventh chapter, picks up and takes further the vertical theme of research as a process of textualization. The chapter begins by considering why, as social researchers, we might wish to apply a close focus to the formal structures of a text. It goes on to explore the methodological gap between approaches to discourse analysis that are mainly interested in the linguistic structures themselves and how they work in social settings and those whose concern with the social is further to the fore. Critical discourse analysis, an approach that claims to mediate between the two, is given special attention.

The eighth chapter, 'Pulverizing policy – deconstructing documents', starts from the premise that the point of policy development is to shape social practice. However, policies will vary in their real coercive power and there may be unintended consequences of policy production and implementation. The effect of social policy may therefore be other or more diffuse than its intention. In this chapter, we look at the policy process and the various critical contexts within which social policy is constructed both institutionally and nationally. We take a particular policy and exemplify the possibility of a transgressive reading through deconstruction. This involves looking not only at content but also at form, genre and provenance, as well as the political and social values that may be embedded within the policy text.

As well as addressing issues about how one re-presents research, the final part, 'Data with destiny – reconstructing text', is concerned with re-examining some of the key ideas of the book as a whole. In Chapter 9, 'Writing research – authoring text', we challenge the idea that research writing is merely a technical activity and we explore the notion of researcher as writer. Modern and postmodern models of the researcher as writer are explored in relation to their significance for the author-ity of text and claims to knowledge. The concepts of authoring and author-ity are examined in relation to issues of representation, truth and legitimation. This draws on some postmodern conceptualizations of the nature and construction of text and applies them to writing research. In particular, the way in which these ideas confront positivistic and empiricist assumptions in research is discussed. A range of related concerns are addressed including intertextuality, audience, reading, form and genre.

Chapter 10, 'The selfish text – research and identity', looks at the interplay of the vertical axes of text and identity, and the centrality of the researcher-self in knowledge production. We examine modern and postmodern models of identity. In particular, the various uses of narrative in constructing identity and the postmodern challenge of a more fragmentary and non-essential sense of the self. These are looked at in the context of the place of researcher identity in the reconstruction of their research texts. This involves us in a critical exploration of agency and determinism, the global context of knowledge construction and the democratization of knowledge production. Through this we attempt to develop a critical understanding of ourselves as constructors of research texts embedded in a dynamic model of identity.

The last chapter, 'Methods and methodology', continues and extends these ideas. It gathers together strands encountered throughout the book and presents ways of conceptualizing research methodology as dynamic and holistic. The aim of the chapter is both to clarify and to problematize questions of knowledge, practice and identity in the social sciences. The chapter acts both as a summary and a stimulus to the reader to theorize their own position. It suggests that a methodological narrative might be both a good way of developing reflexivity as a researcher and of legitimating the positions taken up. *Becoming a researcher* ends by using a recent manifesto for social research as a way of summarizing some of our ideas.

Happy reading!

Part **1**

Distinguishing data – constructing text

2

The logic of enquiry

Finding a place to stand

Brew (2001: 3) suggests 'anyone coming into the research arena or wanting to understand more about the nature of research faces a number of puzzles'. This is caused partly by the fact that 'traditional disciplinary research has to give way to new forms of enquiry, requiring self-knowledge on the part of the researchers' (Brew, 2001: 3). Indeed the issue of what counts as legitimate knowledge, in a world of competing and contradictory research paradigms, is itself often unclear. It is also the case that research is no longer confined to the academy and, in understanding the process of research and its social applications, a wide range of communicative skills are required on the part of the researcher.

Nonetheless, the research process, virtually universally, begins with a concept and ends with a text. The space in between is normally given shape and coherence by decisions we make about how to proceed; collectively those decisions comprise our methodology and this determines what we do as researchers and how we understand our actions and experiences and those traces of the social that we construct as data. The initial idea can take many forms. Partly its nature will be determined by the general discursive arena that researchers, and perhaps their teams, are working within or living within.

The French structuralist anthropologist Levi-Strauss in his investigation of the nature of human being was critical of needs theories of the social. Such theories, which now are associated with socio-biology, suggest that humans create culture in order to satisfy the biologically driven needs to eat, to have shelter and to reproduce and that it was these needs that lay behind our ordering of our knowledge of the world. The implication is that science and reason and the production of knowledge of the world are underpinned by our physical needs and nature. Levi-Strauss (1964, 1966) argued that this simply could not be sustained by the evidence. The urge to study and to classify the world around us and the worlds within us goes way beyond anything we might call necessity. Thus, he suggested that the world was not *bon à manger* (good to eat) but it was *bon à penser* (good to think) (1966). We humans find the world intrinsically interesting and much of our sociality is given over to the construction and the elaboration of those cultural milieux we inhabit. Those social activities we call research can be understood as a formalized expression of our human desire to make ordered meaning out of the chaotic flux of experience.

It is an interesting time to be a researcher and perhaps especially a practitioner researcher, someone who uses the conventions of academe to help conceptualize and often to alter the ways in which we think and act. Scott (1999: 2) identifies a range of 'problems and difficulties' that can be seen as characteristic of the research process and also provide a useful way of modelling it. He suggests that the researcher must work between 'structures/mechanisms of society and the practical consciousness of social actors' (Scott, 1999: 2). Research in social settings is often recursive in nature. That is to say that in understanding what is happening we need to take into consideration contexts wider than the immediate social action in which we are participating. We might draw on Giddens' (1984) structuration theory both to help explain this and to locate ourselves as researchers. For Giddens social structure is analytically, but not actually separate from social action. When I act as an individual, as father or tutor I do not have to think about the wider implications of my action in the reproduction of social structure. However, for Giddens, in acting we simultaneously draw on and construct the social reality that sustains us as individuals and the domain of the social. As a researcher I also produce accounts of the social, which in themselves become a part of our general social understanding. The way in which accounts become part of the social lexicon Giddens calls the double hermeneutic which Scott (1999: 2) suggests 'operates, both as a feedback mechanism and as a two-way process of interpretation'. Where the researcher is operating within a professional setting this is particularly the case.

Scott (1999: 2) also refers to the 'complexity of social settings and the ensuing difficulty this creates for separating out the effects of different variables'. This raises some interesting questions. Is the complexity of any social setting inherent in it or do we as researchers read the complexity into social action? If we consider a simple everyday scene, for example, where a student is in the act of writing, then the potential for analytic description is almost infinite. A range of disciplinary accounts might be had from neurological, cognitive, educational and any number of sociological perspectives, all of which would construct both the person and the activity in sometimes radically different ways. Also, all would select different planes of vision of the same object from the cellular to the social.

The research process and any ensuing accounts would be shaped by the methodological assumptions inherent in the different and particular ways of looking at and representing reality. Also implicit in Scott's reference is the issue of causation, of what causes people to act and to think in the ways they do. As researchers we sometimes work with unexamined and vernacular models of the person. In order to make sense of social action we often make the assumption, and it is worth examining, that people act reasonably within a cause/effect model of social action. For psychologists and phenomenologists the answer is at the level of the individual, while for structuralists of all sorts, from functionalists to Marxists, the individual is largely determined by the wider realities of social forces. For some postmodernists and Foucauldians the subject may be understood as an effect rather than a cause and the subjective experience of self, seen as a power effect of those wider discourses that shape our being.

This issue of agency, of determining both the coercive and the enabling nature of the social can also focus on 'understanding the role of power in social settings and in the production of research texts' (Scott, 1999: 2). What sort of thing we take power to be and how we understand its operation in social settings can critically effect what we choose to see. Two basic theories of power might be termed the possessive (Lukes, 1986) and the discursive (Foucault, 1972). The possessive we might associate with a traditional materialist or Marxist interpretation of the social as comprising classes with power conferred by their ownership of the means of production and classes without power; the one exercising power over the other. A model of domination based on presence and absence. Foucault's (1980) understanding of power is much less subjective. Sexual identity is a good example, there are discourses of sexuality in the human sciences, in biology and psychology and sociology. Through our participation in these discourses we construct our sexual identity. Thus, through our social practice the knowledge that is inherent in the discourses of the human sciences operates to construct our unique individual experience of our own subjectivity (Foucault, 1976). Power is inextricably a part of knowledge and flows universally through our discursive exchanges. One can see here that the model of power that we adopt will have an effect on the way we understand social action. It will shape not only the interpretation of the social events we study but also how we conceive and pursue the social actions that constitute our research. Scott's (1999: 2) final two issues are 'the invasive role of the researcher in their research and its reflexive nature' and 'representing the world in textual form'. The former will be dealt with explicitly later in this chapter and the latter throughout Part 1 of this book and also in Chapter 9.

Our social and working lives are saturated with unspoken assumptions about the nature of the world and how to 'go on' as Giddens phrases our ability to act competently in society. In social research, as we shall see, some of these ideas are systematically formulated and as a result there is a multiplicity of methodological positions that we might adopt, and that will guide and in some measure shape what we think and what we do as researchers. Technical advice on how to organize the many different varieties of social research is readily available in research manuals. However, it is the case that the whole research process is dependent upon the initial opting for a particular version of the nature of the social. Thus, before selecting a manual it is sensible at the outset to know what we mean by social reality and what the implications of this are for different ways of thinking about being a researcher and conducting research.

The nature of the social

This also brings us to the matter of research identity. The idea of the researcher role draws on the theatrical analogy so very fruitfully explored by Goffman (1981). When we take on a role that is both complex and demanding it becomes a part of our social repertoire, it becomes a matter of identity and, to an extent, it conditions both how we understand our selves and also how others see us. The research process is a social process and it has social and affective dimensions and consequences that we will explore alongside the practical, technical and methodological issues that are necessary to the enterprise.

What sort of entity we think the social world is and how we think we can have knowledge of it is a prior and continuing question in relation to the research process. The question is prior because how we answer it conditions the way we set up and conduct our research; and it is continuing because it can be modified by our reading and understanding and by the experience of research. The first area, the nature of the social and our apprehension of it, is about ontology and epistemology and the second area, our self-understanding as researchers, refers in part to what is often called reflexivity. Ontology refers to the nature of being, to how things are in themselves. For the researcher this translates into the question, what is the nature of the social? This is very clearly linked to epistemology, which refers to the nature of our claims to know things about ourselves and the world and to how we justify those claims.

How we understand these ideas has a formative influence on how we conceive and conduct our research. For example, whether one sees the people in the field of interest as collaborators with us in the research process or as subjects to be researched by us reflects our basic methodological orientation. Lather (1991: 7) argues that we live in a time of postpositivist enquiry where the researcher may have as a goal, prediction, understanding, emancipation or deconstruction. These four concerns largely cover the whole gamut of available epistemological and ontological stances. A

simpler division into positivist and interpretive methodologies is characterized by Spradley (1980) as the difference between *engineers*, working in
a basically linear rational manner in a known domain and *explorers* who
see themselves as charting what is essentially unknown (Hitchcock and
Hughes, 1995: 17). Similarly, Kvale (1996), in a discussion of in-depth
interviewing, uses the simple binary images of a miner and a traveller as
metaphors for research. The miner represents the traditional natural scientific model of enquiry into an external and objective world where the role
of the researcher is to go in and extract the information that pre-exists
somewhere in the social strata. Here, researcher and the objects of study
are separated and indeed the nature of the person of the researcher is
irrelevant to the research except insofar as it might be a source of bias or
contamination. The researcher discovers what is there and faithfully
records it in as neutral a language as possible. The image of the traveller
implies a different model of research where the presence of the researcher
is integral to the events being investigated. The implication here is that we
are not dealing with a fixed and exterior social world, but a world of
meaning where the actors are constantly in the process of social construction; and where the researcher is ineluctably one of those actors.
Knowledge is here understood as something that is jointly constructed or
negotiated between researchers and their collaborators.

It is not only the case that there are a range of methodological positions
that can be adopted but those positions in themselves may be differently
understood depending upon the assumptions one makes. The image of the
miner loosely corresponds to the cultural values and social practices associated with positivism, the twentieth-century name for the Enlightenment
elevation of reason, particularly in the form of natural science, as the sole
source of truthful accounts of the world. Currently the position of positivism in the research firmament can be understood as something of an
enigma. For Lather (1991) and many others, the Enlightenment project
of social progress via reason in the guise of science has failed and so we
now inhabit a postpositivist world. From a very different position this is
echoed by Gray (1995: 4) who writes of a post-liberal (neo-liberal) Anglo-
American culture where the 'Enlightenment project that history has
passed by . . . is now significant only as the modernist ideology of the liberal
academic'. Compare this to Scott (2000: 1) in a text arguing for a return to a
modified realism and suggesting that in recent decades 'the dominant
ideology of positivism/empiricism has become perhaps even more dominant'. This tells us that when we look at a methodological orientation we are
not seeing a solid object in the world but something that gets refracted in
the light of other perspectives and takes on differing significances.

Positivism as the basis of a research methodology for generating knowledge of the social has, to an extent, become incompatible with a relativ-
ized and globalized world. However, paradoxically it has taken on a new

lease of life by providing the empirical legitimation of the neo-liberal ideology that underpins the modernist state, which is itself a major sponsor of knowledge production through social research of many kinds. The eclipse of the emancipatory interests of the sociology of education in favour of the apparently neutral psychological accounts of schooling that describe the possibility of higher production of cognitive performances is a case in point. Thus, what we have is an academy that is grappling with the complexity of late modern life and an executive that prefers the simplicities of objectivism, naturalism and neutral, true description. Throughout the public service there is a pervasive culture of vernacular positivism that constructs the social as a single measurable and knowable reality. For many researchers this provides an ideological arena within which they must operate but with which they may not necessarily concur.

Elliott (1991: 119) writes of the 'widespread emergence of *fundamentalism* . . . evidenced in most of the "reforms" now sweeping our social institutions'. One of the key features of this is 'a science of management concerned with the prediction and control of behaviour' and also the requirement to 'refer to concrete, tangible and measurable phenomena'. This is what Mills (1959) referred to as abstracted empiricism where an implicit, and so unquestionable, ideology takes the place of explicit, and so debatable, methodological theory. Again for this to work the social world has to be seen in much the same way as the natural phenomena in a traditional scientific methodology. The culture of vernacular positivism can act as a real constraint on the basic identification of areas worth researching, on the research questions that it is legitimate to ask and on the conduct of the research process right the way through to writing the report and its subsequent reception.

Scott (2000: 11) in a discussion of educational research discerns three current versions of the truth, that is to say conceptualizations of the nature and the links between ontology and epistemology; these are 'naïve realism, radical relativism, and transcendental realism'. Naïve realism is a brand of positivism itself drawn from a traditional understanding of the way in which natural scientists produce knowledge of an independent and objective reality. Because of the culture of vernacular positivism it can be presented as the common sense approach to research and, despite Lather's (1991) assertions, it pervades the general culture of knowledge construction in the public services. This is particularly the case for medicine where the privileged status of the activity is guaranteed by the truthfulness of its scientifically justified claims to know. While it is heavily criticized (Cresswell, 1998; Denzin and Lincoln, 1998a; Lather, 1991; Stronach and MacLure, 1997; Scott, 1999; Scott and Usher, 1996) it would seem that positivism remains a powerful methodological and ideological tool for many researchers.

Positivism and social values

Kolokowski (1972) is cited by Scott (2000: 11) as suggesting that positivism has four main characteristics 'phenomenalism, nominalism, a distinction between facts and values, and the unity of the scientific method'. The first suggests we should be concerned with surface phenomena, with behaviour rather than meaning and with surface effects and not with underlying causes. Thus, if we notice a correlation between social class and obesity the issue is one of the micro-social organization of medicine and not the cultures of capitalism. That is to say that if we are operating in a medical subculture that values evidence-based practice, then that acts as a paradigm that will construct both our questions and answers for us. It can have the effect of cutting the researcher off from other potentially significant wider social contexts. Nominalism argues that the world is full of irreducible factual things whose existence is entirely independent of us and our sociality. Research is the discovery and assembly of what actually is; this necessarily involves screening out our own values as researchers. Nominalism has another important consequence in that it negates and excludes whole swathes of what we might think we know from the realms of knowledge. Not only are statements that might be underpinned by values not real knowledge but all non-scientific areas of enquiry are excluded, including 'aesthetic, ethical and religious statements' (Scott, 2000: 12).

The issue of values in research is contested ground. Not only is there argument about the place of values but it is not clear from the literature precisely what a value might be. It may be something like an opinion or the embracing of a particular emancipatory theoretical position to do with social justice. It may more simply be understood as a matter of the presence of the researcher's subjectivity and its effects on the research process. For Denzin and Lincoln (1998b: 24) 'the age of value-free enquiry for the human disciplines is over'. If it is the case that the person is implicated in knowledge production then research acquires moral and ethical dimensions that can only be ignored where the relevance of the researcher's person is denied. Tripp (1998: 37) argues the case for the role of critical awareness in research with his dictum '*be critical of everything except being critical*'. While warning against the development of a personal dogma, Tripp (1998: 37) suggests that it is axiomatic that 'ultimately no one, not even a critical reflexive researcher can escape making a stand on their values'. Walsh (1999: 51) takes an interesting position arguing that 'human science is constitutively value-engaged in a way natural science is not'. However, this does not automatically imply a loss of the traditional virtue of 'the objectivity of human science' (Walsh, 1999: 51). Walsh argues that 'human science calls for nuance in the matter of value positions' and building on Weber's idea that 'the concept of culture is a *value concept'* he identifies the 'humanity factor' as a more complex issue than that of values. This humanity factor is 'the researcher's operational acknowledgement of those primordial features of the human situation' (Walsh, 1999: 49). This humane awareness 'interacts with the researcher's ideological values, easily or tensely, depending on the stripe of those values' (Walsh, 1999: 49). The question 'how much of our moral, political, religious or educational selves have to be engaged' is answered largely by looking to the social and cultural contexts within which the researcher conducts the research (Walsh, 1999: 53). This leaves aside the sometimes vexed issue of how researchers are to align themselves to those constraining and enabling contexts. The question of to what extent and in what ways might researchers' values legitimately influence their research is not easily answered by appeals to common humanity.

Hammersley (1999: 26), in the same volume as Walsh, is concerned with the maintenance of the validity of research and argues against what he describes as the 'currently influential advocacy of partisanship, which presents research as properly directed towards the achievement of practical or political goals'. Two points are made against this idea of committed research and researchers with defined goals. It is worth remembering here that research aimed at some aspect of change or development describes much current research in the public services and probably most practitioner research. The first is a basically positivist objection that it will lead to biased results as 'the pursuit of the good will not necessarily aid the discovery of the truth' (Hammersley, 1999: 27). Further, he suggests 'the potentially biasing effects of value commitment must be guarded against if we are to maximize our chances of producing sound knowledge' (Hammersley, 1999: 27). The second is that research that is infused with a value position 'leads to an impossible relativism, and thereby undercuts the distinction between research and propaganda' (Hammersley, 1999: 27). Stating his own value position that draws on an Enlightenment faith in the power of reason to reveal what actually exists, Hammersley states 'I believe that social research must necessarily be committed to value neutrality simply because it cannot validate value conclusions' (1999: 27). Hammersley is aware that absolute value freedom is not a human social possibility but nonetheless argues that it should remain a goal of the social researcher in order to provide a basis for collegial scrutiny of research reports in order to reveal possible bias. The objections of Hammersley and others to value-laden research are explored from a more specific angle in Chapter 7.

Thus, we can see that wrapped up in the issue of value freedom versus value commitment are a host of judgements and arguments about the nature of the social and our ability to represent it legitimately. These problems are an integral part of the research process that requires researchers to discover and justify their own position.

Hammersley's objection to value-laden research can be seen in part as about the presence or absence of the researcher in the research. The idea of the unity of method acts to suppress the role of the researcher in knowledge production in favour of a model of the social comprising independent objects in the same way as the natural world. The scientific method that characterizes positivism is empiricism. This suggests that we can rely on our senses to perceive the world as it is and also on our language faithfully to represent our sense experience of what is indubitably real. This is an important element in the construction of much knowledge in relation to the public services. All manner of reports, audits, evaluations, inspections and the whole panoply of bureaucratic control are based in empiricism, which 'denies the possibility of genuine disagreement about events or human activities' (Scott, 2000: 13). Critically naïve realism fails to distinguish between epistemology and ontology 'what is given to our senses . . . constitutes the world as it is' and this brooks no argument (Scott, 2000: 12).

For the naïve realist what appears to us via our senses is what is real, and that is what is impressed on our minds. For the radical relativist, however, mind and world are entirely separate. Not only does this mean that we can have different versions of the world, but that all these versions constitute separate and potentially viable realities. Thus, our theories and ideas about the world have no necessary connection to an independent social reality. This is at once confusing and counter intuitive. While theoretically radical relativism is certainly sustainable as an idea it need not undermine our sense of quotidian reality. It would seem that generally in our social and professional lives we can rely upon the nature of things to remain largely uncontested, if highly differentiated, and we can assume that the world that we live in is pretty much the world that our neighbours inhabit.

However, one would only have to spend a little time with, for example, Swingewood's (2000) account of the history of sociological thought to recognize that between the conceptions of the social developed by Marx or Parsons or more lately Giddens, Bourdieu or Foucault there are fundamental differences in nature. For Marx the dynamic of the social was conflict whereas for Parsons it was the tendency to equilibrium. It may be difficult to reconcile the idea of an objective social realm with either the history or the current condition of social thought. However, the fact that there are different versions of the social does not necessarily imply that mind and world are not linked, but only that they can be linked in different ways. It is possible to notice that what counts as knowledge and the manner of its production differs through both time and space without taking the radical relativist position that therefore we cannot connect our ideas with any real condition of the world. Such a position is also morally disarming because it 'implies that it is not possible to develop criteria by which we can judge one version against another' (Scott, 2000: 13).

Following Bhaskar (1979) Scott (2000: 14) suggests transcendental realism as a compromise position that neither abandons the independence of the real nor insists on the possibility of a single and true account. Here there is a clear separation between ontology, the way things are and epistemology, the ways in which we construct our knowledge of the world. The ontological realm is seen as having its own nature and as being relatively stable certainly as regards the nature of the social. This saves us from the fragmented flux of radical relativism for 'once we constitute an intransitive dimension, we can see how changing knowledge of unchanging objects is possible' (Bhaskar, 1979: 11, quoted in Scott, 2000: 14). Epistemology is rooted in history; it is transitive 'and therefore subject to the prevailing power arrangements in society' (Scott, 2000: 14). In this position we can take for granted the nature of the social as real, stable and partially independent while the construction of our knowledge of this reality is tempered by our position in time and space and by the cultural milieu that we inhabit. This raises particular issues of nomenclature particularly with respect to terms such as 'social constructivist', which can be embraced by researchers with different ontological positions, including both those who are in pursuit of social realities and postmodernists for whom 'realities' is more problematic. This tension is apparent throughout our discussions in this book.

Reflexivity

For Giddens (1984, 1991) reflexivity is a requirement for our self-management in late modernity. What he refers to as institutional reflexivity is 'the regularised use of knowledge about circumstances of social life as a constitutive element in its organisation and transformation' (Giddens, 1991: 20). Modernity's reflexivity 'refers to the susceptibility of most aspects of social activity, and material relations with nature, to chronic revision in the light of new information or knowledge . . . such information or knowledge is not incidental to modern institutions, but constitutive of them' (Giddens, 1991: 20). In the late modern world we need constantly to assimilate new knowledge that alters our understanding of ourselves and the world and informs our social practice. Social research has a special place here as 'the social sciences play a basic role in the reflexivity of modernity: they do not simply "accumulate" knowledge in the way in which the natural sciences may do' (Giddens, 1991: 20). This is part of Giddens' double hermeneutic, the way in which our researches describe the social in accounts that then become part of a new social condition insofar as they help to reform the realities they describe.

Our social performances are informed by references to our self-conceptions and our understanding of others and also by the recursive link between our social action and the structures of the social. This is occasioned, he argues, by the separation of time and space in what is 'essentially a post traditional order' (Giddens, 1991: 20). In the late modern world we are no longer able to rely upon the given nature of social status, and fixed ideas of personal identity, that arguably characterized traditional societies, to guide our social action. Instead, in a globalized world we must be active in our self-construction, reflexively monitoring our own sociality.

The concept of reflexivity as an aspect of research has come to prominence with the critique of positivism offered by developments in qualitative research and with the popularizing of research, something that was once an almost exclusively academic activity. Usher (1996a: 35) defines the issue succinctly as the idea that 'the activity of the knower influences what is known since nothing can be known apart from these activities'. This prompts the question 'are we really finding out about ourselves rather than the subject of our research?' (Usher, 1996a: 35). This is a profound question about our nature and the nature of our claims to know that brings up again the ideas of radical relativism. Partly what we do as researchers is more or less formally organize our experience of any given reality and then find ways of making representations of that experience normally through the construction of a text. Therefore, are we simply locked into recording ourselves rather than the subjects and objects of our researches? I think the answer to this is both 'yes' and 'no'. This approach can be argued roughly as follows. We are individuated through our physical embodiment. Also, generally, it is individuals who write about their experience of the field. However formal our research design and formula for writing might be; and whatever transmutations the data may be put to in order for them to appear independent of us, arguably we can write nothing other than our selves because it is the conscious self that experiences. The danger is this may lead us to an isolated solipsism, where there are no checks or balances to what we may say or how we may construct the world. However, this eventuality is strongly mitigated by the existence of a research community and the coercive power of the social contexts within which the researcher lives and works. Also, as Giddens (1984) points out, the social and indeed our selves partly consists of orderly repetitions of locally recognized performances. As researchers we participate in and draw on a social order that we do not have to generate or sustain individually. This belies the image of the researcher as an isolated individual knowledge producer.

Our educational system reinforces the idea that the lone individuated person is the locus of knowledge production and acquisition. This is assumed in many of the social practices that constitute the public organization of knowledge in all the different varieties of schooling and professional instruction. Notably this is inscribed in systems of assessment that construct knowledge as essentially cognitive and legitimate it through individuated performance in increasingly frequent mass public examinations. However, since Kuhn's (1970) analysis of natural science as a communal activity, indeed as requiring community in order to function, it has been possible to think more about the social dimensions of knowledge construction. As Usher (1996a: 35) suggests, a reflexive awareness in the research process allows us to discern 'the place of power, discourse and text, that which in a sense goes "beyond" the personal'. Thus, while we may work as individual researchers we can only do so within a complex network of social connections. Indeed, for our work to be recognizable as research requires the recognition by others of its location in that particular social category. Research is social activity and for it to be recognized it needs to be held in place by a host of referents to sets of ideas and to people and purposes. It is the social embedding of research that makes it meaningful activity; and while not wishing to reduce the researcher to a mere cipher, it seems that research is identifiable primarily as social activity. The researcher enters, and is borne along by, a pre-existing community of discursive practice.

Reflexivity can thus partly be understood as the recognition of the social conditions within which the researcher constructs knowledge accounts. For Siraj-Blatchford and Siraj-Blatchford (1999: 95) this 'refers to the process by which the observations that we make are dependent upon our prior understandings of the subject of our observations; they "refer back" '. A linguistic analogy may be useful here. The dictionary suggests to us that language is a collection of words that are tied to definitions. That is to say the dictionary model of language is underpinned by a naïve realist version of the world where words and things are intrinsically bound. However, if we think of language as words in action we realize that they not only have definitions but also wider connotative fields. The word research, as it comes to mind, brings with it a penumbra of associations, of other words and images within which it is embedded and that go beyond simple definition. Reflexivity suggests that language is not a collection of boundaried symbols that represent reality. Rather it is something that inheres in social action and plays over our experience in such a way as to enable us constantly to revise our apprehension of ourselves and the world.

Reflexivity works to allow us to make informed interpretations of what we experience and observe and feel. This can be illustrated by a small example from my own research. I am observing in the piazza outside the senior students' building in a large community college. Three boys from the lower school come into the piazza, which is out of bounds for younger pupils, and begin to play football. The head of the modern languages department comes out the senior students' building, notices the boys, tells them off for being out of bounds and sends them back to their designated play area. Peace reigns in the little piazza. Some five minutes later the boys reappear and resume their game. A few minutes later the head of modern languages comes out of the building once more and, ignoring the boys playing football, goes on her way.

What can be said of this vignette of school life; what can I draw on to make sense of these events? First, I might say that the boys are weakly attached to the out of bounds rule and unafraid of the consequences of breaking it. Unlike the rule that says one must attend lessons or sit examinations this one that refers to what I might understand as the geography of privileged access to certain spaces is of lesser account. This alerts me to the way space is used in school to make statements about relative status. The actions of the teacher in first upholding the rule and then ignoring it also point to its marginality and interestingly to the possibility of the arbitrary exercise of power. This is sometimes called a critical incident (Tripp, 1998), which is a significant event, or a single instance that offers a more generalizable insight into the nature of the cultural site being studied. I can reflexively read from it using my knowledge and personal experience of schooling and also attempt a general statement about the nature of power and its exercise that can form a mini-hypothesis that can go on to inform future observation and analysis. If it were the case that I found no corroborating incidents then I would want to reconsider my first reading.

Useful insights into the notion of reflexivity can be gleaned from feminist epistemology as it works from a clearly politically invested position with no interest in creating a distanced neutrality. Tanesini (1999: 15) unequivocally suggests, contra Hammersley, that 'value-neutrality is neither possible nor desirable'. Tanesini identifies three hallmarks of feminist approaches to knowledge creation that distinguish it from traditional positivism. These are 'the centrality given to practical knowledge, the conception of knowledge as essentially social, and the rejection of value-neutrality' (Tanesini, 1999: 15). This last can only 'seem appealing if we conceive of knowledge as a relation between things devoid of meaning and human representations of them' (Tanesini, 1999: 15). This does not lead to a free-for-all solipsism where things begin and end with subjective belief. This is because 'things do not have their significance because individuals in isolation bestow values to them by means of their mental activity' it is rather that 'things have their significance against a background of socially instituted practices' (Tanesini, 1999: 15). And so the world outside us is precisely that but what we do is invest it with meaning drawn from the contexts that are available to us. Thus, the researcher who abandons the comforts of positivism is not set adrift upon an endless sea of relativisms but must recognize that the task of investigating the complexity of the social requires the development of rigorous and coherent frameworks.

In our understanding of the nature of reflexivity perhaps a critical element is pointed to in Scott's (1999: 2) 'problems and difficulties' where he constructs the issue as one of 'conceptualising the invasive role of the researcher in their research and its reflexive nature'. It is the notion of invasion that is the key. If we understand ourselves as automatically a part of the action then our task is how to build that into our research strategy and representation of the research. If we are working from a more positivistic or naturalistic conception of the research process then our presence becomes problematic as it may shape or contaminate the very thing we wish to describe. From our decision on this matter many of the decisions in constructing our research strategy will flow.

The logic of enquiry

Passively sitting, reading, reflecting and writing are not normally thought of as research in the social sciences although, of course, such activity can be just so classified in the humanities. In most social research there is an element of going and finding out, it is field-based and employs some element of empirical enquiry. In order to maintain coherence in this activity we need not only to be aware of the frameworks that we bring to the experience, we also have to organize that experience systematically. This is in order that the different parts and phases of the research process can make holistic sense and be coherently represented in our writing.

Although there are many methodological and theoretical frameworks within which research is constructed it is nonetheless possible to generalize about the research process in such a way that probably all research studies need to have some regard for the following stages in what we might call the logic of enquiry. This sequence describes the research process in real time where each stage is dependent in some measure on the last. Broadly the stages are conceptualization and focus, the selection of a research strategy and theoretical frame, the identification of relevant data and the means to collect them, the analysis or interrogation of those data and the construction of an account. These are identifiable stages but the sequence is not rigidly sequential. For example, if, as is highly desirable, a research journal is kept then writing and analytical notes will be an ongoing feature of the work, which will end with the finished report.

The process begins with a conceptualization that becomes a focus, an area of interest, and this can be precisely or, perhaps initially, only vaguely understood. The genesis of the research might be a conjecture that the world is like this or like that, which would be followed by systematic empirical investigation, or it might be framed within a set of professional concerns with personal development or organizational improvement.

For example, an early years' teacher, with a class of four- and five-year-olds, may have an intuition that the curriculum she is to work with seems not to mesh with the social and emotional needs of the children. From this an area of interest or an inter-relation becomes a focus and also indicates a nascent question – why don't things seem to fit together? We can see that this is a very broad conceptualization and can be followed up in a number of ways. This could be seen as a policy issue, where central concerns with standards have led to a misconceived set of instructions for the classroom. It might be seen as an issue of professional competence with the teacher asking what am I doing wrong or is there something I am failing to do? It might also be seen as a social and political issue about whether a centrally defined and skills-based curriculum can reflect the diversity of groups of real children.

The next step is to decide upon the plane of activity that is to form the focus of our speculation. How we make this decision is unlikely to be simply an abstracted matter but will often depend upon the contexts that bring us into the research arena. For example, if we are seeking finance then the expectations of our sponsors and of the organization where the research will be carried out will constrain our choices. If, given our contextual constraints, we decide that this is a matter of pedagogics, and the focus should be on classroom practice, then that does not exclude our referring to other planes of reality where our object is constructed. The ideological dimensions of a prescribed curriculum, and its implicit assumptions regarding the nature of society and the individual, are certainly germane to our construction of what is going on in the classroom and how that is to be understood and what meanings we are to assign to it.

Having found a focus and an intention we then need to think about how best that intention is to be realized. If we want to investigate the classroom in a systematic way to understand better the processes that underlay our intuition of unease then an *action research* framework may well present itself to us as the best vehicle for our purpose. Such a choice in itself brings with it some key assumptions. Action research assumes that we are engaging in research because we are interested in change for improvement, rather than simply understanding (Elliott, 1998; McNiff, 1988; Altrichter *et al.*, 1993). It also assumes that we are going with Kvale's (1996) traveller in that our research design is likely to be collaborative and may involve colleagues and students as partners in the enterprise. Thus we will be eschewing any strong demarcation between the researchers and the researched as would be the case in, for example, an experimental design. There is a range of models that are more or less sophisticated in their approach to action research but all follow a similar sequence. First, the *reconnaissance* phase where what is happening now is systematically investigated. This is followed by an analysis and the *development of interventions* in the field aimed at improving some aspects of practice. Interventions are then *implemented*. This process is *monitored* in order to learn about the nature and management of change, and subsequently *evaluated* to discover what sort of impact our interventions might have had. The final evaluation can be seen as another reconnaissance and the cycle begins again.

One of the criticisms of action research is that it tends to be merely technical rather than critical and only promotes change at a superficial level. However, if we look again at feminist research then an entirely different logic of enquiry would present itself. Hitchcock and Hughes (1995: 65) refer to the importance of context in understanding social action in that 'why and how an event happens is understood by reference to concepts, systems, models, structures, beliefs, ideas and hypotheses'. This would be true in different ways of any social enquiry but Hitchcock and Hughes (1995: 64) identify a range of distinctive features of feminist research, which determine just how those references are to be made. First, there is a set of assumptions about the condition of society where patriarchy is seen as the major source of gender inequality and so 'the construction and reproduction of gender and sexual difference' (Hitchcock and Hughes, 1995: 64) is an important research focus. Most feminist methodologies reject the separability of theory from practice and work with a notion of praxis, that theory is implicit in action. Private and public are seen as intimately connected especially in the constitution of sexual relationships. These basic assumptions are reflected methodologically in the rejection of much of what is seen as androcentric epistemologies and research practices. Thus disciplinary boundaries are ignored in favour of a unified understanding of the social realm. The claim of neutrality within positivistic methodologies is rejected as a denial of the political nature of knowledge. In contrast there is a 'recognition of the gendered nature of social research and the development of anti-sexist research strategies' that are 'fundamentally participatory' with an emphasis on 'qualitative, introspective biographical research techniques' (Hitchcock and Hughes, 1995: 65).

Thus we can see that the logic of enquiry is by no means self-effulgent. In choosing a research strategy it is not simply a matter of looking in the toolbox for the best instrument for the job, because it is much more than a simply technical matter. Moreover, and even if we would want to argue that it is merely technical, that also brings with it a host of assumptions about the nature of the social and how we might construct our knowledge of it. The logic of enquiry is less certain than the phrase might suggest but it is in facing and negotiating those uncertainties that we become researchers, and it is the nature of those uncertainties that we continue to explore in this book.

3

Talking with people – interviewing

Introduction

The use of interviews in research suggests that the views and interpretations of certain social actors are important to your research questions. Their knowledge about the specified social context, their accounts of that social arena are significant in your research. The inclusion of interviews in a research design is accompanied by the selection of interviewees from specific social groups (for example, mathematics teachers, nurses on medical wards, elderly male Irish immigrants) and/or a range of respondents concerned with specific social events (for example, National tests, medical consultations, basic skills programmes for young offenders) and/or social contexts (for example, populations in a northern town in the UK, a traveller community or a rural settlement in Nigeria). Whichever of the above is fore-grounded in research, the final description of the interview sample will necessarily include reference to social actors, social events and social contexts.

In a research design the predominant concern is often with the empirical arena and the selection of possible respondent groups. In one way or another, the research will focus on certain relationships within the arena. The interview is a very adaptable and powerful method in a broad range of research projects and in its generic form it is not closely identified with any specific research paradigm, disciplinary perspective or substantive field. As a result of this, it is extremely important to be clear about why and how the interview features in your research design and, by connection, for a researcher to consider explicitly their own position in the interview process. Whether articulated in a methodology section or not, it is with reference to these considerations (why, how, who) that the interview as a method of creating text starts to have a specific shape and purpose with respect to the initial conception of the research. As mentioned in Chapter 2, the disciplinary perspective (cognitive psychology, for example) and the plane of vision (for example, individual or institutional) will also be influential in specifying the form and purpose of the interview.

In this chapter we will consider different forms of interview and relate these to the purposes and processes in the research. Although we may make some references to the practicalities of interviewing, our main concern is to highlight the methodological issues. In concert with the rest of this book we focus here on how researcher identity influences the relationship between researcher and respondent(s) and the implications for the kinds of texts produced.

The broad schema

The interview as a research method has multiple forms. As such the interview is a very malleable research tool appropriate to a very wide range of research. The enormous variety of interview types may be considered along these five continua:

```
formal ..................................................................informal
structured .......................................................unstructured
individual ...............................................................group
one-off..............................................................sequential
public ...................................................private (confidential)
```

These continua describe the context, conditions and approach to the interview. Although some combinations may be unlikely, the type of interview used in a research project may be described by relative position on each of these continua independently. A job interview, for example, may be described as formal, structured, individual, one-off and public whereas a session with a marriage guidance counsellor might be less formal, less structured, group, sequential and private. In similar ways interviews within a research project will also have different forms dependent on the research focus, theoretical frame, the empirical context, the research intention and the respondent(s) and the researcher position. More practical aspects like the number of respondents, time constraints and perhaps funding will also impinge on the form of interview appropriate to a specific research project.

Many research methods texts review types of interview and provide tips on technique. Bell (1993), for example, provides a 21 point interview checklist which may well be worth consulting. In general the tips include issues of access, location, timing, communication, recording and exit. There is general consensus that the interview has three main stages; the introduction, main questions and the closure (see, for example, Bell, 1993; Brown and Dowling, 1998). Many writers underline the difficulties in framing interview questions and, similar to advice on questionnaire construction, they advise that complex ambiguous questions are common and should be avoided (Filmer *et al.*, 1998). At the same time the researcher is advised to guard against exclusions or assumptions with respect to the respondents.

The concern about the questions/schedule turns into a focus on communication in the live interview. The order of questions is highlighted as important, more specifically the move from the particular to the general, that is to elicit responses that start with descriptive and move to analytical responses. Other communication issues include clarity, checking responses, avoiding antagonism (by both the interviewer and interviewee), and the preparation of prompts and probes. There is also a concern that the interviewer expresses and engenders interest in the interview focus, responses and the respondent(s).

Whatever the format of the interview, the interchanges, in whole or in part, are usually recorded in some way. This recorded text, which may appear in different forms, for example, written notes or transcribed audio recordings, is then subjected to analysis. The researcher is pivotal, however, not only in shaping the research agenda, but in constructing the interview questions, selecting respondents, the conduct of the interview, the analysis of it as text and the production of the larger research report based in part at least upon this analysis. The researcher (self-) understanding and position are central to representations of the social within the research writing. Researcher identity, then, is critical to the production of knowledge about the complexities of the social world.

Researching is an iterative process in which the choice of method(s) selected as well as the size, scope and focus of the study will need to be justified and reflected upon during and after the study. A research design is constructed to explore certain questions about the social world articulated in the research questions through specified research methods. The inclusion of interviews (often combined with other methods) indicates that the resultant texts are integral to this exploration of the social. The interview exchanges are recontextualized into intermediary texts, which are subject to analysis. Importantly, the question of how the method (interviews) relates to the research focus depends upon how the interview texts will be read (analysed) and recontextualized in the research report. In this way, we can see that the researcher interest and position, although informed by theoretical disciplinary or professional knowledge, mediates the link between the methodology and the substantive concerns. We explore this further in the final chapter of this book.

Interview texts as 'resource'

An analysis that treats interview texts for their content, the information contained in the text, is described by Seale (1998) as analysis of interview texts as 'resource'. This direct reading locates the researcher within a classical, realist position associated with views of objective social reality. Market survey research interviewers, for example, reflect this disposition through their use of a prescribed list of interview questions with a fixed structure and sequence. The highly formalized, structured, individual, one-off interviews, in a standardized format often with a limited choice of response categories resemble oral questionnaires (refer to Chapter 4 for a more detailed discussion). This form of interview is likely to be included in a research design intended to survey a large number of respondents and a large number of interviewers as they lend themselves predominantly to quantitative analysis in a more or less straightforward way.

Pre-selected criteria that shape the interview and questions of reliability and validity demand the strict following of a protocol in which the interviewer remains disengaged from the content and social exchange of the interview. This is a technical approach in which there is a mental/manual divide with the interview treated as a matter of technique that may be improved with practice but is separate from any intellectual work. Within the rather linear research process, the intellectual effort is in the earlier stage in the production of the interview protocol and the later analysis stage. Nevertheless, reference to 'response effect', in which the interviewee makes efforts either to please or antagonize the interviewer, suggests the influence of social interaction on the interview. However, the question of researcher identity in this approach to research remains implicit and their influence on the resultant interview text is construed only in negative terms and as obstructive to the production of true or authentic responses. This approach to interviewing, which Kvale (1996) describes metaphorically as mining is concerned with '. . . how to ask questions, what sorts of questions not to ask and ways to avoid saying things that might spoil or contaminate, or bias the data. This basic model, however, locates valued information inside the respondent and assigns the interviewer the task of somehow extracting it' (Kvale, 1996: 13).

The concern with bias signals the crucial importance of efforts to sustain a separation of the researcher and the researched and for researcher neutrality. In this way the interview is a vehicle for access to the mind of the researched which is expressed in their responses and over which, except in posing the question in the first place, the researcher has no influence. In the same vein, the interviewees have no direct access or influence upon the research agenda; the power to do this resides with the researcher. This includes particular theoretical (disciplinary or professional) perspectives and value positions, either or both of which may not be explicitly articulated even by the researcher. It is the researcher's account then, that is privileged and who is assumed to have access (through the research process) to the 'real' true account, uncovering the facts about the social world. This empiricist tendency is concerned with the surface features rather than a deeper engagement with the underlying social complexities or linguistic nuances.

The analysis of the interview as resource reflects a positivist stance with parallels in versions of traditional natural science research (whose objects are entirely different) and aims to produce knowledge of an independent and objective reality. The social processes of the interview, analysis and knowledge production remain entirely unproblematic. Although research within our social institutions may not appear at first sight much like the market survey described above with limited tick-box interview response categories, the researcher position with respect to the production of knowledge may be fundamentally similar. Views of social reality, the plane of vision and the consequent analytical process in the production of the research knowledge are significant to the researcher position and their activity with respect to the interview text.

The absence of an explicit acknowledgement of the influence of the social in the interview acts to de-socialize and de-politicize research and reduce the plane of vision to the disembedded individual level. The dislocation of the social interaction of the interview and the interviewee from the social and cultural milieu provides enormous potential for the construction of individual pathologies evident, for example, in the dominant psychological accounts in education, in forms of therapy and in evaluations of social institutions. As mentioned in the previous chapter, the rise of managerialism, bureaucratization, incipient vernacular positivism and state dominance of the research agenda within the social services have favoured empiricist approaches to social research. The underlying effort for control and prediction within the ubiquitous inspections, audits and evaluations strongly indicate the use of the interview as resource in which the researcher identity is suppressed and the knowledge produced is ideologically bound with little or no space for reflection on its assumptions and processes.

Interviews as social action

The ideal type of interview as 'resource' constructs images of a rather passive respondent who does not ask questions except perhaps for clarification or affirmation 'Is this the kind of thing you want me to talk about?' and an interviewer whose only unscripted interjections are to keep the respondent within the agenda. This unproblematic vision of the interview process both depoliticizes and individualizes the interview situation as well as what is done with the resultant text. Brief consideration of an interview situation between doctor and patient, employee and employer or teacher and pupil (whether in a research context or not) would suggest that actor identity and their relative social position make a neutral interchange unlikely. Both the researcher and respondent are caught in contemporaneous social dynamics that invade the social space of the interview. A social researcher, who only uses the interview as resource, does not take cognizance of the interview as social action and effectively constructs a separation of the researcher from the social setting of the interview. As a form of action within a social and historical context, the interview itself is integral to the products of the research. This means moving beyond a view of the interview as 'resource' (information) to include the interview as 'topic' in which the processes of the interview, the positioning of the interviewer and respondent are explicitly addressed as integral to the research.

Decisions about method, for example, the form of the interview, need to be informed by the research relations between researcher and respondent alongside the substantive research concerns. So, in addition to the more technical descriptions provided in reference to the continua, briefly described above, questions about how the researcher and respondent(s) will relate to each other in the interview are of paramount importance. This is not restricted to whether researcher and respondent(s) smile at or laugh with each other or where they sit – although all of these non-verbal aspects of the interview context and conduct are important. The social relations of the interview are about power relations in the research. Just as there are fundamental differences in the social relations in the job interview and the marriage counselling interview, scenarios referred to earlier, so there are key differences between interviewing, for example, primary schoolchildren compared to the primary headteacher or patients compared to nurses or doctors. In this respect the researcher position is critical not only to the choice of interview type but in its influence on the kind and quality of the interview text produced. As Stanley and Wise suggest, '. . . researchers' understandings are necessarily temporally, intellectually, politically and emotionally grounded and are thus as contextually specific as those of the researched' (Stanley and Wise, 1990: 23).

There is then a need for the researcher to be self-conscious about their position in the research from the outset, in the focus and design of the research, during the processes of data collection, in making interpretations and in the writing. Empirical work that does not refer to the conditions of its production ignores important epistemological concerns, tends to construct neutral accounts of a highly political research process and removes a significant player – the researcher – from their accounts of social life. The distancing of the researcher from the research products has some resonances with an image of a white-coated scientist peering down the microscope at blood cells, for example. Such 'distance' is untenable in social research with interests in particular aspects of social life in which the interviewer and interviewee are inextricably linked. The claim for objective distance from the objects of social research, which has long been critiqued by feminist researchers among others (see, for example, Oakley, 1981) leads to skewed theory. In the close quarters demanded by most research interviews the aspiration to neutrality and objectivity seems even more implausible.

Ironically, the absence of any consideration of power asymmetries within the classical approaches to the interview places the researcher in the most powerful and privileged position in relation to the production of knowledge (Seale, 1998; Briggs, 2002). This is often expressed in metaphors of 'miner', 'engineer' and 'fishing' (Wiseman and Aron, 1972; Kvale, 1996), which cast the researcher with authority and power in the interview and more broadly in the research. Discursive authority is constructed through the structured, standardized interview designed to extract facts or meaning from inside the respondent's head, which are then judged as being more or less authentic. Framing the interview (and other methods) as contextually located social action, however, demands that the power relations of the process itself become subject to scrutiny. Rather than create distance, the effort is to develop a rapport between the researcher and respondents. Interviewers are advised to show a caring and concerned attitude within a well-planned encouraging format. Far from the dangers of bias and the researcher 'going native', the more conversational and open interview format escapes the alienation of respondents in the classical interview form and endeavours to produce greater trust and more truthful responses (Seale, 1998). In the interview context then, sensitivity and empathy of the researcher are highly significant to the outcomes.

The metaphor of the interviewer as 'traveller' is used to describe this latter position and to raise points of methodological distinction from the interviewer as 'miner'. These alternative genres with different rules of engagement are detailed by Kvale (1996), who presents 12 aspects of the research interview, 7 stages of interviewing, 9 forms of question and 5 considerations about who benefits in his comprehensive texts about 'InterViews'. In more general terms, once the researcher takes on the 'traveller' metaphor, the interview becomes much less controlled and rule bound. It requires the researcher's consciousness of their position within the production of knowledge, care with the social and emotional aspects of the social encounter and attention to the practicalities. All of this cannot be pre-arranged and needs to be managed within the dynamics of the interview and it is this that describes the skill or art of interviewing (Gubrium and Holstein, 2002). Attention is drawn to the practical and ethical aspects of access to interviewees, the social dynamics of the encounter and satisfactory closure. There remains the constant potential for 'wasted' interview opportunities most frustratingly perhaps through failure to record. It is in acknowledgement of these difficulties that many writers suggest that the interviewer leaves time after each interview to think (and make notes) about it as both 'resource' (data) and 'topic' (processes).

Power and process in the interview

In recognition of the power asymmetries and the potentially intimidating encounter of the interview, an informal, conversational style is often encouraged to put the interviewee at ease. Nevertheless, both the researcher's methodological stance and the specific substantive interests make the interview more than a conversation. It is from this research position that the researcher moves beyond polite exchange to encourage deeper engagement in the issues by the interviewees. So, although a conversational style during the interview is often suggested, the researcher is working hard, continually making judgements about interviewee responses and their own action in relation to their research interests. Just as we have centralized researcher identity in the dynamics of the interview (and the whole process of research), so does Kvale (1996) who describes the interviewer as the research instrument.

The combination of more personalized dispositions, encouragement for deeper inquiry and the less stable interview positioning can give rise to explicitly emotional dynamics for all involved. Moving into more therapeutic forms of exchange, however, not only shift the focus away from the social phenomena to the interviewee but also reposition the interviewer. This is altogether a different enterprise that the researcher (except where such interchange is the subject of research) needs to be alert to and ready to handle. The interviewer as traveller then highlights the need for social sensitivity both during and after the interview. This might require the explicit provision of a safe space for the respondent; usually this is accomplished through assurances of confidentiality that they will not be identified individually as the source. In more serious cases involving criminality or abuse this could mean taking the respondent away from the context or some form of debriefing through special counselling.

The effect of the interview on the respondent has been raised by many feminist and social justice researchers. The issue for them is that the interview is neither personally damaging nor exploitative. Beyond a concern for rapport, such researcher positions recursively connect the internal interview dynamics with a broader social analysis of power. This demands that the researcher is sensitive to their own power position and its influence on the interview. Social class, ethnic and age relations among other structures of inequality are brought into accounts of interviewer–interviewee relations. These methodological sensitivities usually indicate a strong association of the underlying researcher interest with political movements and to social change. They often justify the use of interviews on grounds of providing an opportunity for the 'voice' of individuals from marginalized groups to be heard and for alternative accounts of the social world to be legitimated through research. In these circumstances it would be contradictory in the extreme to engage in exploitative relations with respondents in its processes.

This acknowledgement of the researcher power and position has brought new complexities to the interview as a method and produced a plethora of strategies and formats to deal with it. These include the use of sequential rather than on–off interviews to build better trust and communication, recycling of interview transcripts to the respondent, insider researchers, practitioner research, for example, the teacher–researcher, life-history interviews, emancipatory or participatory approaches and focus group interviews. Further examples and advice about these are detailed in many research manuals. As explained in Chapter 1, these developments in which the power dynamics of the interview are made explicit continue to draw critique from the traditional positivist position that describes them as biased and even partisan.

The kind of interview envisioned above is a very different encounter from the archetype of the market researcher offered earlier in this chapter. Forms of collaborative/participatory research are 'playing' with the boundary between the interviewer and interviewee in the creation of the interview text. As we shall discuss later in Chapter 6, this may not necessarily change the boundary between the researcher and the researched in the same way, as this depends upon how the interview text is handled after the interview and in the analysis. Although researchers often pay great attention to forms of validity in the interview and in producing a transcript that is fair to the interviewee, they may then take huge liberties with the way that it is incorporated into the final report. When talking about the boundary between modernism and postmodernism, Stronach and MacLure (1997) suggest that the critical part to explore is actually what lies within the boundary. Similarly we would suggest that the critical part of the interview is not drawing the line between interviewer and interviewed but in their articulation 'within' that line. In this respect the (re-)construction and projection of the researcher identity in the interview, based on the levels of self-knowledge and conscious self-monitoring, are significant to this articulation, the production of the interview text and its later recontextualization in analysis and writing.

Knowledge and power

The explicit acknowledgement of the interview as a social event and of the crucial importance of the relationship between the interviewer and interviewee has been highlighted by Seidman (1998) as a general issue in qualitative research and by Atkinson (2002) with respect to life history research. Both writers are concerned not only to elicit descriptions from the respondent but also explicitly to ask for the respondents' reflections as a way to understand the meanings they ascribe to aspects of social life. Although this appears to be a distinctive move beyond the classical positivist approaches to interviewing, Ryen (2002) in reference to cross-cultural interviewing suggests that these attempts to circumvent the power of the researcher may also be efforts to get more authentic, truer respondent accounts. In effect, the respondent accounts of the social world excavated through the interview are incorporated to bolster the hegemonic views of social reality rather than disrupt them. Moreover, 'Dominated communities are common targets for interview projects, providing both models of difference and objects of surveillance and regulation.' (Briggs, 2002: 914)

In this sense Briggs (2002) describes interviews as a technology to (re-) invent subjectivities and social patterns that conform to, and confirm, dominant views of social reality. In the same way the interview process and text may also be used to confirm rather than critique the theoretical stance of the interviewer. If we consider, for example, a consultation with a medical doctor as a form of interview, although care might be taken to make the interaction comfortable and unthreatening, the patient's descriptions and responses are used to help the doctor locate their dis-ease in reference to a fixed body of medical knowledge (Foucault, 1977). Similarly, clinical interviews used in educational psychology elicit responses that are often interpreted in relation to a fixed theoretical structure, which is reflected back to categorize the interviewee.

It is evident that the power of the researcher is not only in the conduct of the interview, but also in the construction of accounts of social life through the research. In effect this moves the question of researcher identity beyond a purely methodological position to include the interviewer's theoretical position with respect to the substantive issues that are the subject of the interview (see Chapter 9 for further discussion). These interconnected dimensions (methodological, theoretical and substantive) construct the researcher identity and locate the ways in which the interview as text is produced, analysed and incorporated into public comment about social life within the written report. Even if not explicitly articulated by the interviewer all these dimensions have bearing before the interview has even started. It is in this light that we can see the contradiction of the researcher who claims to give 'voice' to respondents from marginalized groups while incorporating these excluded voices in the dominant versions of social reality.

Alongside other attempts to address this contradiction (see, for example, Clifford and Marcus, 1986), work by Lather (1986a), firmly within an Enlightenment framework, described emancipatory research that included collaborative explorations of theoretical and methodological dimensions in research by the researcher and researched. In addition to the 'need for reciprocity' in the interview, she included 'dialectical theory building' with the interviewer avoiding theoretical imposition. The interview becomes a site for interactive knowledge production. It is the assimilation of this new knowledge that constitutes 'emancipation' through the development of revised conceptions of social reality by the researched and the researcher, and new understandings of personal location within it. Researcher reflexivity, a longstanding hallmark of feminist methodologies, highlights the way in which current understandings of the social constitute the interview which at the same time offers the possibility for new versions of the social and ourselves within it. The researcher is required to reflect critically on theoretical as well as methodological positioning in the social interchanges of the interview. Consciousness about the interview demands researcher self-knowledge with respect to views of the social and the way this theoretical position constructs the interview (and the participants) in social action.

The researcher's disposition towards the interview is constructed, either explicitly or tacitly, through their theoretical and methodological position based on views of the social. As indicated by the discussion so far, a notion of power is significant even when the approach to the interview, for example, as 'resource' (information), does not explicitly address this. In an individuated view of the social there is little regard for the influence of the wider social-cultural milieu on individual position and the words uttered by the respondent in the interview are seen as uniquely the product of their individual cognition or affect. Examples of this perspective may be found in dominant psychological perspectives, which focus on individualized accounts in the interview. As we described in Chapter 2, more socially located approaches offer two alternative theories of power; possessive or discursive. For structuralists, for example, adherents of forms of neo-Marxism, operating with a possessive notion of power, respondent accounts are manifestations of deeper structures of inequality, internalized and determined by wider social structures (Lukes, 1986). Emancipatory approaches are included here as they invoke hierarchical notions of the social and use praxis-oriented research to accomplish political aims for social change towards greater social equality. Despite (or because of) the apparent magnanimity, the problems of position in this approach inscribe a social distinction between those doing the emancipating and those being emancipated. Clearly social position and privilege are implicit if not explicit in these emancipatory efforts. This point was highlighted in black feminists' resistance to some second-wave feminist positioning and representation especially in its homogenizing tendency (Elsworth, 1989; Mohanty, 1991; Smith, 1991). Notwithstanding critique, Enlightenment ideals support a strong tradition in social science research especially for those whose interests are in change for greater equity.

However, with the loss of faith in grand-narratives in the social sciences and the demise in many quarters of the Enlightenment project, there has been a broad move away from realist to constructivist views of social reality. For example, postmodernist positions use discursive notions of power, where language becomes significant in understanding subject positions. Rather than seeing language as referential, as a mirror on social reality in direct realist readings, there is a recognition of people as both products and producers of the discourses through which their subjectivity is constructed. Rather than seeing the self as caught in deterministic and hierarchical power structures, attention is focused on the way in which discourses (systems of knowledge and practices) subjectify individuals in localized contexts. The de-centred self is constructed through participation and positioning within multiple discourses, for example, of femininity, Englishness and being a social worker. In this discursive notion of power a universalized and essentialized subject is not tenable. The interview itself is also a situated practice in which power/knowledge flows through discursive exchanges in cultural and historical contexts. From this perspective the metaphor of interviewer as miner is defunct as both the interviewer and the interviewee constitute themselves in conversational activity (Kvale, 1996). To this extent the interview becomes a technology of the self (Gubrium and Holstein, 2002). As we suggested earlier, the focus of the research is on the text created by the articulating activity inside the line between the interviewee and interviewer. The discursive notion of power constructs the social interaction of the interview as productive of position in text. A more fluid and uncertain social with the possibility of multiple subject positions underscores the significance of language and heightens the importance for self-reflexivity by the researcher. Moreover, a crucial issue here is the identity of both the interviewer and the interviewee, not as one-dimensional and fixed entities but as multidimensional, shifting and above all recursively produced and producing discourse, not least the text of the interview itself.

Questions and design

So far we have explored how different dispositions to the social provide different frameworks for research. We have related methodological and theoretical perspectives to researcher identity and the kinds of texts produced in the interview. The process, however, begins with a focus on specific substantive concerns (for example, headteacher leadership, client relations of community nurses or privatization of prison services) that are articulated in the research questions. Through an iterative process that refers to a theoretical, methodological and substantive position a research design is developed. From this position, unstable as it may be, the interview, as part of this design, is structured with reference to the research questions. Although unstructured interviews might have a place in forms of therapy this is rare in social science. Alongside researcher interests, methodological and theoretical positions, however, the context and more practical concerns of access and time will influence an interview structure and focus. This complex and dynamic set of considerations provide a disposition to the interview that will be realized through the researcher action (practice) in access to the respondents and the way in which questions are raised (and developed) to address the substantive concerns.

In using interviews as resource, the framing questions tend to be tighter and more precise. Concerns about bias in the interview responses caution the interviewer to avoid extensive interaction and leading questions. In less formal forms of interview, on the other hand, efforts for a more relaxed exchange demand that the language (verbal and non-verbal) in the interview will require special attention. The phrasing of the questions is then highly important, as is the degree to which the interviewee (and interviewer) may diverge from the original question structures and sequence. A more flexible schedule offers the possibility of extending and deepening engagement in the interview. Whether this is a strategy to obtain more authentic respondent accounts to be read off uncritically against pre-existing theory or whether it provides a space for a more negotiated exchange in which the researcher position is open to critique, constant attention and interpretation is required of the interviewer. As Gubrium and Holstein (2002: 29) suggest, 'Artfulness derives from the interpretative work that is undertaken in mingling together what interviewers draw upon to make meaning in the interview process and what respondents themselves bring along'.

A more open disposition to the interview requires greater flexibility in the form and sequence of the questions, which may need to be revisited during the course of an interview. In short, this is much harder work that brings to mind another metaphor: the smooth movement of the swan on the water resulting from the intense effort and exertion unseen below water level. In more open and discursive formats, the form, pace and direction of the questions are more dynamic and influenced by the social engagement of each interview. Interestingly too, it might be just those 'leading questions', cautioned against in more rigid approaches, that become the substance of the interview. The interview then becomes a discursive text in which challenges to the alternative perspectives and positions are integral and explicit. In practical terms this might mean that further interviews may be required. Different dispositions then, will anticipate different questions and developmental possibilities in the interview, and this in turn will have implications for the larger research strategy expressed in its design.

Summary

In this chapter we have considered the use of interviews in research and highlighted the importance of researcher identity on the creation of text by talking to people. The collection of relevant data through interviews, however, may take a variety of forms, for example, sequential, group or life-history interviews which may also be combined with other methods in social research. For example, questionnaires may be used in an initial phase to identify interview respondents and/or observations may be used as specific examples of professional practice to be taken up in an interview. Not only does each of these methods need to be thought through in its own right, as described for interviews in this chapter, the connection and combination of the resultant texts also needs thought.

4

Knowing with numbers – questionnaires

Introduction

This is the second chapter concerned with asking people questions. Here
we deal specifically with questionnaires, which are strongly associated
with the production of quantitative data and statistical analysis. By connection, this social survey method, and others that produce numerical
texts such as structured observations, tend to be associated with approaches modelled on research in the natural sciences. In many research
manuals and research methods courses the questionnaire is contrasted
with the interview to typify quantitative and qualitative approaches
respectively. As our discussion of interviews in the previous chapter indicates, however, this distinction is not so clear-cut. Indeed, it is possible to
conduct an interview as an oral questionnaire and to produce similar
kinds of numerical texts. In this sense the association of the questionnaire
with quantitative and the interview with qualitative approaches to research is not exclusive. Moreover, this distinction may not be very helpful
to us in positioning ourselves as researchers, dealing with research texts
and understanding the production of knowledge through our social action
in research.

Quantification as scientific inquiry

Quantification is identified with positivism and the application of natural
scientific methods and dispositions in social research. The associated use
of specialized languages, symbols and forms of representation provides
strong indication of versions of positivist/realist methodological positioning. The language of measurement (validity and reliability), experimenta-
tion and control of variables as well as mathematical equations, tables

and graphs all signal the scientific endeavour of social research. As we contended in Chapter 2, the anticipation of data analysis has an important shaping influence on the broad research design and the specific methods used. The intention to quantify produces an emphasis on technique, procedure and precision to safeguard the prized capacity for definitive description (of the real social world) and/or to make inferences through correlation in probabilistic reasoning to allow generalization and hint of causation in worlds beyond the experiment or sample. The testing of theoretical propositions captured in hypothesis testing are added to an approach that is strongly reminiscent of the natural sciences and the possibility of objective social sciences enshrined in positivism. Consistent with this, researchers position themselves outside the social arena of the research.

Many texts and guides to quantitative data analysis present different ways in which to enumerate data and specific procedures for numerical manipulation and presentation (see, for example, Moser and Kalton, 1971; Munn and Drever, 1990; Oppenheim, 1992). The researcher adopts a space outside the arena of the research from where they look in (or often down!). Thus, the boundary between researcher and researched is clearly defined and together with tight procedural regulation in the application of methods, including validity measures, a space is provided for an objective view of social phenomena. The attempts at specification and close definition include the reductive organization and sub-division of the social. In this nomothetic approach the specification of procedures and careful delineation of particular elements of the field of investigation can provide opportunities to permit generalization and the discovery of laws about the social world. The rationalizing, linear and logical order of the recontextualization within the final report, the structure of which often mirrors reports of experiments, is similarly consistent with the appeals for legitimation to natural scientific methods. The widespread availability of computer technology and software packages has produced an even shriller concern for procedure in developing the research instrument (questionnaire, observation schedule or test) and its administration since mistakes can jeopardize its suitability for statistical treatment and the capacity for generalizing.

The production of numerical texts, however, need not include hundreds of respondents and the analysis may be restricted to provide description rather than as the basis for explanation (Tonkiss, 1998a). Enumerated data and statistical analyses may also be used as secondary data within research either in contextual description or in more critical accounts of the social in research. As we shall see, quantification in research is not deterministically related to specific ontologies or epistemologies (Bryman, 1988). Indeed, research with little or no numerical texts, for example, some evaluation studies in the public services or those with bullet-pointed policy recommendations may more strongly claim objectivity and assert correspondence of their research to the real world outside.

The questionnaire as scientific apparatus

A common justification of using questionnaires in social research relates to notions of efficiency. First, they are seen as time and cost effective as they provide the potential to include many more respondents than would be possible through interviews (Oppenheim, 1992). Second, along with other methods that provide quantitative data they are regarded as more efficient for the identification of underlying patterns than more qualitative and ethnographic methods (Bryman, 1988). Both these efficiency rationales point to the importance of the size of the respondent group as significant for the quantification of data produced through the questionnaire. This concern is echoed in statistical analysis in which the sample selection and size are important to the potential for generalizability of trends or correlations 'found' in the data. From the outset the quantification of data implies realist conceptions of the social. Usually the questionnaire is developed and administered with particular forms of quantification and numerical analysis in mind. In this sense it appears to have a different set of referents from in-depth interviewing in small-scale research.

The weight of scientific precision and procedure is borne in the production of the questionnaire itself. The one-off chance of data collection through questionnaire administration bears heavily upon its preparation in which several drafts and pilots are recommended (Munn and Drever, 1990; Cohen, Manion and Morison, 2000). The overall format, question structure and sequence have underlined importance that is heightened as the scale of the research is increased. Its accessibility to more respondents demands that it is easily understood and followed. Once the respondent group(s) have been specified, standardization is required to make data amenable to various kinds of mathematical manipulation. Uniformity and clarity are sought after and enshrined in the objective quality of the formatted written text as compared to the more subjective quality of speech in an interview. These are ensured by care with sample selection, the structure of the questionnaire text, conditions of administration and through various validity tests (Seale and Filmer, 1998). Caution and attention to detail characterize advice about questionnaire development as the means to produce data that will be analysed to reveal truths about the social world beyond itself.

The main purpose of most questionnaires is measurement and as such the researcher needs to be clear about their aims although these may be fairly broad and diverse or more tightly related to a hypothesis (Seale and Filmer, 1998). The focus of most advice about questionnaire construction relates to the various question types, their order and their potential for statistical analysis. The single point of contact with respondents through the questionnaire text places important emphasis on issues of communication especially in terms of clarity, transparency and the avoidance of ambiguity. This requires some reflection on language use and the assumed meaning of words – their transparency. In these terms, both the phrasing of individual questions and their location within a logical structure demand that the researcher divides and compartmentalizes their substantive interests which may be signified by specific side-headings that demarcate the questionnaire text. There is then a great deal of intellectual effort in advance of moving into the fieldwork phase as the questionnaire fixes both the forms of address/relation to the respondents, the tone and register, and a theoretical mapping of its substantive concerns. The fixing of the content and form of the research communication, however, needs not only a comprehensive, compartmentalized and logical coverage of the substantive issues, but it also has to sustain respondent interest.

Although ultimately arbitrary, high proportions of questionnaire completion by respondents in the sample are considered crucial to the power for generalization to the broader population. Issues on non-response are regarded as serious and require special handling. This dependence on the continued respondent cooperation presents another vital function of the question and instrument format (Oppenheim, 1992). Brevity, clarity and a variety of question/response types as well as specific incentives (for example, entry to a large cash prize lottery draw in consumer surveys, the free pen with charity questionnaires and the legislated sanction for non-completion of census questionnaires) are all recommended as ways of ensuring completed returns. Routing techniques (for example, if No, go to question 7) so that respondents answer only relevant questions, providing a space for free respondent comment and providing the return address and a stamped envelope are other techniques aimed at improving response rates.

The production of a good questionnaire is clearly a difficult task that requires juggling the pros and cons of different forms of questions and questionnaire formats to elicit valid responses from a high proportion of a defined sample. Questions of bias are of greatest concern and are raised as possible causes of data contamination. Within positivist approaches to social research, in which its products reflect the real world, it is the issue of bias that is persuasive in the choice of questionnaires rather than interviews. In either case, possible bias has to be addressed, so in addition to prestructuring at the conceptual level, drafting, piloting and redrafting are recommended in the process of questionnaire development. In this way researcher bias through, for example, leading questions may be minimized although the distorting influence of unreliable responses always remains of concern, 'Even children of below-average intelligence can give job descriptions that are very clear and free of humbug. . . . Wives, on the other hand, will sometimes introduce prestige distortion, describing the husband as an "engineer" when he is a garage mechanic, . . .' (Oppenheim, 1992: 133).

In some research, triangulation through mixed method design is devised to deal with respondent 'unreliability'. The constant problem of the 'contaminating' human influence (either researcher or researched) has led to the development of processes of question and questionnaire validation, also through statistical means, that make it a complex and time-consuming method to use effectively with scientific precision. The rewards, however, are great – we can all appreciate the power (and confidence) in being able to state '73% of . . .' or 'only 11.39% . . .'. The efforts to get to the truth and minimize bias and distortion are articulated once again by Oppenheim in his comprehensive text about questionnaire design,

> The function of a question in an interview schedule or questionnaire is to elicit a particular communication. We hope that our respondents have certain information, ideas or attitudes on the subject of our enquiry, and we want to get these from them with the minimum of distortion. If it were possible to do this without asking them any questions and without the respondent having to 'respond' that would be much better, ... Would that there were ways of looking into the mind of our respondents without having to ask them any questions at all!
>
> (Oppenheim, 1992: 121)

Just as in the natural sciences, a strong dividing line is invoked between the researcher and the researched, the scientist and the objects of investigation. The intention, whether through questionnaire or interview (or both) is for the researcher to excavate the contents of the respondent's mind. This reflects a positivist stance, the researcher as miner, in which the information held by the respondent will be extracted, numerically treated and later recontextualized in the research report by the socially and politically neutral researcher to produce accounts of the real social world beyond the scene of the data collection. This front loading in production of quantitative data through questionnaire research has led some to refer to the process of analysis as simply improving the organization of the information (Munn and Drever, 1981) and interpretation as a matter of common sense (Moser and Kalton, 1971).

Constructing the respondent/reader

In previous chapters we have discussed how, over time, dissatisfaction has been expressed with the application of scientific models to social research. From constructivist perspectives the distancing of the researcher, as a social actor, from the social context of the research and specifically from the respondents, provides an inadequate basis for researching social life. In contradistinction to positivist researchers, efforts to erase the hand/mind of the researcher from the method of investigation are highlighted as disingenuous and confounding. The form of the questionnaire demands questions, amenable to enumeration, fixed in advance to address the sub-divided substantive concerns in cognizance of the range of individual responses. Thus the questionnaire text is influenced by the researcher's theoretical and social position, substantive interests and biography, even though these elements of researcher identity may be hidden behind the apparent objectivity of the text. While a positivist position suggests that if respondents complete a questionnaire with an imagined person or organization behind the questions, it may be a source of bias to be eliminated where possible (Oppenheim, 1992), constructivists would see bias as inevitable and therefore incapable of elimination.

The distancing of the researcher from the researched is a particular concern for researchers conscious of the workings of power in society. For post-positivist researchers, the claims to neutrality and objectivity in positivist social research are 'really' a claim to power in which interaction with the researched is circumscribed by both the form and content of the questionnaire. It is evidently a 'readerly' text in which the researcher position is encoded through the referential use of language within the persuasive scientific genre that depoliticizes, naturalizes and neutralizes researcher power (O'Connell Davidson and Layder, 1994). Compared to the oral questions of an interview, the written text of the questionnaire, aided by the explicit structuring, has a more objective quality, which conceals its author through the literary inscription of facticity (Latour and Woolgar, 1979; Ricoeur, 1981; Smith, 1990). Claims for objectivity exclude the personal and emotional, which together with the enumeration of experience deny the (inter) subjectivity of researcher and researched. Even when questionnaires are attempting to establish the respondents' emotional reaction to an event or phenomenon, this is objectified. Moreover, any indication of the emotional response to the questionnaire is very rarely sought.

Unlike the dynamic synchronous intersubjectivity of an interview, the severely circumscribed interaction in distant questionnaire administration and completion deny the researcher the opportunities to engage or observe (and convey) non-verbal cues, alter questions or change their interpretations during the data collection process. The strictures of the pre-structured text do not allow negotiation, clarification or the influence of the respondent outside the questionnaire frame. In the process of questionnaire development, the reader/respondent position is constructed and frozen such that concern about language level, question types (routed or staged) and the range of response categories refer to an implicit idealized respondent/reader (Scott, 1996; Back, 1998; Czarniawska, 2004). In the same vein Dowling (1998) used a semiotic analysis (which followed a content analysis using enumeration), to explore the ways in which 'ability' specific mathematics texts construct and position their readers, the students, within differentiated mathematics ability groups. These approaches to text may be contrasted with the referential use of language assumed in advice about questionnaire construction. The more technical approaches to the questionnaire and the fear of non-response, especially in large surveys, drives a concern for simplicity and transparency of language in an unmediated naturalized text that points away from the author and the textual production of the respondents.

In more specific ways, through standardization, the questionnaire achieves a uniformity, difficult to sustain in interviews, that also instantiates a coercive conformity (Stronach and MacLure, 1997). There is an implied consensuality in which fixed choice and closed questions provide the limits of valid responses with little room for dissent. Compliant responses are then a form of collusion in the researcher's gaze on social life. Although some space may be afforded to the respondent to offer an opinion or counter argument through the introduction of open-ended questions, the addition of an open response category (Other – please specify) and/or the catch-all open question at the end of the questionnaire, 'Is there anything you would like to add about this issue?', the containment of the respondent remains problematic. In the same vein, the quantification of attitudes, opinions and dispositions in 3-, 5- or 7-point Likert scale questions, for example, of agreement and disagreement, are still structuring devices which, although lending themselves to quantification, are mathematically suspect. The approximation of the affective to a linear numerical scale in a self-completion questionnaire is difficult to justify. It raises the question of meaning when scaled numbers are allocated to response categories of 'agree', 'strongly agree', 'not sure' or 'strongly disagree'. Although it has been asserted that quantitative methods can be used to reveal meanings (Bryman, 1988; Hammersley, 1992), the problem for the constructivist researcher relates to the tendency for these methods to deal with the 'what' of social phenomena rather than the 'why' in a 'factual' way that denies its (the researcher's) own power in the (re) construction of accounts of the social world. The values and position of the researcher are captured, solidified and concealed within the questionnaire text.

For constructivist and emancipatory research the prescribed forms of researcher–researched interaction in the questionnaire are problematic as they neither explicitly raise power relations nor offer opportunities to ameliorate their effects in the research process. The imposed consensus and circumscription of legitimate respondent texts offers limited space for alternative perspectives or a more intersubjective interaction. The completed returns leave the researcher with a written text that is most amenable to enumeration and from which opportunities for reflexivity are effectively banished (Usher, 1996). In the writing of a questionnaire the researcher has explicitly constructed the field and the respondents, which together with the quantification of data appear to reflect realities rather than the power processes in their construction. For emancipatory researchers in particular, the acknowledged presence of the researcher is crucial to knowledge production and legitimation.

Theoretical structuring

For many feminist researchers the separation of the research process (topic) from the data outcomes (resource) is itself distorting in research (see, for example, Stanley and Wise, 1990). The unacknowledged author and authority of scientific and positivist research has been a central point in feminist critique (Harding, 1986; Tonkiss, 1998b). For other constructivist researchers too, it is the segmentation of the substantive field in addition to the ossification of forms of researcher–researched interaction that is problematic in the questionnaire and other forms of quantification. The questionnaire fixes the conceptual structure of the substantive field and the preparation of questions requires the researcher to reduce and compartmentalize the theoretical terrain. Although mitigated by the broader research community, this structuring will depend upon personal biography, the researcher's view of the social and theoretical field and it is likely to include historical social categories, for example, of social class, gender and ethnicity. The use of categories over time takes on an independence and a reciprocal correspondence in social reality (Butler, 1990). Such sustained and enduring categorizations have particular force (Smith, 1990), they are important in statistical analysis and in monitoring the social world. Comparisons are best achieved if categories, variables and indicators remain stable over time. Although this correspondence with an external reality can be persuasive (or is in positivist social science) it is at odds with a constructivist view. As Bourdieu (1987: 8) reminds us,

> Whether they have an occupational basis as in our societies or a genealogical basis as in pre-capitalist societies, groups are not found ready-made in reality. And even when they present themselves with this air of eternity that is the hallmark of naturalized history, they are always the product of a complex historical work of construction . . .

In the process of quantification, the imposition of structure through boundaried categories not only separates, for example, fact from value, theory from practice, researcher from researched, it also produces order and hierarchy that can be enumerated and statistically manipulated.

Quantification lends certainty to categories devised in the interests of dominant social groups. In this respect they may be regarded as forms of social surveillance and regulation (Briggs, 2002) that reflect the agencies and practices through which they are generated rather than the phenomena they describe (Slater, 1998a).

Forms of realist social science remain prevalent in research in public services. Here we find the powerful coalition of science and government in structuring the social world and the research agenda (Byrne, 2002) with demands for audits, inspections, evaluations, the production of league tables and quality measures. This is evident in the international scene with major international players such as UNESCO and the World Bank foregrounding various targets and indicators in measures of development and around which considerable research activity has been generated (Dunne, Leach et al., 2005). A political effort to governance/governmentality is evidenced through objective, scientistic research that is reductive of the population in social groups and concerned with prediction and control of social services through demonstrations of cause and effect. In this context the use of quantification, justified in terms of efficiency, may be used to sustain dominant constructions of the social world and the economic imperatives of global capitalism.

Many feminists and researchers with social justice interests have eschewed the use of questionnaires and quantification in research. The pre-fixed and one-off character of their use precludes reflexivity and reifies social relations through the imposition (and reproduction) of social categories and hierarchies that are the antithesis of their counter-hegemonic intentions in research. Efforts for social justice through research, however, are contradictorily implicated in the construction and reification of social relations in hegemonic interests. Attempts to trace back to the authors' positions and interests have realized critical accounts that highlight the ways in which social research (whether realist or interpretivist) (re) constructs categories of, for example, social class, gender and ethnicity (see, for example, Arber and Gilbert, 1992; Modood, 1992; Dunne and Johnston, 1994). Although categories might be described as contingent representations of the social, such imposition of structure, central even in interpretivist research, is similar to that in the questionnaire method and forms of quantification. Whether in the questionnaire or in the final report, research is a process of objectification that seeks order and coherence in the structure of its text (Usher and Scott, 1996). Even in research with emancipatory or social justice interests, the voices of the disempowered are ventriloquized through the interpretive schema of the powerful researcher (Czarniawska, 2004). Ironically the claims to give 'voice' are another form of authorial concealment heavily critiqued in positivism. So despite the explicit acknowledgement of the politics of research in constructivist and emancipatory approaches, it is through the act of writing (the questionnaire or report) that social categories are reified and come to represent a real world that encloses and solidifies subject positions. The assumption of social categories in research and social description is particularly problematic for researchers for whom the social relations of power are significant. As Butler (1990: 2) elucidates with respect to gender, 'Feminist critique ought also to understand how the category of "women", the subject of feminism, is produced and restrained by the very structures of power through which emancipation is sought'.

Despite the distinction of researcher position around the politics of research and knowledge production, research as a social practice is vital to the making of social categories, divisions and boundaries (between groups of people and practices) that may be unreflexively recruited again and again in research. In cognizance of the rules of methodology, through the practice of research (including writing) the researcher imposes an order on the complexities of the social world within and beyond that social practice. In this respect the structuring of the substantive field in questionnaire preparation and/or the anticipation of data quantification is only one way of imposing an order. In using other methods this order may be less explicit at the point of data collection, but the researcher must engage in this ordering at some point in the process whatever the approach used. It is with this realization that objections to the questionnaire and mixed method research designs dissipate, especially in research without the imperatives of a single disciplinary allegiance or heritage (for example, in education or social work).

The polarization of positivist and constructivist approaches to inquiry led to paradigm wars that asserted their incommensurate difference (Bryman, 1988). This war continues to be played out in the distinguishing descriptions of qualitative and quantitative research and remains an organizational feature of many research training programmes. The argument for incommensurability may be sustainable at the extremes; however, elsewhere points of contact are possible. For some researchers who predominantly use qualitative methods, enumeration can be enlisted to indicate the strength or contextual relevance of their findings (Hammersley, 1992; Silverman, 1993). Here qualitative data are quantified through an explicit structured interpretation, which seeks similarities in data and codes responses accordingly. This produces an inevitable loss of detail and has the effect of reducing the complexity of the data, but it also makes responses available to statistical methods. Qualitative empiricism is also possible. The move out of objective social science positions to constructivism, however, introduces a more contingent view of the social that implies that categories/representations produced through research are socially and historically located and subject to change. One can argue that a problem with closed category questionnaire-based research from this perspective is precisely that the categories are fixed and not subject to change. The production of categories through coding of open responses mitigates this somewhat and it may be argued that through the process of coding the researcher enters into some sort of dialogue with the data and vicariously therefore with the respondents. Although, the degree to which this argument might convincingly counter the constructivist reservations about questionnaires might depend on the degree to which the researcher is able to engage the reader of the research report in a reflexive account of the process of categorization, an issue that is taken up in Chapter 6.

Reflexivity can also be developed in 'mixed method' research, which combines quantitative and qualitative approaches. The idea of triangulation (in this case 'methodological triangulation') has often been used to suggest that by using different methods the researcher can compare results to lend validity to research. The analogy is that like the converging lines of the surveyor, which enable the accurate description of a geographical position so the different methods will meet to provide a surer idea of the truth in a social arena. This image is obviously laden with realist assumptions. However, it is possible to change the analogy slightly so that instead of the expectation of converging lines we may return to the idea of planes of vision, which do not meet but leave a discursive space for us to explore reflexively (see Brown and Jones (2001) for a similar approach to 'pedagogy').

These counters to the universalizing tendency of positivism can be seen as one way of rescuing the questionnaire and other forms of quantification from more determinist readings of the social. Another rather paradoxical possibility is that for many emancipatory researchers and critical theorists with interests in highlighting the contingent nature of social categories and changing the existing inequitable dispensation, engagement in and with quantitative/statistical methods, data and research reports would seem imperative (Jayaratne and Stewart, 1991; Dunne, 1996). Through this they seek to produce alternative accounts of the social world that counter the powerful coalition of science and government.

Identification of a method with a specific research position may often seem warranted but it runs the risk of making superficial assumptions. At this level the position is as blurred for questionnaires as it is for interviews (Guba and Lincoln, 1994; see also Chapter 3). Researcher interests, conception of the social, relation to the research community, disposition to research data and the eventual recontextualization within the research report are of greater significance (Scott, 1996; Usher, 1996). It is in this light that mixed method research designs try to produce a synergy of quantitative and qualitative methods and analysis, for example, in identification of specific respondent groups. After all statistics have been used in accounts of the social by conservatives, reformers and radicals (Tonkiss, 1998a).

Deconstruction using questionnaires

Given some of the overlapping problematics, it is difficult therefore to differentiate researcher position through reference only to method. Post-positivist research has played a critical part in blowing the cover of scientific neutrality by making explicit the politics of the research process and knowledge production. Nevertheless, as with the qualitative/quantitative binary, the opposition between positivism and constructivism is neither exclusive nor complete. Both require researcher interpretation that seeks legitimation through methodology. This dependence on methodology has tended to produce rather technicist accounts of research as a 'natural' rather than constructed social practice that contributes to a vernacular positivism (Usher and Scott, 1996). Although making explicit a critique of the power and authority of science, it is through this opposition that they are connected. The reification of dominant social categories and a possessive notion of power solidify contingent relations that structure the social within which researchers and respondents (and the rest of the world) are hierarchically located. For constructivist researchers this produces a rather ambivalent disposition towards quantification and the use of questionnaires. This strikes at the heart of the contradictory position of emancipatory research that tries to sustain the Enlightenment project and yet critique the scientific rationality of positivism and empiricism that it spawned. Researcher views of the social world and the research process within it recursively structure the production and recontextualization of respondent accounts. That the questionnaire explicitly parades the interpretive power of the researcher as process in research, is problematic for constructivist and emancipatory researchers in their interests in the workings of power in society.

However, the linguistic turn offers some relief for research in the social science. With a focus on language, a discursive notion of power undoes the modernist possibility of reflecting the 'real' in language (Smith, 1990). In a widely acclaimed text on gender Butler (1990) describes how language constitutes the 'imaginable and realizable gender configurations within culture'. Highlighting social action and practices, she continues with an explanation of how the gender category has been naturalized and how it might be deconstructed,

> Gender is the repeated stylization of the body, a set of repeated acts within a highly rigid regulatory frame that congeal over time to produce the appearance of substance, a natural sort of being. A political genealogy of gender ontologies, if it is successful, will deconstruct the substantive appearance of gender into its constitutive acts and locate and account for those acts within the compulsory frames set by various forces that police the social appearance of gender. To expose the

contingent acts that create the appearance of naturalistic necessity, a move which has been part of cultural critique at least since Marx, is a task that now takes on the added burden of showing how the very notion of the subject, intelligible only through its appearance as gendered, admits of possibilities that have been forcibly foreclosed by various reifications of gender that have constituted its contingent ontologies.

Butler, 1990: 33

The production of power/knowledge through language practices casts positivist and interpretivist social science as competing discourse. In the same way the questionnaire text constructs and encloses a conceptual and discursive boundary. The certainty and presence in the written text provide the claims to authenticity and the focus for deconstruction. Rather than a paranoid concern with non-response or spoilt papers as detracting from the capacity to generalize a truth or with its possibilities for gaining access to alternative accounts of social structure and experience, it is these limitations that provoke interest. Respondent transgressions in filling out the questionnaire are the rejection of particular discourses and/or positions imposed through it that point to its incompleteness, its (the researcher's) omissions – the absences.

In reference to postcolonial theory and the work of Bhabha (1994), Stronach and MacLure (1997) describe how the native in refusing to return the colonial gaze fails to authenticate the narrative of colonial identity. This is an act of transgression and a rejection of a certain reciprocal discursive production of the subject. Within the questionnaire too, the breaking of the coercive consensuality written into its text provides productive possibilities with opportunities to be reflexive about the theoretical and relational construction of the field and respondents (both of which refer to a world outside the research) and/or to look for discontinuities and absences in transgressions of its form. Such denaturalization exposes the cultural arbitrary (Slater, 1998b).

In this vein, Stronach and MacLure (1997) discuss an inventive form of questionnaire in an evaluation study, though this was in part driven by the performative culture of much contract research. Respondents were asked to indicate agreement (✔) or disagreement (✗) within tracts of headed texts about the course being evaluated. Following this, substantial space was left for the respondents' comments or additions. This offered the opportunity for surface analysis that allowed enumeration through direct counting of '✔'s and '✗'s and through the coding and enumeration of the open qualitative comment. Then, moving beyond the usual treatment of questionnaire data, they analysed responses for ways in which they breached cultural conventions. Their analysis exposed attempts by respondents to engage in more informal, negotiated and holistic terms that pushed away the coercive consensus that typifies classical question-naire formats. Although this is not presented as a model this does suggest that the questionnaire as a method demonstrates the capacity to be used in a variety of approaches to research, recalling the argument above about triangulation. It also raises the usefulness of quantification in research and a freeing of the questionnaire from the methodological bars of previous association. The critical issue returns us to one of researcher identity, their construction of the field and the production of research texts. In this case this refers to the way the questionnaire text and the resultant numeric text are recontextualized in combination with texts from other methods. This might include the secondary analysis of statistics and other numerical texts which, depending on researcher position, might mean reading the author into the text, to expose interests, contingencies and claims to authority by exploring the textual strategies (including quantification and numerical textualization) and discursive practices that (re-)construct powerful representations of the social.

5

Being there – observation

Introduction

The title of this chapter highlights the naturalistic nature of observation as a research method. What the researcher does when observing is superficially no different from what they do in any other aspect of their social life. It is about being there while the action takes place, participating in activities to a greater or lesser extent, by watching, listening and sometimes by speaking, writing or drawing. However, there are important distinctions between everyday social participation and observation as research. Generally what we say and do is ephemeral, in that once said and done, it is as if gone. Although gaining experiences that one may then later reflect on may be part of everyday life, for the researcher it is more than this; it is the central purpose of being there. Indeed, we might go further and say that the essential purpose of the researcher's experience of the setting is to transform into text the experiences they have there. Reviewing the particular processes of textualization that take place in observational research is the substance of this chapter.

When I was doing my doctoral research, I was faced with a problem. Some of my richest data occurred in group interviews. When I tried to make use of these data in the thesis by quoting little snippets just as I did with one-to-one interviews, the complexity of the situation and the meanings that I could offer to the reader seemed to disappear. Reflecting on this, it became apparent that what I was interested in was not just what the individual interviewees said, but the way that they interacted with each other and with me. To ascribe meaning to the interviews, the lines of the tape-recorded transcripts were not enough; the space between the lines seemed significant too. Tape-recorded transcripts made much more sense when viewed in conjunction with the notes that I wrote afterwards about what I thought was going on and with later comments on the interviews by other participants. A statement of Bronwyn Davies who also used group interviews seemed significant to me:

> The interviews were, in an important sense, not separate from life as the children knew it; they were life, brought into the interview room from the classroom and the playground.
>
> Davies, 1982: 2

Although the focus of the data was specific events in the past or the participants' generalization based on repeated events, where as a researcher I was at least in some sense absent, in these group interviews I was present. My problem was therefore that I was thinking of interviews as interviews rather than recognizing that they were more like observations. The important thing for me as researcher was being there. Two stories were being recounted, the story of the incidents that the children were recollecting and the story of their interaction in the interview. My attempt at a practical solution to the problem was, like Davies, to report my data in two columns, where the interview transcript was accompanied by a second narrative taking place in a parallel column. It was, of course, only a partial solution, since the social, whether we are thinking of the incidents or the interviews, is necessarily a dynamic arena, which itself exists from moment to moment and the traces of it that we collect as researchers can never represent its 'reality'.

The same technique was later extended in work with Harry Torrance, where we were dealing with more obvious observational data. A column on the left contained the transcription and an italicized description (*cf.* stage directions) of what was happening, both derived from video tape recordings. A column on the right showed our commentary or interpretation as a further level of analysis (see Table 5.1). This technique enabled us to present a relatively long transcript in its entirety, which was needed for our fine-grained analysis (this is discussed in more detail in Chapter 7), and yet also to highlight incidents of interest as they occurred. Finally, below the columned section, was another level of interpretation and discussion of the incidents that had been recounted.

The illustration of the use of columns to report is partly about a solution to a practical problem, but it has strong theoretical implications and brings to the surface two important issues about observational data. First, the process of carrying out the observational research process is about dealing both simultaneously and in sequence with several different texts; second that the researcher is complicit in the production of each of these (indeed, the derivation of the word text from the Latin word for weaving underlines that it is always a fabrication). The text in the left-hand column was an attempt to 'capture' the action. The text on the right was indicating significance and justifying the editorial function of the selection that had been taking place in turning the action to data. The discussion below the

Table 5.1 Example of double-column presentation of observation data

T *OK* – so – you had three – you happy with that – did you – was there a lid put on the bottle Cs yeah T so what happened next – I've got three bottles now with warm water in – all the same height ~ *T repeats his three-fold gesture and then holds his index finger and thumb apart as if holding a small bottle.* Cs yeah T all the same bottle shapes ~ Cs yeah T so they're all – so it's *fair* is it ~ *T moves his left index finger abruptly from right to left parallel to the ground. The children nod.* T OK – who can tell me what happened next –	Another question to which T does not know the answer but by asking it he assigns significance to the issue. T is restructuring pupils' responses in order to attach significance to the control of variables. This leading question establishes a boundary between the idea of a 'fair test' and other aspects of the investigation. A typical 'framing move' followed by a very open elicitation – but one which is an invitation to bid, perhaps to keep the quiet pupils 'on their toes'.

Source: Torrance and Pryor 1998: 109

columns was more specifically about the communication of ideas to the reader of the research report.

When reporting this work, we used the idea of different, progressively higher, levels of inference. However, one can also think about these texts in terms of the way in which they were telling different kinds of stories. In grappling with this idea of multiple texts, Flick (2002) draws on Ricoeur's (1981b) interpretation of mimesis. This was originally a term used by the Ancient Greeks to denote the way that art imitates life, but was extended by Ricoeur to explain the way that humans make sense out of action. Flick (2002: 34) extends this further by focusing on the way that social scientists make sense out of action through research. He characterizes Ricoeur's three types of mimesis as:

- Mimesis 1: 'pre-understanding of what human action is', the process by which we are able to apprehend what is going on.
- Mimesis 2: the transformation or processing or configuration of action into text.
- Mimesis 3: the interpretation or transformation of the data as text into a report for an audience.

Mimesis in this sense is about the process of turning action into texts, which thus act as versions of the world; it is about the way that one moves from one text to another. Crucially it is also about mediation between the worlds of the subject, the researcher and the reader, and acknowledging the implication of all three of these 'characters' in the research process. As Flick says when describing the post-structuralist position:

> . . . texts are neither the world per se nor an objective representation of the parts of this world. Rather they result from the interests of those who produce the text as well as those who read it.
>
> Flick, 2002: 23

It is important to stress the cyclical nature of mimesis within Ricoeur's conceptualization. The three are not so much discrete stages as intertwined and should be seen as a unity (Verhesschen, 2003). Ricoeur's work is about textualization in as much as he shows that mimesis turns life into narrative, which then transforms action. Social actions encompass all three parts. In this book we have emphasized the process of doing observational research as a social action. In the rest of the chapter I use the image of this tripartite structure of textualization or narration to analyse the methodology of 'being there'. Mimesis 1 concerns processes that shape the way that the social situation is read by the actors in the social situation under study. Mimesis 2 is the process whereby this text is turned into a data set. Mimesis 3 takes place when the data are transformed into a research report. However, it is important to stress here and throughout this analysis that the idea of mimesis is essentially about synthesis of joining 'a world of the text' with 'the life-world of the reader' (Ricoeur, 1984: 160). In this sense, it can be connected to Giddens's (1993) idea of the double hermeneutic which we have mentioned before.

This may be a slightly unusual position to take, since this narrative approach is not one usually associated with observation but with interviews and life histories. However, the premise on which the chapter is based is no less logical for people involved in observed interaction than for those interacting through interviews. The premise is that because human existence is temporal, 'we come to know ourselves by discerning a plot that unifies the actions and events or our past with future actions . . . [which] . . . involves the cognitive operation of narrative structuring' (Polkinghorne, 1988: 149). The other possible objection is that observation is about dramas not narratives. However, the word mimesis is derived from Aristotle who was concerned as much with the dramatic as the epic. Plays and films also tell stories; they are textual, even though the words are put into the mouth of the character and the hand of the author/researcher is less visible.

This chapter will also draw out our theme of the centrality of the issue of the researcher's identity, arguing that doing observational research is about becoming a researcher or, as Lawrence Stenhouse (1975) maintained, teaching a definition of oneself to those one is researching.

Action in the field

The discussion so far in this chapter has emphasized the complexity of observation. This leads many people to say they dislike it as a research method and avoid it in favour of others. However, in many social research projects it is not the actual observation that is avoided so much as the acknowledgement that it has taken place and recognition that data have been produced. As pointed out in Chapter 3, it is impossible to conduct a face-to-face interview without noting things about the interviewee such as their dress and demeanour. If the interviewing context is their home ground, many other things will be not only be apparent but also will be seen as significant by the researcher. A trip to collect documentary data may also be an opportunity for observation and even the process of making contacts or negotiating permission to send out a survey may involve the researcher in observation.

All this relates especially to Mimesis 1, the process whereby the actions and interactions that are the subject of the research are produced. It is about recognizing an action as an action and as significant for the actors, not least the researcher.

There is a very wide continuum in the explicitness with which the observer is constructing the data. So, for example, when you set up a video camera which is left alone and allowed to run, especially when those it is directed on have no knowledge of its presence, there is often a feeling that the data are collected themselves, without the mediation of the researcher. At the other end of the spectrum is the participant observer who is an agent in the events under study and who transforms them into data through the medium of fieldnotes or a reflective journal. Even where there are no physical manifestations of the transformation into data and where production occurs *post hoc*, the thought of the textualizing of the experience is never likely to be far from the researcher's mind. Issues about what is the research focus as well as theories about what are its significant features and where they might be found, feed into decisions about what actions will potentially be visible. These inevitably raise questions about the researcher's identity. Thus, for example, Wong (1995) describes how in order to study in a naturalistic setting whether school students' explanations of natural phenomena were 'scientific', he took a job as a teacher. This presented dilemmas. For example, in a whole-class lesson, he found himself engaged a discussion with a student which was very relevant to his research:

I began to feel uneasy about continuing my line of questions with Toni. The rest of the class was clearly losing interest and I was running the risk of losing the focus of the lesson. However, this opportunity . . . might never present itself again.

Wong, 1995: 23

In this case Wong decided to continue with the line of questions at the expense of the naturalistic practice ('contaminating the data'). However, whether he had or not, it is an illustration of the way that as a researcher his thinking about it was shaped by his ultimate concern for creating an interesting research text.

In that example Wong was an obvious participant in the action. In work on observation a distinction is frequently made between participant and non-participant observation, often based on the notion that they form quite distinct, easily recognizable approaches. However, this has been seen as problematic for some time. For example, Gold (1958) proposed a four-part typology of observer roles ranging from complete participant, through participant-as-observer and observer-as-participant to complete observer. Spradley (1980) proposed a five-part system: non-participation, passive participation, moderate participation, active participation and complete participation.

At a common sense level these distinctions are sound. It seems obviously important to differentiate between, on the one hand, a practitioner researcher who is carrying out their normal job and generating data from notes taken after the event, and on the other, an observer who avoids speaking to research subjects, standing up and looking away whenever they make eye contact (King, 1978). However, there are dangers with both the binary system of participation and the four or five part distinctions. There is often an assumption that the degree of participation is the same as the extent to which the text in the first mimesis, that is the interactions of the actors in the context, is affected by the research. In any situation people act in a way that seems appropriate to the totality of the context. Their actions towards others are affected not just by their understandings of those they are overtly addressing, but by others whom they see as literally or virtually present – their audience, of whom the researcher is one. An active participant is overtly shaping the text that is produced and so is seen as part of the action. An observer who is not heard by a tape recorder or seen by a camera may be outside the formal text, but their presence nonetheless has an effect. It only needs to affect one of the actors for it to feed into the interaction and influence even the text produced by those who are unaware or unaffected directly by the presence of the observer.

Thus, it is impossible to remove the effect of the researcher's presence, and the nature of the effect will be influenced by the identity of the researcher. Who you think you are as a researcher will be important. Just as important, probably more so, will be who they (the other participants) think you are. It is therefore not so much the actions of those that appear to be the subject of the research which comprise the first text, but the interaction of these actions with the researcher.

This inevitability of the observer affecting the research is problematic; but rather than being a reason to rule out observation as 'biased' it means that the issue of identity becomes a very central one in the process of planning research. It means that identity becomes something that one should carefully think about as a researcher and monitor in such a way as to produce the sort of data that one desires. Seen from this angle one is always and inevitably biasing the research, so lack of bias cannot be the determinant of the research quality. Instead, what becomes important is an aspect of reflexivity, that identity issues are seen as problematic and discussed in the research report.

This argument is obviously situated in a discourse that questions the realist and positivist assumptions, which held sway until the last quarter of the twentieth century. It would seem therefore to be articulating a recent preoccupation of social research. In fact this is not really so since at every period field researchers have needed to provide some sort of reason for their presence to the people in the situation. Within ethnographic research it is called 'passing' and has been a central concern, though not necessarily one given great prominence in their accounts of the research.

I shall give a further personal example to illustrate how a researcher might consciously influence their own positioning and their positioning by other participants. The research was aiming to produce an account of how children aged four to seven understood issues of quality in their school work. When an adult researcher is interested in gaining the perspective of children they cannot pass as a child, so some other role has to be assumed. Moreover, as Fine and Glassner (1979) note, children are sensitive to people who pretend to be what they are not. Mandell (1988) approached the issue by playing alongside children in a kindergarten, adopting what she called a 'least-adult' role, whose salient feature was to downplay the power differential between herself and the children. She presents evidence for this having been a successful way of working with pre-school children. However, she found it impossible to sustain when the children were doing work directed by the teacher. With the slightly older children that I was interested in, directed work was the norm so pretending to do it alongside them seemed pointless. Some other role, recognizably adult, but deliberately understating the aura of authority associated with adults in school settings appeared appropriate. The point of such positioning was to lower the stakes as far as possible in what the children said to me as researcher. Pupils' interaction with teachers in schools is such that they are often looking for the right answer (Edwards, 1992).

My policy was to be a participant in the classroom, but with a deliberately obscure role. I did not want the children to see me as an authority figure and certainly not as a teacher, since interviews with the teacher were designed to yield an insight into that perspective. I asked to be introduced, and was known by, my first name, in contrast to all the other adults who were called by their title and family name. Children were told that I was 'from the University' but few seemed to know what this meant and I was hardly ever asked about it. They were more interested in my personal life: how old my son was, whether I supported a football team. Rather than discouraging this sort of conversation, I was happy to respond to it and to talk to children about subjects that they initiated as well as those that derived from the work, partly so that our interaction followed the pattern of conversation rather than that of teaching and learning, and partly because they might initiate speech on issues that might be pertinent to me. To this end, rather than using questions all the time, I also tried to use my own experience as a way of beginning conversation, a strategy which has the effect of handing some of the control over the discourse to the child (Wood, 1992).

Rather than being a least-adult, I was aiming to be a least-teacher. The degree to which I was successful is debatable. Children certainly committed offences against school rules in my presence in ways that they did not in front of members of the school staff. What I did achieve was a different version from that which the teachers gave me and which allowed me therefore to construct a richer account than I otherwise would have. I would not claim that their conversations were natural or that they expressed their 'real' opinions. However, their interpretation of my identity enabled them to read my presence in the situations I was focusing on; this produced a form of text that was interesting to me and, it seemed, more pertinent to my research questions. The issue of my participation was therefore more complex than finding a place on Gold's or Spradley's scale and indeed it varied from time to time.

The discussion above touched on the idea that the researcher's identity, through their involvement in issues of research focus and theories about the significant features of a situation, impacts on the research even when the subjects might be unaware of the research taking place. This raises the question of the extent to which research might be covert. A wide ethical divide is often erected between covert observation and observation where the permission of all the actors has been obtained: the former is seen as immoral, the latter acceptable. However, in practice the issues are not so clear cut as they seem. Covert research is sometimes not only a good idea, but is the only type of research available, especially where the practices being researched are illegal. This point has been debated in many places, a recent example being Herrera (2003), who unusually finds the most problematic aspect of covert research the fact that its anonymity makes it susceptible neither to verification by participants nor by peers. However, completely covert research is unusual for a range of practical as well as ethical or epistemological reasons. What is more likely, are situations where the issues and the identities of the actors are blurred.

Ethical guidelines often talk of informed consent, but when one comes to negotiate this, it is not always simple. When a researcher says what the research is about, what they are focusing on, they may be only telling half the story. In a project about gender issues in groupwork, I was very open with the children about the groupwork issues in the fieldwork primary school; indeed I involved them closely in the research, collaborating with them in designing ways of recording their impressions of interaction following group activity. They even became more intimately involved in data collection by working with me to produce an observation schedule so that they could observe each other working. My observation involved not just my watching and listening to the children as they interacted with their peers, but also conversations that we had about this interaction. At the start I mostly initiated these conversations, but later the children themselves started them just as often. For them, gender was an emerging issue and one that we discussed a great deal, so they knew it was relevant and important to me. However, what I never did was to tell them that gender issues were the filter that I was using to make sense of the groupwork interactions. My data collection was about children's interaction in groupwork, but my research was about gender, because theories of gender led the way that I analysed those data, and ultimately the story they told would be about gender. In other words, I told them the subject of my research, but not the theoretical resources I was bringing forward to make sense of the data.

When I was making my mind up about how to proceed, I wanted to avoid influencing the actions in the classroom unduly by sensitizing the children to gender issues. I was concerned about the naturalness of what was reported, with the idea that these 'natural' data would be somehow better and more authentic. From my current methodological perspective 15 years later I see it slightly differently. Now, I question the naturalness of what was going on anyway. What I was doing was asserting my own desire to decide what were gender issues and to select those events that I deemed significant. Had I said that my research was about gender, the way I would have influenced the interactions between the children would have been such that a different, narrower filter would have been applied to the interactions I witnessed and to those that the children reported to me as having taken place in my absence. In other words, by telling them that I was interested in gender, I would have been relying more strongly on their conceptualization of gender. I would have been asking them, albeit tacitly, to construct a gender narrative whose emplotment, the mimesis 2, they would have accomplished themselves. This might then have excluded elements of later interest to me. My theoretical intention of opening up the idea of gender relations by reading them into the subsequent data set and generating a more interesting (or 'original') research report would thus have been much more difficult.

It is interesting to note that this argument began with mimesis 1, the children's reading of the situations in which they were acting, but it implicated the other two levels, an idea that I shall return to later.

In the case above I was deliberately not telling the whole story. However, even when one is at pains to do so, the meaning of informed consent is problematic. Many research projects explicitly concern themselves with an undertheorized idea whose terminology may occur quite frequently in the discourse of both practitioners and policy makers, but where their understandings are at a taken-for-granted level rather than being explicit. Lack of consensus or clarity makes the research topical. Doing observation in schools, I have frequently found teachers surprised by the choice of incidents I considered relevant.

This is in part a cultural issue where the university-based social scientist might be seen as a member of a distinct cultural group. However, even then there may be problems. People do not necessarily think through the implications of what they are doing. Recently conducting research with doctoral students, I gave them a form to sign, spelling out what we were proposing to use as data. Nevertheless, one of the participants, a university social science lecturer, expressed surprise later on about what we were analysing. When researching in contexts where one is more clearly a cultural outsider, there are even more opportunities for the research rationale and therefore the meanings that might be attached to the data, to be understood differently by different parties, even though every effort is made to have a dialogue about this. This was certainly the case in work in rural Africa where people were very happy to accede to requests to be observed and interviewed. However, as we debated with them issues about communication and cultural exchange through visual media that were in part the focus of the work, it became clear that there were problems. No matter how hard we tried, it was very difficult for people living in a situation where communication media were so different from those of the town and the richer countries, to understand the implications of what was going on (Pryor and Ampiah, 2003).

This means that one cannot assume that even at the level of mimesis 1, the first text, that; people's readings of what is going on are natural or authentic, the issue will remain complex and problematic. We have emphasized the salience of the researcher's presence, but even within research contexts where this is so, there may be moments when they become 'absent'. Cheryl Tilse, interviewed in Darlington and Scott (2002), showed that even though she made a real effort to flag up her presence as a researcher, inevitably over time she 'disappeared'. People frequently noticed her again suddenly and said 'Ah, so you're still here'. When viewing research videotapes one often sees people who have seemingly ignored the camera for several hours, suddenly look up at it and gaze back. Observation over time also involves a change in the relationship with the participants.

In summary, even before the actions become data, they are then affected by the identity of the researcher as it impacts on the social space of the other participants (mimesis 1). However, rather than there being a 'best practice' that can reduce this effect or create a more authentic situation, we are suggesting that you need to think carefully about the issue within each particular context, to problematize it and use it to guide your actions. In this you will be guided by what you are interested in and therefore want as data and how you will give the actions meaning (mimesis 2). Later, when the actions are further transformed (or recontextualized) into a research report, the problems can be discussed (mimesis 3). Atkinson and Hammersley's (1998) dimensions of variation, which they suggest as alternatives to the participant/non-participant dichotomy are a useful framework for such a discussion:

Acquaintance	The extent to which researcher is acquainted with the subjects (participants)
Knowledge of research	Subjects' knowledge of what the research is about
Research activities	Activities in the field and the way that these cause subjects to position the researcher
Insider–outsider	The extent to which researcher positions her/himself as outsider–insider.

From action to data

As we have seen, participants read the social situation, and produce within it a text composed of their actions, words and expressions. However, as far as the researcher is concerned what arises is a virtual and potential rather than a usable text. Except over a very short time, the quantity and complexity of social interaction are such that they are not amenable to being frozen and captured. In order to turn these potentialities into the actuality of a data set, a mimetic process is required.

From a common sense position, there are many attractions to observation as a research method. As human beings we often link knowledge to direct experience – 'I know, because I was there'. Learning things from other people involves second-hand knowledge and one learns quickly that other people are not always reliable. Common sense here maps fairly straightforwardly onto the theoretical position of empiricism. Usher

(1996: 26), for example, in listing the 'leading assumptions of the positivist/empiricist research tradition' puts at the very top 'observation is value-neutral and atheoretical.' The central precept of empiricism is that all knowledge is ultimately derived from experience via the senses, rather than from theory. Bulmer (1982: 31 cited by May, 2001: 11) takes this one stage further by characterizing empiricism by the proposition that 'the facts speak for themselves'. Throughout this book the empiricist position is problematized. Rather than rehearse the ontological argument addressed in Chapter 2 about whether facts can have an existence separate from the observer, in thinking about observation the most salient questions are more practically oriented – which facts are brought into the frame and how do they 'speak'?

This empiricist position is reflected in a great number of metaphors that are used to describe the compilation of a data. The two verbs most often used are 'gather' and 'collect', suggesting that data are like wild fruits or flowers, which the researcher finds in the field and thus have an existence independent of the researcher. A more apt botanical metaphor, which chimes better with our previous analysis, might take place in a garden rather than in the wild. Here, when the researcher goes looking for data, they see only the fruits or flowers that they have grown themselves, whose colour and variety they have already had a hand in. However, even in the wild, before anything can be gathered, it has to be noticed and if abundant then some selection may need to take place. Using a different metaphor of assemblage or collection Denzin and Lincoln point out that the

> researcher-as-bricoleur is always already in the empirical world of experience. Still this world is confronted, in part through the lens that the scholar's paradigm, or interpretive perspective, provides.
>
> Denzin and Lincoln, 1998a: xi

Thus the issue of what is noteworthy inevitably depends on the observer. The personal and professional social experience of the observer give rise inevitably to a mental image of what is being looked for. Bourdieu, for example, talks about referring to a series of mental photographs (Bourdieu and Wacquant, 1992). However, cultural issues are also crucial. A major preoccupation of ethnographers researching other cultures has been to be able to see beyond the exotic to the aspects of life that are important to those they are studying ('making the strange familiar'). More recently, with the advent of insider ethnographies, the challenge has been in the opposite direction, to notice what may be important but is taken for granted – 'making the familiar strange' (Spindler and Spindler, 1982). Indeed this latter problem was identified as a primary concern in social research by Garfinkel (1967) and led to his development of breaching experiments whereby the researcher deliberately set out to disrupt the normal patterns of social practice in order to bring them into sharper relief.

Looked at from this perspective the prospect of capturing observations as neutral, objective data becomes an unattainable goal. The very process of observing becomes loaded with the theories of the world that researchers carry with them. The researcher will have formulated both planned research questions and possibly others that are more tacit, which serve to shape what they see as important. This in part constitutes a theoretical, that is, a methodological position. In other words, what kind of research you have planned on doing shapes the data that you will get, as also does what kind of researcher you consider yourself to be.

Indeed the idea of a fact becomes rather slippery and problematic. Barthes (1981) claims that facts in this sense are tautologies since what is noted is derived from the notable, but the notable is only what is worth recalling, that is, what is worthy of being noted. Elsewhere when talking of historical research he states that:

> The historian is not so much a collector of facts as a collector and relater of signifiers; that is to say, he organizes them with the purpose of establishing positive meaning and filling the vacuum of pure, meaningless series.
>
> Barthes, 1982: xx

The notion of organization to fill in a vacuum brings us back to the idea of mimesis as narration. Some definitions of narrative emphasize the importance of the sequencing. For example, Rapport and Overing (2000: 283) define a narrative account as 'a sequence of two or more units of information . . . such that if the order were changed the meaning of the account would alter'. The implication of the Barthes quotation is that, in order to be perceived as a unit of information, the researcher must already be able to fit it into a meaningful sequence. The observer may not be aiming for a data set that is coherent as a whole. Nevertheless, the selection of things to note implies that fitting data in demands that they be units of meaning, not just units of information, at least in the eyes of the researcher.

In Ricoeur's terms meaning is invested in the data by the researcher through a process of 'emplotment', which includes above all giving a sequence to what is observed so that it begins to tell a story. The observer is thus reading the situation and creating a text by selecting and sequencing.

This argument may appear to rest on the technology used for recording the data, the practical transformation of action into data. It is fairly uncontentious when observation is of overt participation by the researcher and the data are notes recollected in tranquility; also when the researcher is making unstructured fieldnotes. However, the involvement of the researcher may be less immediately obvious when the data consist of electronic recordings. The notion of the researcher as constructor of the text was brought home to me when doing a long period of classroom observation based on video recording. The video camera was left running on a group of children. However, decisions made before filming – which group to point the camera at, the width of focus, where to place the microphone – made a great impact on the usability of the videotape as data. It might be argued that everything that was recorded was part of the data set, but that was of little consequence to me when faced with a large box of tapes to review. The only actions that could be used were those that could be put together to make narratives. When occasionally people might drift into view it was only when they remained for long enough or what they did could be coordinated with others that their actions became meaningful and became in any practical sense data. In fact, the unit of analysis for this project was 'assessment events'. Although we reviewed the whole set of tapes and coded each section, the operative codes were about the level of interest or relevance of the data and therefore only a relatively small number of incidents went forward to be transcribed (therefore made into more literal text) and further analysed.

So far this argument has ignored structured observation, whereby the observer is using a schedule to note down specific features of the situation. It is often advanced as an objective method because it is possible to generate virtually identical accounts with different observers and to demonstrate this statistically. However, an observation schedule is even more reductive than unstructured observation. The schedule is a way of deciding in advance what is noteworthy and especially of excluding everything that does not come under its headings and so subjectivity inheres in the design of the schedule and in the decision to use it (*cf.* the argument in the previous chapter). The data produced may not be so overtly narrative in form, indeed one of the perceived advantages of this approach is that it results in data that are clear-cut (usually they are numbers) and therefore removed from the narrative of the context to which they relate. However, we would argue that observation schedules relate to abstract or idealized narratives of what should or could be going on in the interaction. The story will, of course, re-emerge in the final report usually in a generalized way – 'this is typically what happens'.

Another technology that was referred to above is the writing of unstructured fieldnotes. Advice as to how to write these is usually couched in terms of making them as objective as possible. Given that our argument has been about the impossibility of objectivity in research observation, this raises questions about the nature of this text. Our position is that in writing fieldnotes, one should still aim for as low a level of inference as is consistent with producing a meaningful text, but this is not about making them as 'objective' as possible. Rather it is about creating as open a story as possible, one that is least constraining to further reinterpretation. The transformation of action into data is necessarily reductionist, but to reduce too far is to preclude further meaning making. It is not so much one coherent narrative that is produced as many. In other words, one is looking forward to further restructuring to tell different stories, avoiding the closure which precludes the alternative interpretation (see Stronach and MacLure, 1997). Moreover, the process of mimesis that creates the observational data set looks forward to the mimesis 3 in which a public text is made.

From data to report

Since Chapter 10 is concerned expressly with the nature of research writing, this chapter will not go into great detail. However, to complete the argument it is necessary to look back at the idea of the triple mimesis and to see the process of textualization as a whole. Research of whatever kind, whether it is contributing to a university degree, whether it is commissioned by government, bid for from a charity or funding council or done just to justify the author's position as 'research active', is judged on the basis of its outcome; it stands or falls on the basis of this final text, almost always a written one. Although many aspects may be seen as contributing to research quality, including technical, ethical and other methodical issues, almost invariably these are assessed on whether the research report tells a convincing story. It must also find a fit with the data, but has to be more concise and more ordered and therefore have its meaning more sharply defined than the data (Verhesschen, 2003: 461).

This has a very important bearing on what the researcher does once they have a 'complete' data set. It will clearly shape the process of data analysis and interpretation, and the consciousness that all depends on the research report will be especially sharp at this stage. But the knowledge of this is not confined to the endgame. The thought of the transformations required to create the final text will be with the researcher throughout. This means that though we have been thinking very much in terms of the two positions of researcher and researched, it is important to recognize that the third character, the reader, has been there silently in the background all along. The cyclical nature of mimesis means that not only do we look at the world in a different way, but we also act differently (Ricoeur, 1984).

However, despite this sense of the reader's presence throughout the process it is most clearly evident in the final report. Moreover, there is a special way in which the presence of the reader is important in the text of a research report that is derived from observational data. This is that the extracts from the data tend to be multi-voiced, that is, the stories that are produced are mediated play scripts. Thus, it potentially includes more elements of context, particularly social context, a factor that lends a certain power to the text. This is the power to give readers an enhanced sense of being there themselves. Observational data can be especially strong in engaging the reader and especially of presenting multiple perspectives. A transcript of a conversation between two people does not need to be presented from the perspective of either of them. The research report as a dialogue with the reader may therefore invite an engagement with the perspectives of any of the actors.

Conclusion

Observation, the process of being there, is a highly empirical research method. An aim of this chapter has been to show that it need not be seen as an empiricist approach. The rationale for observation is less that it gives more authentic access to what is really going on, but rather that, like other methods, it generates texts that are potentially rich in their capacity to speak to an audience. It can offer accounts whose plausibility the reader can assess through comparison with their own experience (Hammersley, 1990).

To sum up schematically the propositions put forward in this chapter:

* Meaning accrues from the selection and sequencing of actions into narratives.
* The actors in the research context are seeking to make meaning from the situation, one aspect of which is that they are being observed.
* Observational data result from the researcher's selection and sequencing of aspects of the actions.
* Data are further reduced and recontextualized to form the narrative of the research report.
* The narrative nature of the research report can be explicit ('I am doing narrative research') or implicit but either way the researcher is attempting to tell a convincing story or stories.
* Triple mimesis describes the process by which the texts are created and implicates the three characters of researcher, actors and readers mediating between their different worlds.

The central position of this chapter has been that although not so obviously a part of 'narrative research methods' observation does, in fact, give rise to texts which are essentially narrative in that they involve what Ricoeur (1984) calls emplotment: the selection and sequencing of actions such that they tell a story. The process involves actors, readers and researchers but in all of these narratives the identity of the researcher is a pivotal feature. First, it affects crucially the way that the actors interpret the situation under observation, since the observer becomes an audience or reader of their actions. Second, the theoretical orientation of the researcher as well as their practical preferences shape what is noted and therefore what becomes data. Finally, the identity of the researcher is important in the way that the report is constructed – as a writer one will be anxious not just to tell a convincing story about the substantive issues but also about oneself. As Hammersley (1990) maintains, with ethnographic research as well as the plausibility of the claims, the credibility of the researcher is of great significance to the final reader.

We are aware that our use of these concepts would not necessarily be endorsed by Hammersley as we are using them to describe what is essentially a rhetorical position, whereas his orientation to realism connects them much more firmly to evidence. However, these two ideas of plausibility and credibility give a key to the implications of the argument in this chapter for someone tackling a research project. This is that both can be enhanced by awareness of the ways that you are complicit in the action that the research is about, the data that are collected and the report that is produced at the end. Thinking of what is happening in terms of narrative transformations will help you to gain more critical control of the research process.

Beyond this, a narrative approach to observation, being there, provides many opportunities for establishing *critical empathy*, which we would suggest is an important feature of good research. In my own experience in classroom research I have aimed to use it to establish simultaneous empathy with both teachers and learners and thus to gain more critical purchase on the situations and avoid the guilt which it has been claimed is associated with the participant observer role (Gans, 1982).

Part 2

Dicing with data – deconstructing text

6

Breaking down data – routes
to interpretation

Introduction

We start this section with a chapter about how the texts produced through
fieldwork are handled. It relates to the move from field to text. Although it
can be seen as a discrete and significant stage in the research process, as we
have suggested already, tying research down to a sequence of events is
problematic. Analysing and interpreting data involves both looking back to
the field experience through the resultant texts, and looking forward to
their reconstruction in the production of the report or thesis. In this sense,
texts produced from research activities are intermediary as the researcher
moves away from the field towards the text of the research report.
Although associated predominantly with the period immediately after the
completion of the research fieldwork, interpretation is a necessary part of
the researcher's activity during fieldwork processes and in all research
related decisions even from the earliest design stage (Huberman and Miles,
1998; Janesick, 1998; Seidman, 1998). At one level the activity of interpretation is a constant part of everyday life that enables people to order
and navigate how they 'go on' from day-to-day (Miles and Huberman,
1994; Schwandt, 1998). However, research is a different matter and
interpretations offered need to be made credible, justified, supported and
communicated in more explicit ways (Altrichter, Posch and Somekh, 1993).
    In this chapter we will deal with the more generic aspects of breaking
down data and making meaning. We provide a broad map to indicate
different genres in research with their implications for researcher activity.
In particular, we pick up the vertical themes of the book in highlighting
how researcher identity and text interplay. More specific examples are
provided in Chapters 7 and 8 in this part of the book.

From field to text

Although the birth of the research proposal may have seemed a titanic struggle by this time it will probably seem a long way away. The predicted and unanticipated twists and turns of the research process have had to be dealt with. No matter how many times the researcher has been through it, there are always critical decisions to be made at various points along the way and often with minimal thinking time. These may be in relation to access to particular respondents or during an interview or in an emergency situation in the research setting. Nevertheless, our concerns in this chapter are with how the researcher handles the data produced through the research process after the close of the main fieldwork period. It is the point at which the predominant activity is making sense of the research texts accumulated from the field activity, a period when the researcher sits down to focus on the analysis and interpretation of the research texts. It is important to acknowledge, however, that interpretation has probably been continual and that the boundary between the fieldwork and periods of reflection may be more or less permeable, depending on the research design and developments through the process.

During the fieldwork enormous efforts have been made to collect and record research data from/with a variety respondents and/or settings in accordance with a research design. In addition to the written textualization of the research experience, for example, from the live interview to a transcription, current advice is likely to recommend a researcher diary so that their thoughts and feelings may be included as another research text. It is these written texts that provide the main objects for analysis and interpretation, although some of the speech and interactions will undoubtedly leave traces. The move from field to text is a recontextualization – the texts are moved into a different context for the purposes of analysis and interpretation. This distancing from the field is repeated in a further recontextualization in writing the research report, as writing acts to remove the word from the context of its production (Hodder, 1998) (for more detail, see Chapter 9). The notion of mimesis explored in Chapter 5 is also appropriate here as a way of understanding how activity in the setting is represented in texts for analysis and again in the research report, another textual representation of selected aspects of the 'real' world of the research setting. The issue of representation is a key distinguishing feature of different research paradigms, which we will discuss later in this chapter and also with respect to writing in Chapter 9.

Dicing with data

Ways of engaging with interpretation and analysis come from two directions: first, the research design, as the preliminary statement, indicates a logic for the research; second, approaches to the analysis and interpretation of research texts emerge from the dynamic interplay of the substantive interests, theoretical frameworks and the empirical experiences of the researcher (Coffey and Atkinson, 1996). It is in this sense that researcher identity is intrinsic to the production of research texts from the field, the analysis and interpretation and the eventual recontextualization in the written report. Authorship starts well before the act of writing and may be seen as an expression of researcher subjectivity. It is important to highlight here that although researchers may start with notions of acting within or on a contextual field, reflexivity, experience within that field and/or with particular respondents often produce changes in researcher position and interests. It is this dynamic that may lead the researcher some distance from the substantive concerns and theoretical frameworks that provided the structure for the initial design (Tonkiss, 1998b). Although probably not very welcome in highly bounded projects, as in some government or organizationally commissioned or funded research and evaluations, in postgraduate and 'blue skies' studies, these changes are treasured as integral to the reciprocal learning possible through research.

Research projects, courses and texts are categorized frequently as either qualitative or quantitative and often associated with dichotomous methodological positions, although, as we have suggested in Chapters 3, 4 and 5, there is no necessary alignment of specific methods with forms of analysis or genres of research. It is at the point of analysis and interpretation, however, that the stakes are raised. Even so, there are some parts of the process that are generic. For example, given that fieldwork often produces binfuls of data, at some point certain texts will be selected and others put to the side (Seale and Kelly, 1998). There will necessarily be some form of data reduction and organization in which groups of observation/responses will be coded, grouped and/or themed. The products of the analysis will also be interpreted in relation to theoretical constructs and/or contextual parameters. There are many research texts that go into detail about these processes. For example, Huberman and Miles (1998) suggest 13 tactics for generating meaning in interpretive research. In a similar vein, Altrichter, Posch and Somekh (1993) describe two phases in practitioner research, the constructive and the critical, with the latter devoted to checking findings and the search for counter evidence. These are all the explicit acts of the researcher. However, their significance lies not in the fact that they are generically part of the process, but rather in the way that readings are produced, that is, in how the research texts are read and what kind of a reading is being made. Interpretation is the construction of a reading through processes of refinement and a move away from the field through text towards a reader (Denzin, 1998). It is the attempt to create order and meaning out of the research experience and thus the enclosure of the research texts within a conceptual and discursive boundary.

In the processes of analysis and interpretation, the researcher moves between research texts derived from the empirical field and those from the theoretical. Researcher interests as realized formally in the research questions, play a part in the dialogic process that bridges the discursive gap between the empirical and theoretical fields (Brown and Dowling, 1998). In the iterative cycles between these fields the empirical is objectified. The inevitable recontextualization of research in written texts and their analysis in reference to theoretical or conceptual constructs are aspects of this objectification. It is through this that specific theories are localized in the research context (Brown and Dowling, 1998). The possibility of change is always pregnant in this iterative movement. Edley (2001) gives a good example of this where his research on middle-class masculinities was organized initially around topics like fatherhood, sexuality and relationships. Through an analysis informed by discursive psychology, these categories were transformed into his eventual focus on interpretative repertoires, ideological dilemmas and subject positions.

The ways in which the researcher handles the research texts, the extent to which the emergent categories are theoretically justified, the bases for interpretations and the claims made for the research, are all markers of research genres. Referring back to Chapter 2 we can see that implicated in the production of knowledge through research are notions of the social (especially of power and the 'real') and in particular epistemological position as it informs other aspects of methodology. Researcher position, whether made explicit or not, is fundamental to the interpretive practices that selectively activate the text (Smith, 1990; Usher, 1996b). These interpretive practices constitute a reading of the research texts. As Denzin (1998: 329) suggests, 'The art of interpretation produces understandings that are shaped by genre, narrative, stylistic, personal, cultural and paradigmatic conventions'.

Using the structuring themes of this book, we now turn to different configurations of the confluence of researcher identity and text. Denzin and Lincoln (1998b) describe five moments in qualitative research in the social sciences characterized by positivism derived from methods in the natural sciences, modernism and its emancipatory projects, blurred genres of thick description, the crisis of representation and finally the double crises of representation and legitimation. Through these moments, processes in social science research are seen as influenced by the natural sciences and more recently with approaches from within the arts. It is within this context that they refer to 'multiple interpretive communities each having its own criteria for evaluating and interpretation' (Denzin and Lincoln, 1998b: 30). Further, they suggest that every researcher is biographically located and speaks from an interpretive community that offers the writer 'a repertoire of expressive means and to the reader a repertoire of reading clues' (Czarniawska, 2004: 69). In current times, as we contemplate the sixth moment perhaps, it would seem incumbent on the researcher to locate themselves within or perhaps across interpretive communities in efforts to explicate their readings of research texts which include their analysis (deconstruction) and synthesis (reconstruction) in the report (Ragin, 1994).

Perhaps not . . .?

As rehearsed in Chapters 3 and 4, positivist social science accounts are founded on a realist position that imitates research in the natural sciences. The social distance of the scientist from the objects of their investigation together with the collapse of ontology and epistemology produces the scientist's capacity to 'read' the real from properly conducted research (Guba and Lincoln, 1998; see also Chapter 2). The transfer of natural scientific approaches to social science has produced enormous emphasis on the creation of social distance and strong boundaries between the researcher and the researched (Oppenheim, 1992). The technical and rigorous application of method in a highly structured way with minimal personal engagement, as well as tests for reliability and validity are for these purposes. Excision of researcher bias is fundamental to the demarcation of the researcher stance and the creation of their objective and neutral speaking/reading position. Legitimation of research findings is claimed through the rules of methodology and measures to avoid researcher bias (Altheide and Johnson, 1998). Interpretations may simply involve literal readings from the data that refer directly to and represent the real world (Munn and Drever, 1990). A correspondence theory between the research texts and objects in the field means that questions of representation, which we discuss later, do not arise. The importance of the researcher's scientific stance is underscored and their authority is further bolstered by writing in a scientific genre (see also Chapters 4 and 9). To this effect, the purposive and personal act of interpretation is concealed, as indeed is the author. In reference to interpretation within positivism, Stronach and MacLure (1997: 35) suggest that, '. . . the appearance of artlessness is a rather artful business'.

Experimental designs are archetypal: the researcher manipulates variables in, for example, a pre-post test with specified groups of respondents who have undergone different 'treatments', which may be a drug trial, a form of therapy or a curriculum/pedagogical intervention. In this type of controlled experiment, measurements are collected and compared. This emphasis on measurement of pre-specified parameters and comparison is evident in a range of realist approaches to research that might include tests, questionnaires and structured observations (Oppenheim, 1992; Robson, 1993). In these cases validity and reliability may also be measured through the application of standard mathematical tests. Experimental approaches are usually tightly structured and highly specified. They are often founded on a hypothesis and associated with prediction and control (in the treatment or sample and in the conduct of the research) and look for causes (Byrne, 2002). Tight research designs and the pre-specification of variables are highly prized as characteristic of 'good' research. It is the pre-selected categories that provide the structures by which the data will be broken down and the more closed research designs usually invoke strong boundaries between the fieldwork and analysis. Even though often inappropriate, the remnants of this model of empirical research and writing still inform postgraduate fee and tuition structures in the many universities and research proposal structures in funding applications.

Within this kind of deductive research, pre-selected criteria, often associated with a hypothesis derived from more general theory, are used to organize the data collection. The structure of the questionnaire as a whole and individual items, observations, or interviews are normally related to conceptual maps. These framing criteria provide the rudiments of a coding scheme, which may be collapsed or expanded in the process of analysis. Through deductive reasoning, generalized theories that informed the initial hypothesis are used to interrogate data from the specified sample and context (Byrne, 2002). Coding is part of the process of data reduction, the analytical deconstruction that follows almost directly from the parameters used to structure the experiment or questionnaire (Moser and Kalton, 1971). The advance intellectual effort in designing, structuring and compartmentalizing the research, prior to the data collection, reduces analysis and interpretation to a matter of common sense. As Munn and Drever describe:

> It will be seen that what we are suggesting as a coding process is one of transcription rather than interpretation. . . . The whole process is quite straightforward. You are recording information but not evaluating it. You are doing no more than making the information more manageable.
>
> Munn and Drever, 1990: 43

The pre-selection, when allied with responsive rather than interactive methods, as in the standard fixed-response questionnaire, produces data that tends to conform to the singular account of the researcher. The space for respondent transgression of this structuring of the field of inquiry is limited and also may be factored out in the processes of analysis or enumeration that usually follow from highly structured research methods. Advice on dealing with 'spoilt' and non-response in questionnaire returns, for example, is normally included in texts on quantitative analysis. Enumeration and the use of statistical methods provide an increased aura of objectivity, in which the classifying schemes and the dynamics of the social context are solidified. The operation of probability theories in statistical knowledge is impervious to the specifics of local research settings or the framing theoretical concerns (Brown and Dowling, 1998). At the same moment, the researcher's privileged perspective is preserved and sustained but submerged in the analysis and interpretations. Readily accessible computer applications can now perform complex mathematical procedures on data sets whether meaningful or not. To this extent the production of categories, clusters and their inter-relations may be very easily explored in relation to the original hypothesis, or other theoretically informed analyses, for example, by gender or ethnic origin or in more exploratory ways. Although, on the one hand, this provides the possibility of unexpected analysis and interpretation, on the other, it reifies the researcher's original categories and framing of the empirical field.

Complex realisms

The development of critique of the application of natural scientific methods to the social has taken many forms that have changed the research landscape. By questioning the researcher's privileged position in the production of legitimate knowledge, their position as the disinterested scientist, expert (Guba and Lincoln, 1998) or great interpreter (Usher and Scott, 1996) has been lost. In terms of analysis and interpretation – the deconstruction of social research data – the critique relates not only to the fixed enclosure of the social arena through predefined classifications that freeze the dynamic social world, but also to the way that this tends to compartmentalize and reduce social complexities (Byrne, 2002). Several arguments have been offered in criticism of the naive realist position described above. These demand greater self-awareness of the researcher's part in the social activity of research. In this chapter, this refers particularly to the need to address explicitly the processes of breaking down data and the bases for particular interpretations.

In Chapter 2 we traced developments in social theory and illustrated how these have impacted on the logic of inquiry. Denzin and Lincoln's (1998b) moments over time have been produced in response to critique of forms of social inquiry within qualitative research. The bases for critique are often complex and detailed and draw on arguments from a broad range of domains including many branches of philosophy, ideology and politics, anthropology, psychology, sociology, and so on. As the debate continues, a range of research stances is now available through different configurations of position on these arguments. At heart, however, these refer back to the loss of confidence in the application of scientific method to the social world (Schwandt, 1998; Czarniawska, 2004). If we separate ontology from epistemology, that is the real world and the possibilities of our knowledge of it, we might then come to a position whereby we accept the reality of the world but question our ability to have direct knowledge of it. This then places critical emphasis on the researcher's stance and their interpretations in the production of knowledge about the social world. The researcher, now located within the social realm rather than in a vantage point outside, is dispossessed of the certainty and authority assumed in the scientific realm (although even there it is contentious). That the researcher is part of the world that they investigate collapses any claims to a distanced, objective speaking/reading position. It also points to the inevitability of contamination of the social space that they invade in the research process. As such, their speaking/reading position, especially in the analysis and interpretation, requires some explicit description and broad definition. Researcher identity, their interests and values, are integral to the way that the intermediary texts for analysis and interpretation are derived, brought together, handled and further recontextualized in the writing. The complexities and critique have produced a range of 'interpretivist' approaches to social research that move beyond naive realism to include, among other approaches, critical realism (Byrne, 2002) and transcendental realism (Bhaskar, 1979).

Realist positions are commonly associated with scientistic approaches, the production of quantitative data and statistical analysis. Although still acknowledged as possibly useful in describing *what*, these approaches have been recognized as more limited for addressing *why* and *how* questions in research (Munn and Drever, 1990). Moving out of the straightjacket of traditional science approaches, more open structures in research instruments have provided space for more qualitative aspects of the social world to be incorporated into research. In clarification of the implications for interpretation Denzin (1998) describes the more scientific 'etic' approaches, in which the researchers own theoretical frameworks are used deductively to describe the specific context. These are contrasted with 'emic' approaches where researcher experiences in the field are used inductively to provide more contextually situated descriptions. The introduction of qualitative methods more widely in social research has provided opportunities for more dialogic processes in the development of interpretations, as the observed's views/understandings interact with those of the researcher. Nevertheless, although unusual, there are also approaches to the analysis of qualitative data that are not so open to the field, these use highly structured predetermined networks for analysis that are applied rigidly (see, for example, Bliss, Monk and Ogborn, 1983). This again makes the point that distinctions of method do not distinguish research methodologies.

Anticipation of analysis is an important consideration in the development of research designs and indicates a logic for the inquiry. Tighter designs tend to imply more deductive reasoning, in which the work of interpretation concerns testing or confirmation of hypotheses or general theories in specific local settings. More open designs imply the inclusion of more qualitative approaches, in which interpretation takes place through inductive analysis. These more exploratory studies may involve hypothesis seeking or theory building from the local context to the general (Huberman and Miles, 1998). As Byrne (2002: 148) explains in reference to grounded theory, which he associates with critical realism, interpretivist approaches may combine deductive and inductive reasoning to provide better understandings of the field and build theories.

> The whole process is inherently inductive in that, in principle, theoretical schemes derive from empirical investigation. It is important to note that there are two sources for the construction of components of and relations among the category set. The first is the conceptual apparatus of the disciplines themselves. The second are the in vivo codes, which derive from the language of those observed and/or questioned in any particular piece of qualitative research.

The wider introduction of qualitative data processes of analytical induction and the broader development of interpretivist research may be seen by positivists as unreliable and an attack on reason, truth and objectivity (Denzin and Lincoln, 1998d). However, even with predominantly qualitative studies the claims to legitimation still reflect the vestiges of scientific method. This remains evident in grounded theory that refers to the production of hypotheses and specific modes of verification (Strauss and Corbin, 1998), with research reports punctuated by the language of validity. Qualitative texts are often coded in reference to the researcher's conceptual framework and made available for enumeration and statistical treatment in ways that may not be very different from more closed structures. The usual analytical treatment and interpretations of open response items in questionnaire data exemplify this point. Again, in grounded theory, the dominating influence on interpretation of previous theory rather than contextual experiences connects this approach to positivism (Denzin, 1998).

Processes of analysis and interpretation are similarly reminiscent of scientific methods for legitimation. The coding of qualitative data to allow counting and other numerical manipulation or to detect patterns are efforts to improve validity (Seale and Kelly, 1998). Observed patterns are verified in efforts to confirm or qualify the emergent findings, often through comparison, contrasts and the search for negative cases or counter theories. Similarly, triangulation, which is so influential in qualitative research designs, is intrinsic to the claims for validity and legitimation by the interpretivist researcher (Byrne, 2002). Attempts to replicate findings in case study (Yin, 1984) and efforts to authenticate accounts with respondents, also implicitly refer to the notion of 'social reality'. These are efforts towards an approximate external truth, so a form of realism, in which the incommensurability argument of quantitative and qualitative methods proposed by the 'paradigm wars' (Gage, 1989) becomes unsustainable and the mixing of methods less problematic. Interestingly too, and from a different direction, advances in computer technology allow more complex modelling and manipulation that also has produced greater convergence in analytical processes for qualitative and quantitative data (Byrne, 2002).

Interpretivist repertoires

Despite the spectre of science and constant tensions in research and interpretation, developments in thinking and research practice have given rise to a number of interpretivist modes. These bring sharper focus on the researcher, whose identity and stance remains central to knowledge production through research and its representation in text, albeit in reference to a community of research practice and its range of interpretive repertoires (Usher and Scott, 1996; Altheide and Johnson, 1998).

> All research is interpretive, guided by a set of beliefs and feelings about the world and how it should be understood or studied. . . . each interpretive paradigm makes particular demands on the researcher, including the questions that are asked and the interpretations that are brought to them.
>
> Denzin and Lincoln, 1998c: 26

In contrast to their contrived absence in science, the researcher here is centre stage with their interests and values foregrounded. As we have emphasized elsewhere, the move away from realist epistemology towards constructivism has had a significant impact on the shape and form of research in the social sciences. Constructivist epistemology although in different ways through its radical and social variants, always highlights knowledge as a human production. This has introduced a new significance to the understandings and perspectives of social actors in given contexts. Rather than abstract theory developed by claims to neutrality and objectivity, an emphasis on practice in context has brought participatory methods, practitioner research and other action-oriented approaches to the fore. Critique from feminists about the exclusion of women and other marginalized groups in the production of legitimate knowledge has also contributed to this democratization of research (Harding, 1986, 1991; Fine, 1998).

Within this more complex view of the social, researchers have lost their footing in the vantage point of science, they become more like participants and facilitators (Guba and Lincoln, 1998). The more negotiated and uncertain enterprise has left the researcher with limited resources to make truth claims for their interpretations. The association of constructivism with forms of fallible realism/transcendental realism hinge softer truth claims made through research (Schwandt, 1998). Alongside this, a different vocabulary is used to describe the legitimation process (Guba and Lincoln, 1998). Trustworthiness, credibility, dependability, transferability, confirmability, authenticity and impetus to action provide constructivist versions of validity, reliability and objectivity but still indicate a commitment to good science (Denzin, 1998: 330–1). This is made explicit by Miles and Huberman (1994: 245) who, speaking from a transcendental realist position suggest that 'the critical question is whether the meanings you find in qualitative data are valid, repeatable, and right' and that use of numbers in research might be useful, 'to verify a hunch or hypothesis; and to keep yourself analytically honest, protecting against bias' (Miles and Huberman (1994: 253). Despite efforts to the contrary, these criteria for legitimation are highly reminiscent of science where the interpretive power of the researcher suppresses the dialogic dimension of a more contextual focus (Schwandt, 1998; Czarniawska, 2004).

Issues of power in the research process and analysis of the social world have been significant, even if in contradictory ways, in the move away from positivist social research. Structuralist theories of power inform critical theorists who connect local social formations to the power networks of global capitalism. And, although often motivated to produce counter-hegemonic argument within specific contexts,

> the person is merely the 'speaking object', a user of codes and symbols who selects among preconstituted options, voices, and programs. Structures exist at the organising centers of social action; persons are in every sense not only the creations of such structures, but manifestations of elements and rules created by social structures.
>
> Manning and Culum-Swan, 1998: 255

The imposition of this theoretical edifice with its possessive as opposed to discursive notions of power provides a deductive interpretative framework for the researcher that dominates the readings of different contextual perspectives. In this sense, research becomes a means by which grand theory is further substantiated, often through using quasi-scientific methods for legitimation by an unreflexive researcher. Despite this, the spirit of the approach together with the movement to democratization in research and views of the social that offer more human agency, have provided a space for identifiable forms of emancipatory research. Action, rather than unreflexive theoretical verification, becomes the legitimation criterion. The researcher becomes an instigator and facilitator that gives 'voice' to multiple, marginalized perspectives and provides the impetus to action in context (Guba and Lincoln, 1998). The action orientation provides what Lather (1986a) called 'catalytic validity' which 'points to the degree to which research moves those it studies to understand the world and the way it is shaped in order for them to transform it' (Kincheloe and McLaren, 1998: 289).

Clearly this assumes participatory forms of research that underscore the politics of knowledge construction. However, modes of analysis and interpretation remain unclear (Denzin, 1998). As such, even those researchers with emancipatory interests see research as a technical rather than constructed practice (Usher and Scott, 1996). The question about how analytical constructs and interpretive frameworks emerge through research brings us back to researcher identity. While founded on theoretical and practical insights and experiences, it is the researcher interests that inform the research intentions and approaches to analysis and interpretation (Altrichter, Posch and Somekh, 1993; Usher, 1996b; Byrne, 2002). With the demise of validity measures of objective epistemology, researcher politics and values are highlighted in interpretation (Lincoln and Denzin, 1998). Along with reference to the community of academic and/or professional practice, ethics also may be introduced to suggest limitations to the analytic and interpretive freedom of the researcher (Altheide and Johnson, 1998). Although we may attempt to produce what might be coherent, methodical and sensible, disciplined accounts (Atkinson 1992), it is in the later recontextualization in writing the report that we hope to persuade the readers of the veracity of the account. Nevertheless, the researcher's imposition of order on research texts in analysis, interpretation and writing is still an act of power (Usher and Scott, 1996).

The placing aside of measures of validity and objectivity and the foregrounding of the moral and political position of the researcher in processes of analysis and interpretation has led to long and agonized debates. Researchers who 'confess' political perspectives, with interests in social justice, multiple perspectives and heterogeneous voices from the social world are termed as partisan by social researchers who want to sustain some sense of objectivity and political neutrality (but not the correspondence theory of truth implied in science) through, for example, Hammersley's (1990) 'subtle realism'. The tension seems irresolvable,

> . . . no simply neutral or value-free position is possible in social research (or, indeed, else where). The partisans for truth just as much as the partisans of the 'underdog', are committed to an absolute value

for which there can be no purely factual foundation. . . . Even the commitment to scientific (or rigorous) method is itself, as Weber emphasizes, a value. Finally, the conclusions and implications to be drawn from a study are, Weber stresses, largely grounded in the moral and political beliefs of the researcher.

Silverman, 1998: 90–91

This impasse has been described as the crisis of legitimation in social research, which begs the question of what and how the researcher claims for their interpretations. As we have indicated above, the way the data is broken down (and recontextualized in the writing) is related to the interests, values and politics of the researcher – researcher identity.

Reflexivity and representation

At this point many researchers reach a stage of distress and a crisis of confidence about their emergent interpretations. Finding a naked emperor and unable to distinguish their claims to 'truth' from those of the proverbial 'women at the bus-stop' sends many to the jaws of despair. That the world is a different place from where they started the research and indeed, that they are different people, adds to the general confusion about the rules of the game. Rather than submerging or deflecting attention away from the researcher as pivotal in research accounts, reflexivity explores this relationship. In constructivist epistemology and in a transcendental realist position, accounts of the social are fallible and subject to constant revision. We can then no longer take for granted the given nature of the social world and fixed, essentialized identities. As researchers, we need to monitor our own sociality within a more fluid social as this informs how we make sense of our research experiences and represent them in texts. Echoing some feminist positions, what we 'find' through research is a product of the process (Stanley and Wise, 1990; Usher, 1996b). So reflexivity provides the space where, as researchers, we critically reflect upon the social conditions in which we have constructed our accounts. In this sense the accounts 'speak back' and confront the researcher in ways that demand self-reappraisal (Hodder, 1998). As such, reflexivity works to allow us to make informed interpretations of what we experience, observe and feel.

Our conscious critical awareness draws attention to our social performances as researchers with respect to the field of investigation (and the social actors within it) and our researcher reference group (Tanesini, 1999). This context for our social action works against the free-fall into relativism, once the shackles of positivism and empiricism have been cast aside. Self-knowledge of the bases for our judgements and performances through the processes of constructing and deconstructing research are excavated through critical reflection on theoretical and methodological position (Hodder, 1998). Researcher reflexivity highlights the way in which research is constituted by current understandings of the social and at the same time offers the possibility for new versions of the social and ourselves within it. This is a critical aspect of the double hermeneutic in which our accounts of the social, that are intertextually derived, then become part of a new social condition as much as they produce reformed accounts of the social context that they describe (Giddens, 1991). Reflexivity then asks us to consider how '. . . frameworks and categories, all the basic intellectual "tools" of research, are implicated with power' (Usher, 1996b: 48).

The power of research and researchers to provide descriptions of the social, especially in accounts that claim a correspondence to the real as in positivism, has been highlighted particularly by feminists. The focus on the politics of research and inevitable absences have been the basis of critique that points to the partiality of theory and method (Mohanty, 1991; Pattai, 1994; Dunne and King, 2003). Against the monologic universalizing of grand theories, the emphasis has been on localization to provide more historically and socially located research that invites multiple perspectives on social life in context. In addition, for many, a key purpose attached to research is some form of social action or change in the context. This characterizes emancipatory research and action research and is enshrined in the notion of catalytic validity (Lather, 1986b). This may provide further discomfort to researchers who, despite their focus on actors in a specific contexts, realize that the social change appears to be limited to their own gaze upon/readings of the social world. Although this alone should not be underrated, in a research world framed by policy imperatives and characterized by vernacular positivism, the temporality and uncertainty of research 'findings' can be seriously disconcerting. It is in cognizance of the strictures of the broader research scene that we can understand the reservations articulated by Marcus (1998: 395):

> . . . reflexivity opens the possibility for the so-called polyphonous text or the completely collaborative project, but often as not, it ends up reinforcing the perspective and voice of the lone, introspective field-worker without challenging the paradigm of ethnographic research at all . . .

The democratization of research has witnessed the proliferation small-scale local studies outside the academy and in a broad range of fields. The emergence of practitioner research in the many professional public sector spheres is but one example. The small scale and its contextual specificity demand that the researcher gets much closer or immersed in the action of the field that they are investigating. Both the context and first-hand observations are highlighted as significant for the purposes of understanding rather than the control that is associated with more scientistically informed research (Denzin and Lincoln, 1998b). The closeness to participants in the field of inquiry typifies insider research and ethnographic studies and is not unproblematic. Strong contextual circumscription, following the symbolic interactionism of Mead and Blumer (Schwandt, 1998), has produced a form of ethnographic realism that has long troubled anthropologists. In addition to the problems of legitimation described above, there are also problems of representation in ethnographic research. The latter refers to how 'others' are incorporated/represented in research. Several aspects of researcher identity are germane, their relationships with the researched, their interpretive frameworks and the recontextualization of research texts in the written report. In addition to the selection of particular texts for analysis and interpretation, the processes of writing textualizes the rich experiences in the field and as Denzin, (1998: 322) observes 'meaning, interpretation, and representation are deeply intertwined in one another'. Writing, then, is integral to interpretation (Coffey and Atkinson, 1996).

So, from an understanding of interpretation as making a reading, we now come to see that interpretation is also a writing (see also Chapter 9). More specifically to our concerns here, the questions focus on how the researcher represents their experience and the social actors in the text of the research report. We are now at the edge of the linguistic turn as the realities of the research and social context slip away through their recontextualization. The critique offered against the correspondence theory of positivism, again comes into play against a version of the world where words and things are intrinsically bound (Altheide and Johnson, 1998; Czarniawska, 2004). Similarly, the rejection of a correspondence between texts and reality throws into relief the researcher/author, and their speaking position.

In ethnographic research and some forms of participatory and emancipatory research, the research texts are intended to provide thick descriptions in which voices from the field speak through/in the research text. Nevertheless, whatever the intentions and desires, the inclusion of 'other' voices is subject to conditions imposed by the researcher (Eisner, 1993; Altheide and Johnson, 1998; Seidman, 1998; Wetherell, Taylor and Yates, 2001; Czarniawska, 2004). These conditions include the criteria for analysis and interpretation and the textual construction of the account, which is discussed more fully in Chapter 9. However, as Czarniawska (2004: 61) expands, '. . . rendering somebody else's story in one's own idiom. No matter how well meaning the researcher is, such translation is a political act of totalizing'. These acts of ventriloquism involve the researcher in problematic representations of the 'other', the social actors and their context, in the narrative of the research. Although sometimes stylistically different, the politics of representation, writing the 'other', remains a key issue for the researcher today as much as for the colonial anthropologist (Geertz, 1988). As researchers, we fashion the research texts, acting as a bricoleur to construct versions of the social actors and their social world such that inevitably analysis implies representation (Coffey and Atkinson, 1996: 108).

Processes of analysis, then, are far from simple even when ever more flexible and sophisticated compluter applications for quantitative and qualitative data are readily available. The intellectual work of moving from field to text is full of problems that interact as we move through interpretation to writing. Different genres of research suggest different ways to navigate this journey and the relationship between researcher identity and text. Perhaps over-summarizing, Czarniawska (2004: 101) suggests that analysis

> . . . will depend on the theoretical affiliation of the scholar: the objec-tivists will refer the answer to relations of power, the subjectivists to the workings of the human mind, and the constructivists will show that 'how' contains a 'why'. In other words, a narrative analysis forms another narrative that, in order to become a fully fledged story, needs to be emplotted. Theory is the plot of a dissertation.

Forms of writing in social science research also require the gloss of ration-ality on what is often an emotional rollercoaster marked by struggles in the field, with/in the texts and with yourself (Denzin, 1998). This rem-nant of a science of the social additionally demands the construction of a fluid, tidy and complete research story in which ambiguity, unevenness and challenge are dispensed with, irrespective of the experience and sense of self of the researcher or the researched (Stronach and MacLure, 1997).

For the poststructuralist, the text, as an occasion of the interplay of multiple voices, is the focus for analysis (Manning and Culum-Swan, 1998). The search is for the way that meanings are put together. Texts and contexts are in constant tension, as in the hermeneutic cycle, texts and contexts reflectively define and change each other (Denzin and Lincoln, 1998d). Given that there is no correspondence between words and worlds, no referential use of language, the authority of the text has to be accomplished. Its verisimilitude is the mask through which it attempts to convince its reader. Rather than freezing the text and producing a meta-text (and a meta-contextual researcher position), the analytical effort is in addressing the mobilization of meaning. It is in the trajectories of meaning that power/knowledge is disseminated. This is a discursive notion of power, as opposed to the possessive kind that privileges the foundational fantasies of grand theory associated, for example, with crit-ical theory (Stronach and MacLure, 1997; see also Chapter 2). The attempt is to look at the instability and ambiguity of meaning, for rupture in the narrative and for transgression in the unruly text. Rather than the one true reading, multiple readings are always possible (Fine, 1994, 1998; Lather, 1994; Stronach and MacLure, 1997; Denzin and Lincoln, 1998d; Tonkiss, 1998b). Examples of this may be seen in Gilligan's re-reading of Kohlberg (Gilligan, 1982) and Walkerdine's re-reading of the psychological production of the child as a cognitive subject (Walkerdine, 1988).

The linguistic turn has invited literary influences on social science research. The invitation is for researchers to make readings of their research texts that highlight its inadequacies and discrepancies rather than closure and completion (Stronach and MacLure, 1997: 111). This might mean re-reading the spoilt responses on a questionnaire or the awkward interviewee as attempts to transgress the enclosure offered in the research encounter and perhaps in anticipation of the totalizing way the encounter might be (un-)represented in the research report. Some forms of discourse analysis and deconstruction associated with this genre, which we address in the following two chapters, hope to explore these possibilities. Rather than a retreat to a pure science of the social, researchers are now looking forward to the blurring of boundaries not only 'between the science and art of interpretation' but also between 'fact/value, subject/object, knower/known' (Schwandt, 1998: 250). Some embrace the possibilities of more literary forms through metaphor or in poetics (Lincoln and Denzin, 1998). The task remains to work with the mess between and within politics and social research, to ask unsettling questions about theory and research (Fine, 1994), trying to make sense of our lives without framing the researcher as the final arbiter (Schwandt, 1998).

7

Worrying at words – discourse analysis

Introduction

There had been tension between Esther, a friend of mine, and her line manager for a number of months, so she was apprehensive about the appraisal interview. When it actually happened though, she did not think it passed off too badly. She had been able to say what she thought the problems had been and her appraiser had noted them down. However, when I met Esther a few days later, she was incensed. She felt that the report form the manager had prepared was not at all a fair representation of the conversation appraisal interview. 'Just you read it,' she said. 'It's not so much what he says, though that's bad enough. It's how he says it. Even things that pretend to be complimentary create the impression that I'm to blame for everything that's gone wrong. I've got to respond to it, but it's just so hard to get to grips with.'

The issue Esther was wrestling with was that something was going on, which was readily recognizable to her, and she feared, to anyone who would be reading the appraisal records kept by her employer. *What* was happening was only too apparent, but in order to defend herself against it, she had to try to understand *how* it was happening; this might involve interrogating the text much more closely than was possible at a simple reading.

Esther's purpose was the professional one of defending herself against the negative consequences of what she felt to be an unjust appraisal. However, appraisal within the public services is also a very suitable topic for research. At some level, the information contained in the previous two paragraphs might be seen as an adequate starting point in order to construct a case study of Esther's appraisal. This might take the form of an interview with Esther focusing on her side the story and follow-up interviews with other interested parties, say, the manager and other people he appraised. We might expect this to produce interesting data, whereby Esther, and possibly her colleagues, described their thoughts and feelings about the appraisal process and in particular how it became inscribed in a report. In Esther's case, her main point would be that her manager had unfairly manipulated language to create a false impression. However, just as Esther was angry about the way that this had been achieved, so a researcher might be intrigued by this effect and might therefore seek fuller understanding. To do this would involve examining much more closely the particular language that the manager had used.

An interest in the language through which social interaction is accomplished runs through this book and indeed through much of the social sciences in recent decades (the 'linguistic turn'). The key notion in this is discourse, the term that links both language and social life. However, the nature of this linkage is problematic as the word discourse means different things to different people. A dictionary definition that might apply to everyday, non-technical usage would have discourse as synonymous with talk or conversation. It is therefore clear that at root, the word is about language in use and in that sense involves the social world of speakers and listeners, writers and readers. Thus, following this definition, discourse analysis might involve the scrutiny and interpretation of language which is being used to some purpose and therefore bringing into the field of play the purpose intended and effect of the language on both those who produce it and its audience.

However, we have already used the word 'discourse' in this book many times. Generally we have used it to denote something rather more extensive than the dictionary definition, often with reference to the work of Foucault, which has been very influential in this. The fundamental idea behind the extended meaning is that language is not only central to the way that social life is enacted, but that the forms of social life and of language are mutually constitutive. This means that discourse now encompasses much more than just the language that is used to constitute knowledge about a particular topic, but also the practices that are associated with it. For Foucault, knowledge and power are closely associated, so a discourse also includes the 'rules' governing what is legitimate and what is not. Moreover, rather than discourse being seen as the creation of the speaker, Foucault sees discourse as actually producing the subject position of the individual. Thus, discourse analysis here might involve studying texts in an attempt to ascertain the rules of formation of the discourse.

Between (and possibly beyond) these two approaches to discourse, there are many more different possibilities some of which will be discussed in more detail in this chapter. In an earlier book in this series on discourse in educational and social research, Maggie MacLure (2003) writes what she calls a sketchy overview of definitions of discourse. She recognizes the multiplicity of positions, but in common with many other commentators, identifies an important boundary which gives rise to only two distinct traditions. The first derives from European, especially French philosophical and cultural study (including, of course, Foucault) and the second is heavily influenced by Anglo-American linguistics. After a review of each of these she concludes that there is something of an impasse between the two and quotes Pennycook's (1994) suggestion that they may be 'incommensurable discourses', that is ultimately irreconcilable ideas. A key difference is that the two traditions are represented by different people, who have been shaped by different academic identities and allegiances. Implicated in this we might also include their political and social contexts as well as their disciplinary affiliations, which give rise to different academic interests and thus as researchers to different questions guiding their inquiry. However, the strongest boundary between them appears to be epistemological: 'Where linguists generally assume that it is possible to jump clear of language, to see it clearly and "capture" its regularities, many poststructuralists would see themselves as obliged to work from inside the textual fabric that holds them in "an enfolded entrapped relationship with the real world" ' (Bal, 1999: 24; MacLure, 2003: 190).

We are generally in sympathy with MacLure's position and in this chapter we will explore the idea of incommensurability. MacLure's conclusion is that an integrated discourse theory appears to be impossible. This may well be so; however, the function of this book is less to point to ways of formulating integrated theory than to raise issues about particular research practices and whether they have anything to offer to readers who are developing their identities as researchers. In exploring discourse analysis and what people from different positions have to say about it, we intend to show that at the level of *method*, the incommensurability may be less than it first appears. In other words, it may be possible to appropriate some of the techniques used by researchers whose identities are in many ways quite alien to us. Nevertheless, on the level of *methodology* (or at least its non-practical elements – we will discuss these distinctions in more detail in the final chapter) the differences will remain clear cut. Positions on the relationship between language and the real, the ontology of discourse, link up to the epistemological distinction in the quotation from Bal and seem to be irreconcilable. Lines may also be drawn on political issues, though the border may be drawn in a slightly different place.

In doing research, our concern is about how to make meaning from the texts we are studying. In this chapter, we pick up on the idea raised in Chapter 4, to explore the extent to which the starting point of analysis, the analytic method, may be similar for researchers who are developing very different methodological identities, and whose interpretation is leading them eventually in very different directions. To go back to the example of Esther's appraisal, there might be a variety of purpose and ultimate conclusions to be drawn. One might be to adopt a Foucauldian position and to investigate the way that the manager's position and indeed her own are produced by the management discourse of the public services. Another might be seeking as a 'critical' social scientist to improve the lot of the oppressed appraisee. Another would aim at improving management practice by looking at the psychology of the work place. Yet another might be interested in comparing the language use of managers in different places and of different types. However, no matter which of these disciplinary perspectives or planes of vision fit most comfortably, we will still be interested in how the effects, however they are construed, were achieved.

Various typologies of discourse analysis have been proposed. A particularly extensive one, which begins their source book of examples, comes from Wetherell *et al.* (2001) who enumerate six discourse traditions: conversation analysis and ethnomethodology; interactional sociolinguistics and the ethnography of communication; discursive psychology; critical discourse analysis and critical linguistics; Bakhtinian research; Foucauldian research. Nevertheless, they acknowledge that there are others, for example, the particular form of pragmatics derived from Sinclair and Coulthard (1975), an approach which has been very influential in much research into classrooms (Mehan, 1979; Edwards and Mercer, 1987; Edwards and Westgate, 1987). It would not be sensible to describe in detail the different traditions of discursive research as outlined by Wetherell *et al.* (2001) or according to some other typology. Instead, in the rest of this chapter we will borrow a structure from another text by Antaki, Billig, Edwards and Potter (2003). This article from the journal *Discourse Analysis Online* represents an attempt by the authors to identify shortcomings in work that purports to be discourse analysis. What is significant is that although the authors are colleagues, they stress that they disagree on many matters; their core discipline might be psychology, but they relate slightly differently to the various traditions of discourse analysis. Thus, they have to chart a rather careful course around the six different 'weaknesses' in analysis that they identify. These are:

1   under-analysis through summary;
2   under-analysis through taking sides;
3   under-analysis through over-quotation or through isolated quotation;
4   the circular identification of discourses and mental constructs;
5   false survey; and
6   analysis that consists in simply spotting features.

Antaki *et al.* claim to have derived their typology of weaknesses from journal articles that they have reviewed. However, what is interesting is that their critique is more than a technical exercise, it contains arguments which both position the authors with respect to various traditions of discourse analysis and also engage with many of the issues of method and of methodology that are relevant to the field. Discussing each 'weakness' in turn, I shall characterize the criticism of Antaki *et al.* and also use this to open out some wider issues.

Transcripts and summaries

Antaki *et al.* claim that presenting a summary of text in a discourse analysis report is not enough, because it 'flattens' the text: it tends to omit features such as laughter and may also miss out on the structure of the content, and the detail of rhetoric. The implication of this is that offering of a text (a whole text?) is a necessary condition for a proper analysis to have taken place. Unless the text starts life in written form, a transcript will then be needed. From this critique, we can deduce several things about their conception. First, it positions discourse analysis firmly in the linguistic frame, where the discourse to be studied means actual concrete examples of language in use. They appear to be differentiating themselves from traditions that see discourse as a wider cultural entity. However, although placing a great deal of the discursive research, which draws on a Foucauldian model outside their definition, it by no means forecloses on all of it. So, for example, MacLure's book is itself replete with transcripts (of, for example, a home–school interview). The question is what is seen to be of most interest and significance.

Transcripts allow fine-grained analysis, where inferences about the meaning of the text are built around details that are unlikely to be apparent in a summary. The issue is about where the analysis starts, and here the researcher's stance may determine not just whether there is a transcript, but what its nature is. For example, conversation analysis usually employs a very complex series of symbols including markers of intonation, breathing patterns, other non-verbal signs such as posture and facial expression (Chandler, 2004). Even for a text that may have been performed in a very short amount of 'real time', this then gives rise to a long transcript for a text. The very process of preparation involves a theoretical input from the researcher in deciding what is and what is not noteworthy. That will then be reflected in the analysis, which can only point to those features that are included in the transcript. Moreover, this epistemological position about what is knowable and worth knowing is connected to a technological one about what can actually be apprehended, a connection, which is taken up in the final chapter. Linguistic analysis of written text has always been possible, but it was really the advent of electronic recording, which took some of the hit or miss element out of transcription that turned attention towards the spoken word.

At the other extreme it is possible to have transcripts whose form models those of a novel or a play. These still allow a level of analysis but different features become salient. So, for example, one of the leading exponents of critical discourse analysis (CDA), Van Dijk (1993: 312), suggests that 'few levels of analysis are as revealing and relevant . . . as the semantic study of local "meanings" including the propositional structures of clauses and sentences, relations between propositions, implications, presuppositions, vagueness, indirectness, levels of description, and so on'. None of these necessitate (though they may be accompanied by) any special symbols or codes, though they are clearly linguistic features. Another possibility is represented, for example, by Maybin (1993) who supplies transcripts in conventional literary form, but in her interpretation below adds extra details. So, for example, she tells us that the speakers 'create voices' for the characters and describes how a boy raises the pitch of his voice, rather than indicating this through typographic symbols in the transcript.

At some level one might think that a very detailed transcript would denote the researcher's reluctance to position themselves within a realist ontology. By bringing in other formal features and elements of semiotic systems, such as intonation or even facial expression, they seem to be recognizing the slipperiness of words and that meaning cannot be read off unproblematically from a transcript of the words alone. However, this assumption is not necessarily warranted. A researcher will often compile a very 'technical' transcript because they believe that if they can capture enough of the detail, they will achieve the precision and accuracy to pin down what the text is really about. Although this recognizes that the written forms of words as signifiers are not the same as what they purport to signify, it seems to suggest that if enough signifiers are piled up, then the way through to the signified is less problematic.

Returning to Antaki *et al.*'s contention about analysis and summaries, I am struck by an issue raised by my own work for a conference paper I am writing at the same time as this chapter. The paper is reporting on a whole three-year research project, during which we used discourse analysis on part of our data set, some online discussion forums. However, the breadth of the paper meant that, rather than present the analysis, we had just to summarize what we had inferred from it through one or two short examples. Thus, although analysis had taken place, it may not have satisfied Antaki *et al.* because the status accorded to it in the report was lower than that of other forms of data analysis, which were given more space. Overall our project, like much discourse-based research was ultimately concerned with more than the language, and thus did not have a unit of analysis that was fine enough to be recognizably within what they understand as discourse analysis.

Finally, the privileging of transcripts seems to suggest that a transcript is somehow more 'real' than a summary. As we argued in detail in Chapter 5, although a lot of effort may go into creating the transcript replete with very fine semiotic detail, it remains an interpretation and is shaped by the concerns of the researcher.

Critical?

Antaki *et al.*'s second weakness, under-analysis through taking sides, addresses what is perhaps the most contentious area in the whole field. This is that some researchers have embraced an approach which they term critical discourse analysis (CDA) (Van Dijk, 1993; Fairclough, 1995). Like many of the theoretical approaches that label themselves 'critical', its salient feature is that it does indeed take sides. One reason they advance for this is epistemological and familiar from previous parts of this book, namely that a neutral analyst is not possible, and that objectivity is itself a form of subjectivity that masks the position of the researcher. However, the main argument for CDA proceeds from the view of language as discourse, which does something in the social world. The emancipatory agenda of CDA researchers is to ensure that the something is as positive as possible. As Kress (1996: 15) outlines:

> from the beginning [critical approaches to language] had a political project: broadly speaking that of altering inequitable distributions of economic, cultural and political goods in contemporary societies. The intention has been to bring a system of excessive inequalities of power into crisis by uncovering its workings and its effects through analysis of potent cultural objects – texts – and thereby to help in achieving a more equitable social order. The issue has thus been one of transformation, unsettling the existing order, and transforming its elements into an arrangement less harmful to some, and perhaps more beneficial to all the members of a society.

Political engagement seems then to be a necessary condition for critical discourse analysis. However, Antaki *et al.*'s identification of 'taking sides' suggests that they do not find it a sufficient one: 'sympathy and scolding (either explicit or implicit) are not a substitute for analysis'. Beyond supporting or attacking the position of the text, analysis involves identifying how the position is achieved. However, other issues lurk beneath the surface of this criticism. Because the analyst approaches the text with an engaged political aim in mind, particular texts are chosen and particular features of the texts are focused on. Critical discourse analysis applies a close focus on language. It is technical and is clearly within the linguistic end of discourse analysis. Certain linguistic features are therefore identified which are particularly likely to be ideologically significant and these are focused on. This can be seen clearly in the way that CDA is concerned with, for example, modality – defined as the means by which speakers or authors commit themselves to truth or necessity. Although modality is very much part of mainstream descriptive or applied linguistics, it is also obviously central to a preoccupation with issues of social justice, as the modality of a text links clearly with its power to persuade.

This is what gives rise to the criticisms: a political view of text may preclude other analyses and therefore it is 'under-analysed'. Worse, from this perspective, if the analyst is taking sides they may be biased towards or against the speaker and because they are 'politically rather than linguistically motivated, . . . find what they expect to find, whether absences or presences' (Stubbs, 1997). In other words, what non-critical linguists find unsettling about CDA is that critical analysts, because of their political project, may not 'bracket' their own opinions and therefore reach findings that are not in the text. Burman (2003), in a response to Antaki *et al.*, counters this by suggesting that a further kind of weakness, not mentioned in the original argument might be due to under-contextualization, a corollary of a neutral position. She adds that an analysis is not complete without contextual information such as 'historical moment, cultural setting, institutional position . . . gender (as well as other structural positions) of participants'. These other structural positions bring neatly back into play the politics of both the author(s) of the text and, presumably, the analyst!

Ultimately this argument is not capable of being resolved, as we are up against the incommensurability mentioned above. Here the methodological line is drawn on political rather than ontological lines, but once again the incommensurability is not really one of method, since critical and non-critical discourse analysts use similar tools in their analysis. The difference lies in their research focus and questions. A focus on issues of justice and injustice – 'the role of discourse in the (re)production and challenge of dominance' (Van Dijk, 1993: 249) – is liable to be reflected in the questions which guide analysis and therefore in the inferences drawn from it. A CDA project is unlikely to have addressed its questions if it is not able to make political conclusions, and as Hammersley (1997) points out, is liable to be seen as methodologically defective in this case. For him, it is this attitude rather than the actual taking sides that is difficult, the fact that 'advocates of CDA treat the validity of a critical approach as obvious, and as providing an unproblematic basis from which to criticize more conventional kinds of work' (Hammersley, 1997: 237). What he is critiquing is less the taking of sides and more the methodological under-theorizing of the analysis. Taking sides does not necessarily entail under-analysis, but the researcher would be well advised to adopt a reflexive approach which acknowledges that there may be other different things to say about the text and which holds the position of the analyst as well as other textual subjects as problematic. If not they run the peril of 'decontextualized and objectivist claims to knowledge that discourse work . . . was formulated to critique' (Burman, 2003).

A final danger in taking sides is the tendency to dichotomize and to conduct analysis through forming binaries. This is seen as undesirable both by realist linguists (e.g. Stubbs, 1997), whose interest is in the complexity of the language, and by poststructuralist discursive researchers, who are seeking to disrupt both linguistic and social certainties and who see analysis as a way of opening up rather than closing down the meanings in a text (Luke, 1995; MacLure, 2003).

Uncritical?

Antaki et al.'s third weakness, under-analysis through over-quotation or through isolated quotation, is somewhat less complex. It represents an opposite position to the previous one, whereby the analyst avoids not only taking sides but also engaging with the text at all, seeming to feel that the text speaks for itself. Over quotation involves extracting parts of the text without much by way of comment from the analyst. Thus, there is no argument. Isolated quotation involves making an argument, but not connecting it up sufficiently to the quotation from the text.

My suspicion is that through this weakness Antaki et al. are policing the border between experts and beginners rather than the one between approaches or traditions. Nevertheless, isolated quotation does raise a problem that is not directly addressed by Antaki et al., namely that all linguistically-based textual analysis faces issues in determining the boundaries of the text. Deciding where a text starts or finishes, in time and space, is already part of the analysis and the necessity of presenting fine-grained analysis means that inevitably boundaries have to be set on what constitutes the discourse to be analysed. The context must therefore either be narrowed to make the analysis manageable, or presented in summary form, which, as we have seen, is not acceptable to Antaki et al. This idea then raises issues about the micro- meso- and macro-focus of discourse analysis, which are confronted even more strongly by the next of their weaknesses.

Reference outside the text: circularity of argument

Antaki et al. do not dissent from the central tenet of discourse-based research, that the specific language of a text is derived from wider, socially shared entities, whether they are termed 'repertoires', 'ideologies', 'discourses'. The problem comes when the analyst links particular features with the wider phenomenon and then claims the presence of the feature as evidence of the existence of that phenomenon. They quote Widdicombe (1995: 118) who talks of:

> the analytic rush to identify discourses in order to get on with the more serious business of accounting for their political significance

may be partly responsible for the tendency . . . to impute the presence of a discourse to a piece of text without explaining the basis for specific claims.

However, there is some considerable width in the way that one might interpret 'the basis for specific claims'. A good way of looking at this might be seen from looking at a specific example. This comes from a journal article by Widdowson (2000) in which he makes a distinction between 'applied linguistics' which is properly seen as a way of mediating between linguistics and other disciplines, and 'linguistics applied' under which he includes CDA, and about which he is very sceptical. As Fairclough (1995: 2) attests, CDA does more than mediate since it involves: 'analysis of (spoken or written) language texts, analysis of discourse practice (processes of text production, distribution and consumption) and analysis of discursive events as instances of sociocultural practice'.

Widdowson takes to task what he sees as CDA's oversimplification of the relationship between grammatical features and textual significance, and goes into much more detail about the way that interpretations of lexical items are 'read off' by the analyst. His particular target is Fairclough's (1995) work. This criticizes a television documentary on world poverty by saying that it presents the poor as passive rather than active. Fairclough substantiates this claim through several examples, but Widdowson (2000: 17) finds one of these unconvincing. This is where the poor 'inconveniently take on the semantic role of Actor' being described as 'flocking to the city'. Fairclough's analysis is that the word flock is associated with sheep and sheep are notoriously passive. Widdowson counters by saying that Fairclough is engaging in circular argument: 'flock' only has passive connotations because Fairclough has already read them in. He backs this up by consulting the British National Corpus. This is a computer-based collection of samples of written and spoken language from a wide range of sources, designed to represent a wide cross-section of language in use. Widdowson claims that in the large sample of cases he retrieved from this database not only was flock not always associated with sheep, but that it carried no implication of passivity.

This is interesting to me because neither position seems quite tenable. One might agree with Widdowson that 'flock', especially in this verbal usage, does not imply literal passivity. According to his research (p. 18) 'pretty active unsheepish people flock, so it is wrong to characterize the word in this way'. However, one might agree with Fairclough that the use of the word was not necessarily dissonant with the portrayal of the poor as passive, but that it suggests something slightly different, namely that the decision to move the city is not taken actively by each individual, but is collective. Moreover, it may not be a reasoned decision, so much as the result of a desire not to be left behind. Thus, a more nuanced analysis of this particular example, avoiding a straightforward active–passive dichotomy, might have been advised for the original analysis. Above all, the connotations of 'flock' in this particular example are affected by the context of the statement, what has already been said in the text. The neutrality of 'flock' in other contexts may then not hold here. However, the debate goes beyond this. Widdowson seems to be suggesting that to avoid circularity of argument one needs to adopt a form of analysis that goes back to the natural scientific model. Inductive reasoning produces a hypothesis, in this case about the passive connotations of the word 'flock', which then needs to be tested normatively by reference to a large database.

This seems to hold some very dangerous assumptions. First, it takes the word as a unit of meaning, whereas many would argue that meaning derives from the interaction of the language with its context (Foucault (1972), for example, suggests that meaning derives from both the situational and linguistic elements of statements). Second, connotative ideas are of their nature shifting and impossible to tie down; to infer them from a huge database assumes not just an evenness of contexts, but also a lack of differentiation between speakers of British English. (The flock seems to have been placed in a connotative pen!) It seems therefore methodologically unsound to claim that all members of a speech community would interpret something similarly. Indeed, elsewhere in his article Widdowson is careful about delineating the possibilities of corpus linguistics and his main conclusion that, rather than 'reading off' significance from the data, problems of this nature should send one back to the context, seems at odds with his analysis of this particular example.

Again this whole question seems linked to issues of epistemology and interest. Fairclough's intention is to investigate how a particular discourse is represented in actual texts and how discursive effects are textually enacted. The fact that he may not be able or may not wish to prove the universality of an interpretation does not preclude him from making suggestions and offering them to the reader. Moreover, within CDA there is some acknowledgement of the possibilities of different readings, whereby 'the reader' of the text is not idealized and essentialized but rather has to do a job of establishing a fit between the text and the world (Fairclough, 1989).

Widdowson's criticism of the way that CDA reads interpretations off unproblematically seems also to ignore another aspect of the approach, which is its interest in intertextuality, discursivity and genre mixing, whereby the relationship of one text to others is explored. Thus, the way that the text refers to and invokes others is seen as an important means of analysing its effects. Even here though, CDA is not immune from criticism. For example, Stubbs (1997) also contrasts his systematic use of a corpus with what he sees as CDA's more speculative approach to which texts may be intertextually invoked for different readers. Interest in intertextuality is also apparent in other less overtly linguistic approaches to discourse, especially in the field of literacy and cultural and media studies. Indeed intertextuality is a pivotal concept for post-structural approaches. However, the way in which the idea is used indicates some difference.

Critical Discourse Analysis looks at the concrete forms of discourse and describes discursive practices at the micro level. Thus it often analyses the way that the rhetoric of politicians is produced and what effect this has. Norman Fairclough's core project is the analysis and exposure of the discourse of globalism as articulated by New Labour within the UK. His analysis therefore confronts the way that its leader, Tony Blair, self-consciously weaves together different identities by invoking different texts and different genres (2003: 181–3). By referring to discourse and genres, the emphasis is placed on the text rather than the agency of the speaker. Nevertheless, Fairclough also has a robust view of social agency whereby speakers are left 'with a great deal of freedom in texturing texts' (2003: 22). Similarly, he recognizes that poststructuralists have objections 'to placing too much emphasis on authors' but refers to authors himself 'without getting too much into those complications' (2003: 12).

In fact, post-structuralists problematize the whole idea of the author, whom Barthes declared dead, and analysis of text becomes as much as anything the discussion of the relationships between texts. The argument is that any text owes more to other texts than to its own author (Chandler, 2004). This is also consonant with those who share Foucault's view of discourse, where, rather than the author producing the text and the text producing the discourse, discourse produces both the text and the subject position of the author. The text is thus 'caught up in a system of references to other books, other texts, other sentences: it is a node within a network' (Foucault, 1972: 23). This argument also gives rise to a political difference. Although both Fairclough and Foucault locate power within discourse, the latter is reluctant to take anyone's side (see Chapter 2). For him power, rather than being just repressive, and therefore inherently negative, is much more complex. What makes it 'hold good, what makes it accepted is simply the fact that that it doesn't only weigh on us as a force that says no, but that it traverses and produces things, it induces pleasure, forms of knowledge, produces discourses' (Foucault, 1977: 61).

Indeed, Foucault's definition of discourse is very strongly implicated in Antaki et al.'s concern with circularity in analysis. They state that:

> circularity can occur when the analyst is working with a more macro concept than 'attitude', such as a Foucauldian notion of 'discourses'. The analyst may claim that the texts that are being studied show evidence of a particular discourse, i.e. they may say the writer/ speaker is using 'the faithfulness discourse'. It would then be circular to explain the particular texts on the grounds that they have been

produced by this 'faithfulness discourse' if the texts themselves were the evidence for the existence of that discourse.

Antaki *et al.* 2003

The issue here is about the nature of analysis and argument. The Foucauldian notion is that discourses are not so much produced by speakers as that speakers occupy discursive positions and with identities that are produced by discourse. Antaki *et al.* seem to be suggesting that for them discourse analysis is about building arguments from scrutiny of the text. Working with this premise the situation they describe is indeed circular. However, within the Foucauldian framework although texts are studied, indeed analysed, the analysis is of the whole discourse that is connected with the texts, not just the specific language. Discourse, as we saw above, is not a micro-level concept and therefore needs inevitably to be referenced to situations outside the micro context under study. Indeed, in terms of analysis, what is more important is the idea of discursive formation, and of finding what are the *rules of formation*, the connections and disconnections between things. Within this scheme and this approach to analysis, it is the rules of formation that are the conditions of existence rather than the details within the texts themselves (Foucault, 1972).

Thus, much non-linguistic discourse analysis in the Foucauldian tradition points to the macro by reference to the micro examples. CDA, by contrast, is more directly concerned with linking the micro with the macro, what Fairclough (2003: 2) refers to as 'oscillating' between a focus on specific texts and a focus on 'order of discourse', to reach relatively firm conclusions about both. This certainty may not only trouble more overtly postmodern discourse analysts, but is also disturbing to realist methodologists such as Hammersley (1997). He attacks its 'extra-ordinary ambition', since, as well as seeking an account of discursive processes, it also offers an understanding '. . . of society as a whole, of what is wrong with it, and of how it can and should be changed. As a result, it faces all the difficult methodological problems with which more conventional kinds of research have to deal, plus many others as well' (Hammersley, 1997: 245).

Thought and language: more circularity

As well as finding circularity in references outside the text, Antiki *et al.* also suggest it results from over-interpretation of the text. This involves interpreting text 'as the expression of some underlying realm of thoughts, ideas, attitudes or opinions, where the nature of those underlying thoughts and opinions is given in the talk itself'. What they are saying is that thought and language are not the same thing. The notion that thought can be straightforwardly adduced from language is therefore seen as inimical to discourse analysis. They find some discursive psychologists at fault here and suggest that, if anything distinguishes discursive analysis from other approaches, it is that it sees in text much more than an expression of views, thoughts and opinions. In this they receive support from MacLure who sees the suspension of 'belief in the innocence of words and the transparency of language as a window on an objectively graspable reality' (MacLure, 2003: 12) as the defining principle of discursive research.

Once again, though, this agreement masks some differences in position. For linguists, the salient idea is that 'locutionary force', the propositional content of the text, does not match its performative function, its illocutionary force – the meaning – which is acted on by the listener. This may, however, still be part of a realist or positivist approach to analysis, whereby the analysis enables us to adduce the illocutionary force and so to discover what the language is 'really' doing, even though we do not know what the speaker is thinking. For MacLure and post-structuralists, however, it is more about the slipperiness of language, the impossibility of certainty and closure and the implication of the researcher in the text (Stronach and MacLure, 1997).

This particular issue is a very delicate one for Antaki *et al.* since one of the authors has written a number of papers on discourse analysis and the unconscious. These draw on Freud's ideas concerning the unconscious and repression, suggesting that analysis of dialogue and attention to what is absent can indicate how repressions are 'themselves dialogically and socially constituted' (Billig, 1998: 11) and by suggesting what is present can give insights into what is being repressed. However, in this it is only clear that repressions are being enacted when one has access to other texts – in this case Freud's books and case notes. So, whereas these papers are not guilty of this weakness, they may be uncomfortably close to some of the circular argument criticisms.

Generalizing

There is less to say about Antaki *et al.*'s fifth form of under-analysis, the false survey. Indeed, some of it has already been said in our argument with respect to critique of Widdowson's (2000) of CDA. What they are identifying here is that discourse analysis has little in common with quantitative research and any attempt to generalize unproblematically from the discourse of one or several members of speech community to that of all of them. The distinction made by Stenhouse between cases and samples might be worthwhile making here where discourse analysis is concerned with cases. Antaki *et al.* imply that these generalizations are often made through inattentiveness to the researcher's own language.

Nevertheless, Stubbs (1997), for example, is concerned about doing analysis on a representative of samples and describes using a corpus to 'check' on universality.

Spotting features

The final example of under-analysis is again not very complex and concerns just identifying features of the text rather than analysing them. At some level analysis is indeed about identifying the constituent parts of something, but it must mean more than just the process of dissection. If there is no interpretation then it becomes little more than disjointed description. It resembles therefore under-analysis by over-quotation.

This weakness may again be an example of Antaki *et al.* policing the expert–novice boundary – 'descriptive' is often the most damning word of the reviewer. Nonetheless, there is also here an implicit criticism of those who see language in technical rather than social terms and those whose pursuit of objectivity seems to prevent deeper engagement with the text. They are suggesting that even those linguists least concerned with social issues, if they are concerned with language as discourse, need to take responsibility for saying what the language does (or does not do). On the other flank, there may also be a criticism here of critical linguists whose argument about the politics of text may involve spotting the features that are associated with their preoccupations (e.g. nominalization which hides the agency, Fairclough (2003)).

Discourse analysis and researcher identity

What linguistic analysis does is useful to social researchers. This is the premise of Fairclough's (2003) book, which is written largely for social researchers who want to look more carefully at language. However, to go along with his argument completely, you have to accept his critical theory or to believe in the possibility of emancipation that it offers. Fine-grained linguistic analysis can be a way of 'closing down' a text, a way of identifying the parts, defining them and pinning them down. However, it can also be a way of opening up. As Widdowson (2000: 24) suggests: 'the discourse of linguistics, then, provides a version of reality which in certain essentials is different from that of other discourses.'

This difference can be a starting point for further work. If you are prepared to keep asking questions and to deconstruct the text that accrues from the analysis, incommensurability of the discourses becomes less of a problem and more of a boon. It enables you to use methods that are not normally used within your disciplinary or methodological context.

Examples of this can be seen in MacLure (2003) Chapter 3, where she uses what are clearly linguistic analytic methods as part of a deconstructive approach (see the next chapter for more on deconstruction) to the discourse of home–school relations. Within work on formative assessment I have used linguistic techniques as a starting point for analysis, but have seen them as producing only one version that might then be problematized by others. For example, in the TASK project (Torrance and Pryor, 1998) we began to analyse classroom interaction using the model of Sinclair and Coulthard (1975). They had derived this from fieldwork that they carried out in school classrooms, not because they were interested in the social field of education, but initially for practical reasons – schools provided a captive group of speakers. Sinclair (1990: 7) in a later summary articulates very clearly his interest in terms of linguistics rather than education, differentiating himself from 'some people in education who have aims beyond just understanding the process'. They were concerned with the structure of interaction and identified a fairly rigid sequence, enabling speech acts to be classified and defined. Following Edwards and Mercer (1987), we interrogated this structure using an analysis drawn from Vygotsky's (1978) theory of learning, which was in turn put under pressure by looking at psychological theories of motivation (especially Dweck, 1989). However, these in turn were critiqued from the perspective of a number of sociological theories of interaction, to open up the psychological understandings (Pryor and Torrance, 1998; 2000). Similarly, in more recent work with Barbara Crossouard, we have been using analytic methods derived from CDA to identify aspects of assessment interaction in higher education. However, rather than producing knowledge about language, we have used the results of the analysis to track traces of the way that the positions of student and teacher are produced in doctoral study and to question assumptions about power (Pryor, 2004). The theory of formative assessment that emerges from such work is a much less clear-cut one centred around issues of power, which are troubling rather than reassuring to practitioners and policy makers and leave formative assessment as a much less comfortable idea than the version presented by many other researchers. In turn, the theoretical perspectives employed are opened up to critique.

Fairclough (2003) points out that no analysis of texts can be considered an exclusive approach, but one amongst many. It provides only pointers to the involvement of texts in meaning-making and is often best used in conjunction with other approaches – he suggests, in particular, ethnography. Some of the exclusivity and the mutual critique of the various protagonists of discourse analysis discussed in this chapter may be about an attempt to maintain 'field position' (Bourdieu, 1988). It is not that it is impossible to cross the boundaries, but to do so might involve compromising their academic identity. This might not only feel awkward, but would also mean that they would lose the advantage that their expert status, knowing the rules of the game, affords them. Thus, viewed socially and politically, preserving the distinctions is in their interest (see Hodkinson (2004) for a related discussion with respect to the educational researcher in the UK). At the level of text, analysis can be a starting point for both linguists and other discursive researchers, but the latter will want to take the analysis somewhere else and do more with it.

As an educational researcher who came from a background in language and literature, I find the work of linguistic discourse analysts appealing. They use techniques that are interesting to me and suggestive. However, as a social researcher I am not concerned with knowledge about language as such, but with attempting to understand of the social world. Therefore, although it seems a good stratagem to engage with the specifics of language, I wish to go further.

As authors of this book we have at least three different identities, however, what we are trying to do is to tell a story so as to give some kind of coherence to the reader. Within the frame of academic writing it is helpful to see the inconsistencies not as faults but as challenges to the storyteller. It is in the gaps and the inconsistencies that the space for manoeuvre (creativity?) lies. Davies and Harré neatly encapsulate an aspect of this:

> Because of the social/grammatical construction of the person as a unitary knowable identity, we tend to assume it is possible to have made a set of consistent choices located within only one discourse . . . struggle with the diversity of experience of ourselves to produce a story of ourselves which is unitary and consistent. If we don't others demand of us that we do.
>
> Davies and Harré, 1990: 64

The last sentence here is important, however, in that for the researcher those who are demanding consistency are often examiners and referees and the penalties of not satisfying them are considerable! However, where this argument is leading is that the main constraints on the construction of an approach to the analysis of discourse are concerned with researcher identity. Drawing from different approaches may be risky, since a rehearsal of the canonical positions of one discourse will no longer suffice. We have to see our identity as a researcher as fluid, a 'constant process of becoming' (MacLure, 2003: 19) and to tell it as the story of the research. In other words, reflexivity becomes a necessity.

In summary, the job of researchers is not just to analyse, they must go further than that. The image of research used in Chapter 5 as triple mimesis involves the researcher entering into dialogue within the social situation, with the data and with the reader. Our approach in this book has been to see social events as texts and our job as researchers to transform or to recontextualize them by turning them literally into texts, making them objects to be studied. As the texts are language, it makes sense to see them as linguistic forms and to analyse them, generating from them a series of questions and so deconstructing their form. However, deconstruction goes beyond the form, which is immanent, to what is latent. It is concerned both with what is absent as well as what is present in text, it asks questions of the text and then asks questions of the questions.

Returning to the issue of Esther's appraisal, we can see how attractive a discourse-based approach might be to making meaning from the experience. The words appear to offer us a window on social life. Depending on our perspective, however, the analysis might clarify or problematize, and the window may be construed as a single transparent pane or composed of many pieces of stained and frosted glass, just as the dance of light on it means that what we see may be a fugitive reflection.

8

Pulverizing policy – deconstructing documents

Documents represent a particular form of data. Research manuals will often have a section devoted to their nature, collection and analysis. There is a particularly comprehensive treatment of documents in Hitchcock and Hughes (1995). What should be included in the category document? Clearly it most often refers to a written text, but we might also include artefacts that can tell us something about our area of investigation (Hodder, 1998). It might also encompass other semiotic systems such as self-presentation and school or hospital architecture. What we want to do in this chapter is look at the notion of policy, which produces particular sorts of documents. Picking up from where the last chapter left off, we focus especially on the idea of deconstructive analysis.

I will begin by trying to unpack the concept of a policy and by looking at policy as social process (Hammersley, 2002). In doing this, I shall use examples from English education because they are most familiar to me. However, although the detail may refer specifically to the English context, the methodology is more widely applicable. One way of conceptualizing the policy process is as discursive practice (Foucault, 1972). That is to say it is the totality of all that is thought and said and acted out around a particular social site such as education or health. While the example I draw on is English, the regulatory machinery I describe is part of the Western reconceptualization of education within the neo-liberal frame. The American 'No Child Left Behind' act or the International Monetary Fund's 'Fast Track Initiative' could equally be the site of deconstructive analysis. With the idea of policy the coercive element in discourse is particularly clear, as normally there is an intention to make something happen, to change the course of events in some way. Policies often aim to reorder our real worlds and our social practices and what they mean. This intention is encoded in policy documents that have a special relationship with reality: ideally what is real will come to mirror the desires that inhere in the document. However, there is no ideal social space and this makes policy documents open to different sorts of analysis and the one I want to illustrate is deconstruction.

Policies exist to determine our relations with other states and to govern the economy, but many departments of the modern state are concerned broadly with internal matters of social welfare, transport, housing, health, education and employment. What is a policy and how and why should they become the objects of our research? Many texts understand policy more or less solely as an instrument of state. While that is in general the case, the idea of policy has spread with the increasing bureaucratization of public life and so now companies and corporations, schools, hospitals and universities all have policies that are documented. The ubiquitous processes of accountability are also documented. In the public sector policy development has been a growth area in recent decades under the impact of the scrutiny of a range of government agencies ostensibly engaged in securing the optimal performance from the servants of the state (Mullard and Spicker, 1998; Ainley, 1999). At this level, policy is concerned with regulating social practices and providing an ideological justification for them. So, for example, in England the Office for Standards in Education (OfSted), the regulatory body for schools and further education colleges, has become the best known of the scrutinizing agencies. Its mission is to standardize provision and to ensure ideological conformity with the values and approved practices of the state. It is therefore both a manifestation of policy and a means of pursuing it.

Social policy often declares a concern for justice, which can bring with it a certain homogenizing tendency; for example, all children have the right of access to the National Curriculum. The logic would seem to be that if all children need to access the same knowledge, then schooling provision must also be standardized. This can go along with a contradictory celebration of consumer choice (Gewirtz, Ball and Bowe, 1995).

The point of policy is not simply to support or reproduce the state but, particularly in the case of social policy concerned with welfare, it aims to address a need. Social policy, whether socialist, neo-liberal or third way is constructed in general with the idea of securing some sort of improvement to the current state of affairs; to improve pupils' learning by providing for more teachers, to enhance public safety by building more prisons or to improve public health by the reorganization and increased funding of the health service. As can be seen from these examples, one aspect of public policy is about the competition for the command of finite resources.

Policy can be understood at another level as being about conceptually ordering reality and by so doing helping to construct our identities. Policy attempts to determine what it means to be a social worker or a patient in hospital or a lecturer in a university or an inspector of schools. Policy construction is not normally a random activity or the product of whimsy, although Ball's (1992, 1995) accounts of the policy process that led to the English National Curriculum contain elements of both. Usually under-pinning the policy process are sets of political values. Policy construction 'is guided by (albeit sometimes rather opaque) values, principles and objectives' (Drake, 2001: 3). Policy is informed by 'concepts such as free-dom, equality, justice, rights, diversity and citizenship' (Drake, 2001: 3). These values and their political contexts have important effects in deter-mining the shape and content of social policy and also the methods of implementation.

During the decades following the Second World War, education policy in England was broad brush and largely consensual between the two main political parties. In short, it was conceived of as a public good and there should be more of it for more people. However, the coming of the first Thatcher administration in 1979 and the importation of neo-liberal or neo-conservative ideas made education policy a key site for ideological contest. Within the new government were those who believed that educa-tion should be linked to the economy, controlled by a Department for Education and Employment, and that it would serve the people best if organized along market lines. Opposed to them, but outside government, were those who believed that equality of opportunity should be the aim of education and this could not be achieved through market mechanisms, but was the responsibility of the state. Drake (2001) makes a useful dis-tinction for understanding the contexts of policy between policies con-cerned with processes and those concerned with outcomes. Governments of the right that favour the minimal state concern themselves with pro-cesses. Such an administration 'may have no truck with the redistribution of wealth' and would be unlikely to support 'any thoroughgoing social security system to protect the poor from destitution' (Drake, 2001: 2). Rather the focus would be on social processes, for example, 'laws to pre-vent fraudulent contracts'. Governments of the left are more likely to use policy that concerns itself both with processes and social outcomes. An administration may 'wish to limit the extent of social inequalities in a society or secure fresh opportunities for some disadvantaged groups' (Drake, 2001: 2). And so we need to ask 'by what principles (if any) do political parties claim that their policies are guided?' and also 'how do governments conceptualise the principles to which they claim allegiance?' (Drake, 2001: 3).

Policy and process

Policy can be more or less detailed in its prescriptions. Before the advent of the centralized and statutory curriculum the only subject that English schools were bound to provide was Religious Education. The National Curriculum gave statutory force to a range of traditional subjects and most recently to the construction of the political person through Citizenship Education. Recent administrations have extended the scope of policy as an instrument of control by attempts to regulate teaching as a social practice. This is achieved partly through the administration of teacher education and professional development. Also, policy works inside school through the determination of the contents of subjects and ways of teaching. For example, the National Literacy and National Numeracy schemes under which the methods of teaching and the time spent on various aspects of a particular lesson were prescribed. This is an interesting development, because it is clearly at one level a centrally determined, politically motivated policy, but it is presented as a common sense way of improving the measurable performance of both teachers and pupils, which itself is constructed as an unalloyed good. It is an example of the way that doing 'what works' is the justification for policy but the means of defining 'working' is externally directed and closely controlled.

In the modern state the principle organizational form is bureaucracy. Bureaucracy is the application of reason to social function. Following Weber, Brown and Lauder (1992: 11) list the attributes of bureaucracy as 'precision, speed, clarity, regularity, reliability and efficiency achieved through the fixed division of tasks, hierarchical supervision, and detailed rules and regulations'. The shift in culture in the public service from collegiality to a semi-commercial bureaucracy has made those engaged in the provision of services more amenable to control through policy direction, particularly because in a bureaucracy the person is subsumed under function, which can be clearly delineated as text. This brings us to the idea of the policy document.

While traditionally the medium of a document is a piece of paper, the advent of the electronic document has had an impact on both form and function. Nonetheless, there is a constant stream of paper-based policy documents that move and shape public service and public servants and their clients. Documents are to be read and they are produced to achieve an effect. Reading is not a natural activity but is socially constructed within different cultural and political contexts (Street, 2001). Reading the Qu'ran as a poetic and dramatic performance is different from scanning the papers for a committee. For most people reading is part of schooling. In school, reading is constructed as a cognitive activity to do with the decoding of text, its reality is psychological not political. Implicit in this approach to reading is a model of language and reality that coincides with the vernacular positivism of the modern state, the privileging of rationality and with it the belief in a single plane of knowable reality that is represented in a one-to-one or mapping fashion by language. The idea that language corresponds to what is real is an important element in understanding the nature and status of policy documents. In the perfect policy document there would almost be an assumption that in some way it was the duty of social reality to reflect the contents of the document. The inspection manuals of inquisitorial bodies such as OfSted are themselves active policy documents and reality is tested against them with the ideal being a perfect representational match between the official meanings and the social object that is being tested.

As Drake (2001) suggests, while it is important to concern ourselves with the intended outcomes of policy, the policy process is more complex than we might at first perceive. While the idea of policy assumes rationality, 'policy principles may be neither harmonious nor mutually reinforcing' (Drake, 2001: 4). The rapid expansion of the higher education sector in recent decades fulfils the aim of greater participation, but may have an adverse effect on the pursuit of excellence or the maintaining of academic standards. There is also an issue of political power: when policy becomes statutory, then mechanisms within the bureaucratic culture of the state evolve to monitor and evaluate those social practices the policies aim to create or control. A key working assumption of this process is that the social is in some sense objective and that it exists on a single plane and can have a singular meaning.

For example, in recent times in England there have been cases of small rural primary schools radically failing to meet the criteria for a successful OfSted inspection and thus being threatened with closure. The school may be locally esteemed by pupils and by parents happy with the education their children were receiving. However, their truth was not the objective truth that was constructed by the authoritative text of an inspection report; a text that has the power to define reality. The person who authored the text is seen merely as the operator of a system for generating standardized true accounts of educational reality. There are also unintended consequences of policy implementation. It is not OfSted's intention to traumatize whole communities for substantial periods of time, which is a common result of the inspection process, but more reasonably to monitor standards in schooling.

Outside of the world of policy and its implementation and evaluation it is generally recognized that social reality is not a natural object, but a human construct and that another account is always possible. Also policy aims may themselves be ambiguous or contested, for example, 'securing citizenship, promoting equality, preserving the freedom of the individual, furthering justice and pursuing equality of opportunity are open to question' (Drake, 2001: 4). What we have in these a/political practices is the use of positivist empiricist culture to validate a particular reading of the real and to invalidate other readings. Interestingly, the inspection process blurs the difference between itself and research by adopting research-like practices and writing remote and apparently context-free reports drawing on the model of scientific writing. These texts are not alone, but form part of a wider state discourse on education that includes a whole range of abstracted texts, some apparently authorless, and particularly policy documents which not only define the empirically real but also attempt to constrain and define future realities.

Deconstructing the text

Deconstruction is not a concept that is normally associated with the analysis of public policy although Ball (1994) and Stronach and MacLure (1997) are notable exceptions. In general it is about inverting the obvious. Foucault (1990), for example, inverts the received wisdom of our under-standing of the Victorians by his claim that the age was saturated with sexual discourse rather than characterized by its absence or by reticence. Absence is a key term here. As we shall see, what is significant is not only what a document contains, but what it omits.

Deconstruction as a method was explored by Derrida (1973, 1976) as part of a larger critique of Western metaphysics. Some of its features have a direct bearing on the ways in which we can approach policy documents. Binary opposition privileges one term above another, positive/negative being both an example and the methodology. That is to say, the terms are not only oppositional but the first term is positively privileged in rela-tion to the second, which is its inferior. The binary that Derrida considers is presence/absence. Presence is the first term and absence is its subordinate. What Derrida does is to invert the opposition and so absence becomes the privileged category. And so speech, which is about presence in both space and time, gives way to writing. Foucault (1984) asks the question, what is an author? He notes that some pieces of writing are not authored and appear to be the product of human agency in general, but in the case of policy documents this also serves to give them an objective quality. Their genesis in the desires of real persons to bring about a particular state of affairs is sequestered by the rules of the genre (*cf.* Chapter 4).

Deconstruction as a method is explored by Parker (1997: 68), particu-larly in relation to critical reading and the construction of social action as though it were a text:

> Deconstruction is a *strategy* for examining texts which works within the text's own system of beliefs and values. The text provides the fuel for the process of deconstruction; in deconstruction we borrow devices from *within* the text to use them *upon* or *against* the text . . . deconstruction is *always* concerned to show up or exploit *weaknesses* . . . like satire or Semtex it is for anyone to use.

While negativity is not a valued position in research in the public services, it is not the inevitable accompaniment of a deconstructive reading. In the example of deconstruction that follows I am reading into the text the political and ideological dimensions that constitute its connotative field because their sequestration by the text means that they are not available to the reader for scrutiny and critical engagement. As Brown and Jones (2001: 6) suggest 'by adopting poststructuralist frameworks [in research] and by engaging with practices of deconstruction, attempts are made to break away from inappropriate or inadequate category systems'.

The Spiritual, Moral, Social and Cultural curriculum

What now follows after some contextualization is an analysis of a part of the 'affective curriculum,' the Spiritual, Moral, Social and Cultural curriculum (SMSC) (Best, 1996, 2000; Yates, 2000b). The focus is on what might be termed the intermediate documents that are positioned between the policy and its implementation and are created as guides to conformity. One of the interesting aspects of this particular policy initiative is that it very largely failed and was rapidly taken over in the affective curriculum by the imposition of statutory Citizenship Education.

In the school curriculum Ball (1995) argues that cultural restorationism, the nostalgic attempt to re-form education in the image of an imagined golden age, dominates educational thinking with a 'regressive traditionalism applied to all facets of educational practice' (Ball, 1995: 87). This orientation represents, 'a hard line, old humanism based on a discourse that links education strongly with traditional social and political values and with social order' (Ball, 1995: 87). In the restorationist discourse, tradition is evoked and equated with the morally good but ' "traditional education" (and traditional values) is here a pastiche, a policy simulacrum – the identical copy for which no original has ever existed . . . this simulacrum coincides perfectly with the broader agenda of restorationism and the neo-conservative project to re-establish *order and place*' (Ball, 1994: 45). It is within this context that the discourse around SMSC can be located.

Policies require the consent of those to whom they are directed if they are to be successful. Thus, part of the policy process for SMSC was to create something that it could be argued was relevant to all pupils and all schools. A critical issue for the legitimacy of SMSC was that it would enshrine national values and in so doing become universally applicable. However, even the concept of what a value might be is contested and elusive (Halstead and Taylor, 1996).

Rationality and consistency and conformity are highly prized virtues in the bureaucratic culture of the state, which generates policy and this is reflected in monitoring by inspection. Halstead (1996: 11) quotes the *Handbook for the Inspection of Schools* where 'a school is said to be exhibiting high standards in the area of pupils' personal development and behaviour "if its work is based upon clear principles and values expressed through its aims and evident in its practice" '. Standards have two important elements, uniformity in application and conformity in expression both of which deny the importance of difference in persons and groups most particularly evident in those aspects of the person referred to in SMSC.

Ball (1995: 100) is critical of the monoculturalism implicit in the National Curriculum, which he describes as 'a fantasy curriculum', which fails to construct reliable knowledge of the world but attempts to 'conjure up and reproduce a fantasy of Englishness, classlessness, authority, legitimacy, moral order and consensus'. In this discourse the past is more real than the present, which is constantly seen to fall short.

Ball quotes Pascall as chairman of the National Curriculum Council expressing a unitary and fixed view of culture where 'the culture of a society is defined by its political and social history, its religious and moral beliefs, and its intellectual and artistic traditions' (Ball, 1995: 100). Current realities seem not to impinge on the vision of a 'dominant culture', which is constructed by 'the Christian faith, the Greco-Roman influence, the Liberal enlightenment, romanticism, the development of modern humanism' (Ball, 1995: 100). As Ball (1995: 98) notes, 'we are to face the future by always looking backwards'. Pascall's notion of culture as 'a process of intellectual, spiritual and moral development' removes school knowledge from any connection with the cultural realities of pupils' lived experience (Ball, 1995: 98).

Analysing key documents

Before looking at the Qualifications and Curriculum Authority document, *Draft Guidance*, there are two preliminary documents that begin to set the tone and map the territory that SMSC will occupy. The National Curriculum Council (1993) discussion paper attempts to unpack the spiritual and moral domains into a set of standard prescriptions. It is a classic document which while apparently addressing concrete reality touches no known social condition at any point. For example, spirituality 'has to do with the universal search for individual identity', a statement at odds with most theological, anthropological, historical and psychological understanding but consonant with neo-conservative or neo-liberal notions of the primacy of the individual.

The content of spirituality is a catalogue drawn from modernist religious education and includes beliefs, a sense of awe and wonder, feelings of transcendence, a search for meaning, self-knowledge, relationships, creativity and feelings and emotions. The rationale of this collection is not given, nor is there any justification for their being constituted as valid knowledge within the school curriculum beyond the word 'spirituality' appearing in the preamble to the 1988 Education Reform Act. The authority of the text derives from its documentary form and its provenance in one of the agencies of the state. The School Curriculum and Assessment Authority's (SCAA, 1996a) statement on spiritual and moral development continues to address the same problem and is in the same genre. It has a clear concern with standardization, though this is presented as achieving consensus, a matter of no concern in the drawing up of the original National Curriculum (Ball, 1995). In the statement 'spirituality should be seen as a form of skill or aptitude', the limits of its conceptualization are rather firmly set (SCAA, 1996a: 6).

Under the heading of 'Defining Spirituality' Pascall's neo-liberal agenda is confirmed. Throughout the document there is no recognition of the autonomy of the social sphere; it exists only as a medium upon which the agency is to inscribe its will. Thus it asserts that in order 'to enable productive debate, key terms such as "values", "attitudes" and "morality" should have broadly agreed definitions' (SCAA, 1996a: 5), which is rational but unreal in the sense that it can only be asserted but never achieved. Similarly, 'traditional approaches to Personal and Social Education lack rigour', is unexplained but clearly pejorative (SCAA, 1996a: 5). The social is presented as a unified actor in thrall to the agency in the notion that 'society must express and affirm values and behaviours it expects schools to promote' (SCAA, 1996a: 5).

The QCA *Draft Guidance*

The implementation of this neo-liberal model of the person in society embedded in school curriculum was pursued by the Qualification and Curriculum Authority (QCA) through a series of documents framed as *Draft Guidance for Pilot Work* (QCA, 1997). The documents attempt a bureaucratic construction of the spiritual, moral, social and cultural curriculum and this is made clear not simply by the words but also by the form and structure of the Guidance. It comprises nine (unpaginated) documents, two devoted to justification and description, two to the role of subject teaching in the main phases of schooling, one to 66 briefly sketched case studies of 'the promotion of pupils' spiritual, moral, social and cultural development', a list of resources and two matrices, one illustrative and one empty, subtitled 'a management tool' which, 'will be a complete statement of school policy in this area' (QCA, 1997). Lastly, there is a set of instructions on how the documents are to be used in order to create an enactment of their content and its own documentary legitimation in a whole-school policy. In short, the Guidance documents are a do-it-yourself policy construction kit.

The guidance is not constructed in continuous prose, which might encourage careful consideration, but in double columns of bullet points and boxes, a form which evokes the imperative mood and which belies the frequent exhortations to reflection. There is an immediate conflict between the often repeated message that these documents are merely aids 'designed to stimulate schools' own thinking in this area' and the level of comprehensive, and often prescriptive, detail contained in them (QCA, 1997). Instructions for use begin with an 'executive summary' which justifies the activity within a specific image of the school and lists seven advantages to the organization which 'the successful promotion of pupils' spiritual, moral, social and cultural development' can deliver (QCA, 1997). The first is that it will 'enable the school successfully to fulfil its statutory obligation(s)' and the second is that it will 'contribute to success in OfSted inspections' (QCA, 1997). Thus, the exercise is immediately set within a forensic and coercive framework of legal duty and promised surveillance. It will also make people work harder by 'increasing pupil and teacher motivation' (QCA, 1997). The puritan virtue of hard work in the form of increased motivation is a constant reference throughout the documents. The affective areas of the person are referred to only once and in terms of an ideal and empirically meaningless end, that of ensuring 'that everyone in the school feels valued as an individual' (QCA, 1997). The notion that SMSC can make a 'contribution to school ethos' suggests that ethos is a planned and achievable condition rather than an undercurrent of school culture. This is explained by the last statement, where achievement of this 'promotion' is to 'ensure that the values enshrined in the school's mission statement permeate every part of school life' (QCA, 1997). This last is a description of the perfectly rational bureaucratic organization where all idiosyncrasy is submerged under the weight of internalized and normalizing pressure.

The route to this perfect condition is carefully mapped and presented in the form of rational management manuals by 'a six step process towards success'. This describes the process as one of establishing goals, turning them into Key Stage objectives, planning implementation and monitoring and evaluating outcomes. This will enable the filling in of the empty matrix and defines the activity as one of policy production, the creation of the perfect document, which will in an undisclosed way order real-life social action in its image. In this process of conforming SMSC to the restorationist curriculum, the possibility of equivocation in these complex and diffuse areas is addressed through the provision of a 'Glossary of Key Terms'. This may encourage clarity, but also functions to regulate the meanings of words and thereby the boundaries of the discourse they produce and ultimately the meaning of the social action that they refer to.

The question of values and their legitimation as a policy tool is seen to be a key issue. The School Curriculum and Assessment Authority set up

The National Forum for Values in Education and the Community in order first, to establish a list of consensual values, and second to 'decide how schools might be supported in the important task of contributing to pupils' spiritual, moral, social and cultural development' (QCA, 1997). The deliberations of the National Forum, a group of 150 people largely drawn from 'national organisations with concern for young people or education (sic)', resulted in the identification of four value areas; these were self, relationships, society and the environment, each with an associated set of 'principles for action' (SCAA, 1996b: 5). Within the guidance, these principles are translated into a series of moral prescriptions under the four areas. First, the self, where, for example, 'we should: develop self-respect and self-discipline' (QCA, 1997). Second, relationships, where 'we should: respect the privacy and property of others' (QCA, 1997). Third, society, where 'we should: support the institution of marriage' (QCA, 1997). Finally, the environment, where 'we should: understand the place of human beings within nature' (QCA, 1997). The neo-liberal privileging of the individual over the social is established from the start in the statement 'the ordering [of the four value areas] reflects the belief of many that values in the context of the self must precede the development of the other values' (QCA, 1997). The idea that the construction of the self can in some mystical manner precede our sociality can in no way be verified but is an ideological assertion. While our embodiment is individuated any notion of the dimensions of the self can only be constructed within a socially generated lexicon. (For a fuller discussion see Chapter 9.)

As the guidance itself suggests 'these values are so fundamental that they may appear unexceptional' (QCA, 1997). And indeed they very largely do, and so it is unsurprising that a poll of adults and a survey of 3200 schools and 7000 'organizations' overwhelmingly agreed with the values (although we are not given the response rate). A critical question here is why is there a need to establish a consensus on basic social values when we can be fairly assured of their content and existence? The National Forum was set up as a consequence of the SCAA conference, Education for Adult Life, which considered 'the spiritual and moral development of young people' (SCAA, 1996a). The 'key points' to come out of this conference were a neo-liberal unpacking of the spiritual and moral around the implicit theme of social order where values became 'values and behaviour', which were the subject of an unsubstantiated 'current confusion'. Thus, the National Forum was to remove the confusion by establishing a national consensus. It is worth noting that such a consensus could only have moral authority within a populist political framework. Despite this, the demonstrated consensus is then used to remove the burden of the legitimation of a normalizing curriculum policy from the QCA to an amorphous society. Thus, 'Schools and teachers can have confidence that there is general agreement in society upon these values. They can therefore expect the support and encouragement of society if they base their teaching and the school ethos on these values' (QCA, 1997).

The two propositions in the last sentence do not follow, but are in line with the frequent references to 'community' and the need to establish 'business partners'. The preamble to the statement of values is in exhortatory mode with an underlying appeal to social order, 'their [the values] demanding nature is demonstrated both by our collective failure consistently to live up to them, and the moral challenge which acting on them in practice entails' (QCA, 1997). And so the development (which is the word used where one might expect to see 'education') of the pupil is towards perfect consonance with a moral condition determined by a government agency and expressed as a set of rational prescriptions. Given this, success might well be seen in terms of the degree of conformity that schools can manage to engineer.

The document on 'The promotion of pupils' spiritual, moral, social and cultural development' gives advice on how to move through the six steps to a full matrix. This is headed 'the how', and is preceded by 'the why' and 'the who'. 'The why' reinforces the organizational boundaries of the project by emphasizing the point that the 'promotion' of spiritual, moral, social and cultural 'development' is 'an essential ingredient of school success'. The original orientation of the SCAA conference that this curriculum area was to be primarily concerned with preparation for life outside school is lost. The advantages are confirmed in output terms as increased motivation for both pupils and teachers. 'The who' locates responsibility for the curriculum area with the senior management team and outlines the necessary personal and professional attributes of a co-ordinator.

The bulk of the document is given over to detailing the process of policy production. The empty matrix is even suggested as a conforming device for schools 'with well-established policies' who 'may find completing the empty matrix useful for auditing their existing practice' (QCA, 1997). For those who know schools and teachers well there is a credibility gap between much of the advice contained in the guidance and the assumptions it makes and the actual conditions of teachers' lives and work. The echo of consensus is here translated as success being dependent upon 'consistency of pupils' experiences and relationships' (QCA, 1997). The references to consistency in the guidance may have more to do with the aesthetics of regimentation than with the preparation of pupils for adult life. Part of the achievement of local consensus is consultation with the social segment called 'the community'. In 'extended' form this comprises an apparently random group of 'parents, employers and business partners, local shopkeepers, religious and faith groups, youth associations, the legal and emergency services and the local media'. It is assumed that all these groups can be enticed to 'evening meetings at which people can discuss these issues face to face'.

The advice on Key Stage objectives is to turn them into a prescriptive socialization programme by identifying 'the knowledge and understanding, skills, qualities and attitudes that pupils should be acquiring if they are to be developing those identified in the school's overall goals', which will 'facilitate a secure and practical understanding' for all concerned (QCA, 1997). The aesthetic of rational consistency in the bureaucratic model of the pupil is again evidenced by the advice to ensure 'breadth and balance' so that 'pupils' social development is not promoted *at the expense of* pupils' spiritual development' (original emphasis) (QCA, 1997). What would constitute evidence of such an unbalanced state of affairs in order to determine its existence is not ventured.

The review of current practice is to be thorough and is to include not only 'subject areas' and what is referred to as the 'broader curriculum' (a phrase which brings the informal aspects of school under official gaze) but also 'school structures, systems, processes and rules' (QCA, 1997). A range of advice on how to do this is given including teachers spending a whole day shadowing a pupil. No advice is offered on what to do with the fruits of this experience. However, perfect knowledge of the organization is the aim as the co-ordinator should be able 'to make sure that every part of school life is scrutinized and that everyone is clear about their contribution to this work' (QCA, 1997).

'Planning and implementing change' repeats the need for consistency; suggests that business partners and others in the community might 'lead and manage certain changes' and gives advice on bidding for sponsorship from local and national businesses. The fifth step is evaluation, which urges the need for 'reliable systems by which to gather, analyse and interpret evidence' (QCA, 1997). There is an assurance that 'reflection on lessons . . . is good professional practice', and that 'systems and processes designed to test the collective mood of the school can boost morale' (QCA, 1997). These are to include informal mingling of 'staff and management', or us and them, where they might have a 'chance to unwind together'. On the difficult matter of detecting pupil development, the illustrative matrix suggests that annual reports to parents might be based on 'regular questionnaires, quizzes or short exams of pupils' acquisition and development . . . as outlined in the statement of concrete goals for the appropriate educational stage' (QCA, 1997). This is clearly a description of a process of cognitive acquisition as opposed to engagement with what might be considered valuable, but necessarily open-ended, discursive knowledge. Neither here nor in the illustrative matrix is there any reference to the wealth of advice on monitoring and evaluation to be found in the many practitioner researcher manuals designed for schools such as Altrichter, Posch and Somekh (1993) or Hitchcock and Hughes (1995).

The final step is 'recognising and rewarding pupil and adult achievement'. Within the illustrative matrix rewards are justified on the grounds of increased motivation (QCA, 1997). Within the guidance clarity of exposition as to what this might mean in practice masks the real difficulty in determining what achievement in these areas might look like. The list of rewards reinforces the ideal of conformity to organizational goals through offering greater participation as recognition for achievement. These include 'the right to do coveted tasks . . . to achieve status and reward by taking on responsibility . . . to represent the school at public events . . . to take responsibility, with teachers, for press coverage of school activities . . . become members of committees that have real power' and, most blatantly demonstrating the notion of reward as trusteeship of the organization and its goals 'to cooperate with teachers and senior management in the practical aspects of running the school'. These last used to be called prefects.

This is followed by a section headed 'A Discussion'. After disclaiming the prescriptive authority of what is to follow there are four sections devoted to the development and promotion of the spiritual, moral, social and cultural curricular areas. In the discussion of the spiritual area, any notion of consistency is abandoned in an equivocal set of references to social order and the metaphysical. It is asserted that spirit 'is our essential *self* (original emphasis), which moreover 'when it is strong, enables us to survive hardship, exercise fortitude and overcome difficulties and temptations' (QCA, 1997). Temptation is a clear theme. Evidence of moral development is seen in being 'able to deal effectively with moral conflict and temptation' (QCA, 1997). The point of moral development is that it will 'help them [pupils] exercise their will in resisting temptation' (QCA, 1997). Similarly the internalization of 'rules' will, 'enable them to resist the temptations they inevitably face' (QCA, 1997). The human essence or spirit of self becomes reduced to mood with a reference to 'spirits', which can be high or low. The work ethic is appealed to in that 'spiritual growth is the key to human motivation' and its presence can be detected by 'learning and striving throughout life' (QCA, 1997). This undeclared, and vaguely protestant, individualism runs through the whole discussion which is full of exhortations to be motivated, to work harder and to be obedient. For example, evidence of moral development is 'a determination to obey rules' (QCA, 1997). There is reference to pupils discussing, reflecting and analysing, but only as a route to conformity and within a barely mediated transmission pedagogy.

> Pupils will make these values [identified by the National Forum] their own only if they have been encouraged to discuss them, to subject them to criticism and see *why* these values are the ones that, in the light of reason and fellow feeling, they *should* hold and *why* obedience to these rules is a necessary condition of social harmony (original emphasis).
>
> QCA, 1997

It is difficult to see the educational value of organizing so closed a discussion where the object is to maintain social order through conformity. However, this may be avoided as 'teachers uncomfortable with a discussion-based approach to moral issues' can replace the possibility of discursive or cooperative knowledge construction through their own demonstration of obedience: 'the example they set in their own behaviour' (QCA, 1997). An example given is doing 'marking promptly' which demonstrates to pupils that they are valued. This possible reluctance of teachers to move into the affective realm is raised again in the section of the discussion that addresses potential objections. Amongst 'common concerns' expressed by 'heads and teachers' is 'difficulties with feelings, emotions and the need for personal disclosures' (QCA, 1997). At this point the advice is that 'discussions of feelings and emotions can seem intrusive' but pupils need to 'learn to use their emotional, as well as their academic (sic) intelligence' (QCA, 1997). The model offered here has a repressive dynamic because 'the ability to understand, express and control feelings appropriately is the basis of the ability to form good relationships' (QCA, 1997). The reluctant confessor is again reassured that 'personal disclosures are not essential', but as with obedience, the message can be coded in that 'teachers can indicate that all adults have wrestled with the kind of choices and dilemmas that face young people'.

A section of the Discussion (QCA, 1997) is headed 'Relations between the four areas', which it is asserted are interdependent. Interdependence is demonstrated with a range of assertions which are both reductionist and sociologically and psychologically naive. The spiritual is linked to the moral via individualism. Moral development is achieved by the projection of self-love onto others. This moral development 'underpins social development', which in turn depends upon 'this sort of moral reasoning'. The links between the moral, spiritual and cultural are established through our capacity for sentimentality: 'those moments when we are carried away by the sheer beauty of a piece of music . . . enable us to understand the greatness of the universe'. The argument veers sharply from romanticism to social order in justifying the links between cultural and social development. The case put is that 'social cohesion depends on individuals being culturally developed'. The combining of the notions of culture and development is difficult to conceive of, as a culture normally refers to a construction of what actually is, rather than something that we might incrementally instruct others in so as to cause recognizable or measurable development. While clearly aspects of socialization can be purposive and organized, for example, teaching table manners or the rules of public worship, this is part of a diffuse pattern of social reproduction rather than a mass induction controlled by the state. Society is a complex idea that is variously understood in the academic disciplines which seriously address its nature. However, in the Discussion it is reduced to being 'important . . . in virtue of its having clear moral values and a strong sense of shared cultural inheritance'. Protestant morality is here briefly abandoned in favour of hedonism in the statement that '[society] creates the conditions in which human creativity, imagination and insight can be exercised in their highest form, in creation for the sheer pleasure it brings'.

In a separate document, 66 case studies, selected by OfSted for QCA, are categorized within the six steps to completing the matrix and the four areas identified by the National Forum. No indication of the criteria used for this assignment is given. The cases represent sometimes moving testimony to the creativity of the human spirit in the real capacities of children to organize and maintain their micro-communities and in the willing engagement of teachers in their pupils' sociality. However, this humane discourse is absent, because the guidance construes these activities as valuable only insofar as they produce rational cognitive performances that meet 'concrete objectives'.

There is a radical confusion here of performativity and conformity with the exploration and expression of what it is to be a human person. The easy fusion of the behavioural, which is to do with conformity, with the moral, which is to do with distinguishing the precepts that guide social action, turns what might be engagement with the responsibilities of autonomous selfhood into a simple exercise in obedience. This may produce social order, but represents a developmental cul-de-sac. Throughout the documents, what relationship might exist between social order and spirituality can only be guessed at.

In this unauthored document, the disembodied voice of the state gives rational advice on school policy development. The deconstructive reading is made by making present the ideological and political absences within the text. What emerges is a neo-liberal and communitarian concern with conformity and social order. This suffuses the documents, which superficially speak with a naturalistic voice that resists equivocation.

What we have tried to illustrate here is the possibility of a transgressive reading, one that goes beyond the text itself by reconceptualizing and inverting its apparent intention. Barthes' distinction between the 'readerly', that is the passively accepted, and the 'writerly' or re-formed text is apposite here and is more fully explained in the next chapter. In general we have constructed policy as a mass idea, it goes along with Foucault's conception of 'bio-power'; the ways in which the modern state thinks in terms of populations, aggregations of largely undifferentiated bodies that are the subjects of the inscription of the will of the state. However, the broader concerns of policy to create specific universal social states or conditions can focus on the control of the individual's ways of thinking and acting. Foucault (1988: 19) coined the term 'governmentality' to refer to 'the contact of technologies of domination of others and those of the self'.

The example we have focused on is from recent curriculum policy in England where the social practices of the teacher in the classroom have been minutely prescribed through pedagogic instructions and through predetermined meanings of language and action. These prescriptions were presented as natural common sense, and as though they were actually conferring autonomy. However, the deconstructive reading suggests that it can be construed as the freedom to do as one is told. As Barker (1998: 64) suggests 'Governmentality is an attitude that relates to the governing of oneself in order that others may be governed'. This does not suggest that teachers are robotic apparatchiks. However, the policy can be seen with hindsight to have failed: practice was not changed at the level of detail, but it is perhaps arguable that such documents contribute to a more overarching discourse of subjection. Finally, it is important to bear in mind Mills's (2003: 47) caveat that 'the most productive element in Foucault's analysis of power is the fact that he sees power relations as largely unsuccessful, as not achieving the goal of total domination'.

Part 3

Data with destiny – reconstructing text

9

Writing research – authoring text

In this chapter we focus on the nature of research writing. We pick up several ideas that have been raised in earlier chapters, though they are approached here from a slightly different angle. Our main concern is to move away from writing conceived merely as a technical support for research activity. Instead we want to examine the idea that researchers are primarily writers. Within the literature on research writing, or academic writing more generally, there is a wide variety of approaches. These give more or less emphasis to technical and philosophical or methodological concerns. There is plenty of advice on matters of technique related to different research traditions. However, there are epistemological and methodological issues associated with writing that are contested and oppositional and that relate to the nature of language and of reality and to the role of power and of politics in determining what is to be taken as a representative picture of the real.

In Western schooling, literacy is largely constructed as a set of decontextualized cognitive skills. Reading is the decoding of previously encoded language and writing is the act of encoding. In research practice this often means that the writing up of the research is seen as largely unproblematic. One simply has to write the results of one's endeavours. This entails the reconstruction of one's direct experience of the field; an experience that has been systematically organized by recognized and reliable methods of data collection. These data can be seen as providing accurate reflections of the reality from which they were extracted. The task is to represent that reality as faithfully as possible within the constraints of an appropriate genre of research writing. Thus, the major issue as conceived by many researchers is perhaps that research culture demands that they write within the prescriptions of a particular genre, particularly in order to ensure the validity of their account. That is the idea that the account is true or that it conforms to the reality it purports to represent. However, it follows from the previous argument of this book and especially from Chapter 5 that research writing cannot necessarily be understood as merely a simple mapping operation of language onto a reality that can be accurately represented by a single account.

There is a range of questions that almost immediately come to mind around the issue of how we construct ourselves as the researcher/author. Central to this enquiry is the question what is language and how does it work? What is a text? To whom is the writing addressed, who are the prospective audience(s)? How does what I am writing relate to other writings; in what ways is it dependent upon them? This is the issue of intertextuality. What sorts of writing devices are acceptable; can I use playlets and poetry as well as graphs and pie charts? Who or what is governing this choice? What sorts of contexts are relevant to my writing and how am I constructing them? Am I producing legitimate knowledge and how does this relate to the subjects/objects of my research? Am I attempting to mirror reality and what is the epistemological status of my account? What do I understand by the terms 'meaning' and 'metaphor' and how might this affect the truth of my account? How do I understand reflexivity and my role as researcher in relation to my writing? Am I writing about me or reflecting a truly independent reality?

Writing and the real

One of the areas to consider is the matter of whether the objects of research are lodged in an independent reality or whether they are social constructs, an idea that shifts the grounds of reality to consciousness and language. Writing is inextricably linked to the way we see the world and the methodological frame that we find ourselves working within. It is this that determines the way in which we construct the relationship between what we write and the reality or the objects that our writing represents. There would seem to be three basic models of research writing; these might be termed the objective, the subjective and the socially determined. The first would be writing in a naturalistic and scientific frame where the writing attempts to mirror the reality it describes. The second would be based on the assumption that we can only write our own experience; and the third would largely deny the role of the author and give primacy to language, discourse and text.

This suggests that one way of understanding ourselves as writers is through the idea of agency and Foucault's (1984) question, what is an author? How far and in what ways is the research writer as an essential individual the author of the text? The objective paradigm is the traditional science culture of modernity, that is positivism and its variants. As we have seen positivism is thought on the one hand to be no longer credible

(Denzin, 1998) and on the other the dominant paradigm of choice (Scott, 2000). There is also postpositivism exemplified by grounded theory, which has both qualitative and quantitative elements, but this retains the essential positivist premise of an objective reality. The growth of interest in ethnography in recent decades has brought both constructivism and hermeneutics into the research field although a general assumption persists that there is an independent reality and that it is the researcher's role to represent faithfully that reality. More recently postmodern excursions into social research indicate a shift away from a clearly independent empirical realm and so the significance of language, and especially writing, is set at the heart of the endeavour.

This brings us to the issue of representation, the matter of how what we write relates to the realities our research aims to portray. This is critical to understanding the operation of discursive power and the establishment of the real. Usher (1996b: 44) suggests that 'it is writing that makes realism possible'. That is to say, that it is writing that supports representation of the real, and via verisimilitude, the truth. It is this formulation that Usher (1996b: 33) makes problematic: 'writing is not a set of abstract transcendental marks but rather a concrete, material activity located within particular textual practices'.

The writer is never entirely free to write what their genius inspires, but is always subject to the simultaneously constraining and enabling contexts of culture and genre. Texts are artefactual. In the context of applied research 'there is always an intertwining of theory and practice, its writing cannot slip free from practice to live within a timeless, decontextualized world of general theoretical knowledge' (Usher, 1996b: 33). However, that very division between theory and practice normally privileges the empirical. Generally in applied fields such as education, a separable theoretical realm has not simply to explain, but also needs to be justified by its contribution to (improved) practice. Research is seen as a potentially coercive tool, it must accomplish something other than itself. It is understood as analogous to a tool in that it is often said to have 'users' whose existence legitimates the activity and also helps to define what is thought to be researchable. These are cultural constraints imposed by the ways in which one becomes a researcher. Usher (1996b: 33) sees educational research writing as a classical modernist text where 'writing is seen as simply a neutral vehicle for transporting the "truth" '. Consequently 'the *textuality* of research "falls away" ' with writing appearing as simply an unmediating means for communicating a reality that is "outside" the text' (Usher, 1996b: 33). Thus, we have the movement from reality via research to text with a maximum correspondence between the phases, the point of the text being to represent the object of research. Within this process in Usher's term the text is 'repressed'.

Usher notes that research is legitimated by the research community and cites reflexivity as a necessary element in the research process, where this points to the way in which we understand the researcher as a part of, and not apart from, the research. Usher further argues that this is not sequential; one does not do the research and then reflect upon the process, but that the researcher's presence is part of the process. The ramifications of the idea of research occurring within and being dependent upon a community, which includes the researcher, are important in constructing the nature of writing. Individuals may often be researchers but 'the very notion of the "individual" is a *subject position* produced by a certain kind of discourse' (Usher, 1996b: 36). Research then is individual in that it is a matter of identity, and it is social because that is the arena in which that identity is formed; and the one is always present in the other. Given this, the issue of representation becomes interesting, because methodology is there to help guarantee true representations of the world. However, if it is the case that research is a 'discursive practice of "languaging" ' (Usher, 1996b: 39) then the issue of the nature of representations and their relation to the reality they point to becomes not automatic but problematic.

Where the text is a technical production, the social conditions of its construction are obscured. Lacey (1970) and Willis (1977) were both Marxist ethnographers who declared their engagement with a particular ideological frame that constructed for them the real and the true. But this is still not the case with much social research. There are many current texts that appear to be unproblematically engaged in securing progress to perfection through the creation of rigorous and innocent accounts of natural and realist settings. For example, within the literature on performance management or on school effectiveness and improvement the critical voice is massively overwhelmed by technicist discourse. As with inspection reports, much of what is written appears to be context free. Truth value is established via the adherence to approved methodological rituals and is located in the correspondence between text and its objects. Writing is simply the realization of the truth of the process. The text is a dependent naturalistic representation almost automatically constructed within a subgenre of academic writing that seems to aspire to the status of a report, that is to say an account of what actually is. As Usher (1996b: 44) notes, realist narrative texts 'point away from their writerliness' and indeed 'the most important effect of writing is to conceal its own being as writing'. Two things follow from this. First, that there is no research without writing, indeed that research is writing; and concomitantly what becomes obscured is 'the significance (and significatory power) of the representational means or system, the context of language, writing and its textual "strategies and devices" ' (Usher, 1996b: 43). The writer here is sovereign, but also floats with the text, partly authored by what it describes. However, 'the individual researcher not only writes but is also *written'* (Usher 1996b: 43). All writing is located and embedded in ideological worlds and sets of conventions that are recursively productive and constraining. One cannot simply write. Thus, it is the ways in which the processes of textual production are hidden that allows texts to be constructed as realist accounts. This obscures and limits understanding of the nature and the power effects of texts as discourse.

Art and science

Can the researcher's text innocently correspond with actuality in the way that some natural science writers assume? Part of the research culture of positivism is to see the text as in some sense neutral, almost naturally occurring. In this tradition research texts 'seem to be predicated on the discovery of social realities through selectively unproblematic acts of engagement and inspection' (Coffey and Atkinson, 1996: 122). Researchers perhaps rarely see writing as their primary activity, although the text is the place where the research is realized. Most often, the text is the only semi-permanent trace of the human activity that constitutes field-based research.

Coffin *et al.* (2003: 48) in a discussion of academic writing construct an 'academic knowledge continuum' that comprises 'sciences – social sciences – humanities'. Science is reported to be 'hard' and the humanities 'soft' while between these poles 'are the social sciences which have adapted much of the scientific method and applied it to different and less predictable types of data' (Coffin *et al.*, 2003: 48). They note that 'we do know that different approaches to what constitutes knowledge in a subject area are usually implicit rather than explicit' (Coffin *et al.*, 2003: 48). A continuum with three points might be understood as a binary opposition with a central synthesis and the terms hard and soft introduce another binary with hard as the privileged form of knowledge and soft the weaker form. This privileging of natural scientific method as the guarantor of the account that perfectly corresponds with actuality underpins much of the discussion relating to qualitative research writing. As we shall see, a radical approach to language and reality is required before the researcher as writer can establish an alternative position from which to write. Hitchcock and Hughes (1995) note a breaking down of disciplinary boundaries and the impact of feminism and postmodernism on research writing and our understanding of it in relation to reality. Citing life history as an example they suggest that 'self-consciously researchers are becoming more concerned with the "art" of their work as much as or more than the "science" of their endeavours' (Hitchcock and Hughes, 1995: 337).

There is an issue here for the writer trying to discover which language game to write within and the rules of textual production. This problem partly derives from the blurring of boundaries between traditional academic subjects and the rise of hybrid disciplines such as cultural studies (Sardar and Van Loon, 2004) that are associated with a field of interest rather than a distinctive set of methods and modes of writing. This hybridity is not accidental but comes from asking questions and formulating interests that cannot be dealt with inside traditional disciplinary frames. The model for this approach comes from the revolution in literary theory in the last half century 'where it has been possible to ask of philosophy, linguistics and psychology, as well as literary study, questions that they have been unable to ask of themselves, from within their own disciplinary boundaries' (Derrida, 1990: 82; Stronach and MacLure, 1997: 3) Critically 'it is precisely the *im*purity of literary theory – its resistance to containment within its "own" disciplinary field, and its infidelity to the fences erected around others – that, for Derrida, constitutes its power to question the axiomatics and foundational principles of disciplines' (Stronach and MacLure, 1997: 3). Bartlett, Burton and Peim (2001: 247) would locate the study of education in just such a volatile condition:

> A tradition running from Nietzsche in the nineteenth century to Richard Rorty at the end of the twentieth century has challenged the claims of official forms of knowledge to truth. These discourses and others – such as feminism, deconstruction and post-modernism – have deliberately sought to problematize the nature of truth and knowledge . . . this can give rise to 'hybrid' forms of knowledge . . . (which) means that the boundaries of education study are not fixed.

These conditions of knowledge construction are inevitably reflected in textual production so that writers often feel compelled to confront their subjectivity and its effects upon the status and validity of their accounts.

One remedy is a variation on the central methodological gambit of grounded theory (Glaser and Strauss, 1967). From this position, qualitative research is valid insofar as it can satisfy at least some of the criteria by which we recognize the validity of the natural scientific method.

If what we are trying to represent is the reality of other people, is the scientific method the sole guarantor of validity? The pioneering work of anthropologists Clifford and Marcus (1986) brought to the fore the issue of 'how can we write the reality of the other?' This became known as the crisis in representation. The classic model of anthropological writing was close to the omnipotent author. Fieldwork provided the experiential base upon which the anthropological account was written. The objects of the account, those people who actually constituted the field, were only present through the voice of the anthropologist. Coffey and Atkinson (1996: 122) describe 'classic works of ethnography that adopt a single dominant perspective – that of the author/observer'. One might suggest that this is in some sense a necessity, since someone in the research community has to do the writing. But then, how do we understand the relationship between what actually occurred, the plurality of voices that make up the field, and the single voice of the ethnographer? Does the account represent the preoccupations of the researcher and her community? Alternatively, does it try and represent the reality of the field, where the voices of the objects of research are unlikely to include the Western research agenda and its conventions? Clifford and Marcus also highlighted the issue of the politics of power in representation, a dimension of the social that can be lost within a realist image of the research process. For example, we can see discursive power at work in the discourses of educational psychology, which can construct a pathological or non-normal identity for a student, an identity with which the student may not be in sympathy. However, within school this psychological representation is the more powerful discourse. It is taken as real, or more real than the students' construction of themselves. Consequently, this apparently neutral or objective representation is the one that is acted on as the real account of the Other. While the student may not concur with this official definition, it is validated by science and has more power to define what is real than has the subjectivity of the pupil. For the writer this illustrates the further complication of the existence of plural and, not necessarily complementary, accounts of the same sets of experience. What are we to write and which is to be taken as real? This might be termed as the terrorists' and freedom fighters' dilemma because what we take to be real depends upon what set of interests we align ourselves with.

Writing the real

Within the realist paradigm, research methodology functions to guarantee the truth value of the representation and this is not mediated by the nature of language, but is somehow truly reflected in the text. Importantly, what is produced is in some ways secondary to the manner of its production. The integrity of the text lies in its methodological underpinning rather than in the meanings that the text may contain. The value given to positivistic systematic reviews of applied research in health and more recently in education would be a case in point. The methodology or rules for production of text are here seen as the core of the activity and the guarantee of validity. These rules for textual production can be both baroque and prescriptive as in the recipe for producing systematic reviews of research (refer, for example, to the Eppi Centre which produces systematic reviews of education in the UK – http://eppi.ioe.ac.uk/EPPIWeb/home.aspx). More generally within realist research, as Scott and Usher indicate:

> ... the key questions are always concerned with the extent to which research outcomes, as reported, are adequate, correspond to, or truly represent the reality investigated. The effect of this concern is therefore an emphasis in research on outcomes and method.
>
> Scott and Usher, 1996: 39

However, in writing our research we are inescapably at some level inscribing our experience, however that is conceived or mediated by research design and methodology. Kuhn (1970) coined the term 'paradigm' to refer to the discursive world within which scientists constructed and solved their puzzles. A more general term might be 'research culture'. This could refer to the paradigms of research that exist and also to their embeddedness in social and political forms. Giddens's (1991) distinction between practical and discursive consciousness is apposite. The distinction is between those things that we know and which inform our social practice but which we never need to bring to the surface, our practical consciousness; and those things that we consciously articulate in our construction of ourselves and our social worlds, our discursive consciousness. In much practitioner research, we find that realism is almost seen as a part of practical consciousness. It is too obvious to be articulated. Scott (2000: 19) sees the key realist assumption as positing that: 'there is a real world out there which does not depend on how it is understood or articulated by any human being. Furthermore, there is a uniquely best way of describing it, which is not dependent on history or society.'

Atkinson (1990: 41), however, suggests that in research writing 'explicit citations of cultural knowledge blend almost imperceptibly with implicit interpretive reliance on everyday knowledge of a diffuse sort'. That is to say that in both our writing and our reading of research texts, we employ both practical and discursive consciousness.

Qualitative empiricism

There are many forms of phenomenological and constructivist research. A recent influential set of texts around qualitative research is that edited by Denzin and Lincoln (1998a, 1998b, 1998c). Key ideas here are hermeneutics and story or narrative. It is useful to note that hermeneutics is a borrowing from theology where it is the attempt to reconstruct the truth of sacred text and, through systematic engagement, to discover the real intentions of the author. This requires breaking into the hermeneutic circle which is analogous to finding words in a language, or semiotic system, that will allow one to break the code and to invest a text with meaning. Within hermeneutics, both encoding and decoding are sites of theoretical interest. Denzin sees both reading and writing as necessary parts of the research process. In the process of creating an interpretation, or narrative of experience, the reader is a necessary context. Just as the writer works within a matrix of texts and draws on them in a variety of ways in creating an intertextual text, so the reader brings their own intertextuality via knowledge and experience to the interpretation of the text they read.

The key issues for Denzin (1998: 318) in writing are 'sensemaking, representation, legitimation, desire'. Sensemaking is the process of reflection and analysis that creates the text. As Denzin has it 'interpretation involves the construction of a reading of an event, both by the writer and by the reader' (Denzin, 1998: 316). The writer 'creates' a text and Denzin (1998: 316) sees the movement from 'field to text to reader' as a 'complex reflexive process'. Denzin (1998: 319) constructs the writing process as existing in various stages of refinement from the text of field notes 'and other forms of anticipatory interpretive writing' to the finished monograph. This process is driven by efforts to make sense not simply of the field itself but the researcher's experience as well, and so the researcher as subject with agency holds a central position. The final phase is where the writer goes public with a text 'which embodies the writer's self-understandings, which are now inscribed in the experiences of those studied' (Denzin, 1998: 316).

However, in the pursuit of the hermeneutic 'best reading' of a text (that which most nearly approximates the writer's intention) there is always doubt, for while we may concur that 'a good interpretation takes us into the center of the experiences being described', there is always the problem of discerning that centre (Denzin, 1998: 316). Denzin quotes a passage from Rosaldo (1989) depicting a family breakfast and describing the male head of the family by employing the metaphor of 'reigning patriarch . . . just in from the hunt' (Denzin, 1998: 317). These are images that predispose us to a particular construction and as Denzin suggests may not be significant for the actors themselves. Another element of the hermeneutic approach is the provisional nature of text: 'if the paradigm is constructivist, the writer will present a text that stresses emergent designs and emergent understandings' (Denzin, 1998: 318). Paraphrasing Holstein and Gubrium (1998), Denzin suggests that this 'emergent' quality is recognizable where 'an interpretive, or phenomenologically based, text would emphasize socially constructed realities, local generalizations, interpretive resources, stocks of knowledge, intersubjectivity, practical reasoning' (Denzin, 1998: 318).

Representation is thus understood firmly within a phenomenological frame that veers towards the solipsistic, for Denzin (1998: 319) 'representation, of course, is always self-presentation'. Denzin (1998: 319) quotes Kreiger (1991) unproblematically claiming 'when we discuss others, we are always talking about ourselves. Our images of "them" are images of "us" '. The problem of the Other and the recognition of the Other's voice is recognized but seen as almost irresolvable, 'even when "we" allow the Other to speak, when we talk about or for them, we are taking over their voice' (Denzin, 1998: 320). Reality is here located within the researcher as subject and indeed seems to be circumscribed by that writing subject.

Epistemology

An area of real anxiety for many researchers is the epistemological status of the texts they produce. If one is trained as a researcher in the normal fashion of universities through reading for degrees, then it is likely that one will have striven to meet the rigorous criteria normally set for the validation of texts and their assessment that is the standard form of entry into the research community. Generally we are taught to look to the methodology rather than the writing as the source of our knowledge claims. Denzin (1998: 320), however, uses the term 'legitimation' where traditionally we might expect to find validity: 'this is about how a public text legitimates itself or makes claims for its own authority'. One of the paradoxes of globalization is the increased significance of locality and the revival of local identities. On another plane this is reflected in scepticism towards claims to universally valid knowledge. This would be particularly true of the human sciences and to an extent the humanities. The truth value of natural scientific method depends upon it having universal significance. However, can we validly set our writing within the grand narrative of science, Denzin's (1998: 320) 'view from everywhere'? What is advocated in its place is a form of knowledge that admits to its position in time and space as a condition of its validity. This is Lyotard's *petite histoire*, a way of knowing that is both 'local' and 'pragmatic' (Denzin, 1998: 320). This accepts the relativist stress on context as the necessary social referent for understanding the meaning or significance of events. Postcolonialism also bears on this issue of universal truth because it points to the more contentious notion of the decline of the hegemony of the West and with it the foundations of modernity in a universalizing rational science.

Denzin (1998: 321) translates Barthes' (1975) erotics of writing, which are collected in a fragmentary text that emphasizes the impossibility of real presence or plenitude in the text, as a celebration of the subject, arguing 'for writers to put themselves into their texts, to engage writing as a creative act of discovery and enquiry'. This makes the development of stable criteria for comparison of versions of the world impossible and suggests aesthetic judgements of quality to discern what Denzin (1998: 321) calls the 'vital' text 'that invites readers to engage the author's subject matter' in 'a text that does not "bore" us'.

However, adopting elements of a relativist epistemology and what one might think of as a sort of aesthetic realism does not absolutely imply that all we can write is our own subjectivity. In being a research writer, simply through our intertextual engagements, we participate in an enterprise that radically transcends that subjectivity. And indeed, the fact that we can have broadly consensual readings of one another's writing, could be cited as evidence for some sort of shared reality and thus for a type of foundationalism even universalism. The nub of this issue, however, takes us back to the problem of whether or not we are writing the real. Scott (1999, 2000) is reluctant to abandon the real, but is susceptible to the arguments against an omniscient science constructing objective truth and turns to a variant of realism that manages to admit both history and an independent reality. However, it might be the case that 'it is still possible to make a number of statements about the world, shorn of values, which reflect the world as it is and are not dependent on the personal viewpoint of the knower' (Scott, 2000: 12). As we saw in Chapter 2, Scott uses Bhaskar's (1979) conception of transcendental realism as a middle way between the solipsistic and relativistic tendencies of varieties of constructivism and the unsustainability of empiricism, because 'empiricists conflate the knowing of the world with what it is'. Epistemology and ontology, which are conflated in empiricism, are here separated. Epistemology is always situated in cultural and historical realities that determine its form and meaning. For the writer this means that the text is a part of the flux of social meanings, both we and it are subjects of history. However, the social is not universally experienced as madly chaotic and so we can think of social being as a state that 'is relatively enduring' (Scott, 2000: 14).

Thus, the writer maintains an element of agency even subjectivity in representing events and experiences that are subjects of history. This is achieved within a relatively independent real world, where events occur regardless of the significant witness of a knower. As researchers we will write from a particular paradigmatic position, but all research is addressing the same underlying reality.

Language and the real: writing and postmodernism

The philosophers Lyotard, Foucault and Derrida are key figures in the development of postmodern conceptions of research. For Foucault human agency can be understood as something that results from and occurs alongside the discursive regimes of the human sciences. The researcher as subject could be seen as constructed through power/knowledge and discourse/practice. The truth value of what is written is not for Foucault an issue of how closely it represents an independent reality, but is a matter of the power element in knowledge. Thus, the issue of the truth value of one set of research technologies over another is principally a function of discourse. The current battle between knowledge as evidence of the real in the public services, exemplified by the systematic review, and knowledge as ideologically formed representations of the empirical, exemplified by the research monograph, can be readily understood in these terms as competing sets of discursive practices.

Derrida refers to 'the end of the book and the beginning of writing' (1976) and that is a distinction that we shall now examine. The social activity of research, much of which revolves around data collection, 'that hunter gatherer's fantasy of epistemology' as Stronach and MacLure (1997: 99) put it, has finally to be re-presented in writing. Experience, and that includes reflection, becomes text and it is the nature of text in relation to its objects that is critical to the power effect of discourse to define what is real and to enclose it within a conceptual and discursive boundary. The fact of enclosure can rule out of bounds other ways of constructing the real. This is partly what defines realism where 'meaning is use transcendent . . .' and where the concepts embedded in language '*if true*, (are) required perfectly to describe, represent, correspond to, standards which are inherent in the nature of a determinate reality which is fully independent of our attempts to describe it' (Parker, 1997: 102). And so for the realist empirical researcher, whether phenomenological or positivist in orientation, the ideal is a replication of actuality in a language frame that is transparent, in Foucault's term, 'innocent', that is to say it obscures its coercive intent.

There is a problem with innocence in language that has been made much of in postmodern writing. Derrida in particular in his interrogation of the foundations of Western philosophy has reinvented language and most particularly the text. The problem of metaphysics that much postmodern writing more or less directly confronts is the transcendent nature of the sign or concept/word and the way in which we trust it to be faithful and true to what is. Very simply, for modernity the word replaced God as the guarantor of the real. Logos is the metaphysical site of truth, an undivided point of origin. This foundational concept underpins the work of most empirical research.

Some relevant ideas of Derrida's (1973, 1976) may be summarized as follows. The West in recent millennia has been phonocentric, that is to say thought is represented by speech and speech is represented by language, and in modernity from Rousseau to Saussure speech has been understood as closest to thought. Speech is privileged in courts of law (where justice is secured through truth) and *viva voce* examinations. Speech is about the presence of truth or being. Art is meaningful because we interpolate the presence of the artist or her intentions between the object and ourselves. Some modern non-representational art is called conceptual; this links it to language, to presence and the intention of the artist. A recent Turner prize-winning entry was a room where the lights go on and off automatically. This evades the meaningful presence of a linguistically recognizable intention and is difficult to conceptualize or to think about because it fails to articulate an intention. There is nothing to interpolate between our experience and the work itself.

As we saw in Chapter 8 deconstructive method can involve inversion. This is what Derrida does with the opposition between presence and absence and between speech and writing where both presence and speech would normally be seen as the primary or positive categories. And so speech, which is about presence in both space and time, gives way to writing. Writing has significantly different qualities and is characterized by a series of absences, of the writer, the writer's mind, any necessary reader or real presence. Writing for Derrida is about distance, delay, opacity and ambiguity. Absence is not to be understood as a closed category because there is always the *trace* of presence, and so there is a constant sliding between presence and absence within the text. And so rather than meaning being based on presence/truth Derrida substitutes for this an *undecidable* presence/absence. What this does for the research text and also critically for the writer and his identity as researcher is to make the connections between experience and its representation enigmatic. It recovers that ambiguity that positivist empiricism denies by making problematic both the experience of an event and its representation. The undecidable, like the trace, is a presence/absence 'it is a ghostliness "that render[s] all totalization, fulfilment, plenitude impossible" '(Derrida, 1990, quoted in Royle, 2003: 5). What this does to the concept of agency is to make intentionality, in Derrida's terms the 'decision,' radically fugitive. The undecidable in a sense characterizes experience, it 'remains caught, lodged, at least as a ghost – but an essential ghost – in every decision, in every event of decision' (Derrida, 1990, in Royle, 2003: 5). This contrasts with positivist empiricist research and the narrative realist texts that represent it through an exclusive discourse that works with a true/false binary opposition. This can have an important power effect. Usher (1996b: 46) refers to 'power relations . . . the outcome of which is the production and consumption of "powerful" texts, texts which frequently become part of regulatory mechanisms in the domain of governmentality'. Stronach and MacLure (1997: 5) suggest something of a synthesis or resolution in suggesting that contradictions are not necessarily to be resolved but to be recognized as part of the research landscape. They argue for openness and openings: 'we try to practice this kind of strategic uncertainty . . . our aim is to mobilize meaning rather than to fix it' (Stronach and MacLure, 1997: 5).

The above has concentrated on issues that deal with the idea of the primacy of writing as the primary product of research and thereby with the idea of the researcher herself as primarily a writer. To complete this section we want now to turn to some of the contextual concerns that flow from this understanding and that help to contextualize the researcher/writer.

Audience

The writing of our research is the moment of making it public, when the text leaves our control and operates as a text in the world. The form or genre will partly dictate how we write. A book or a journal article is different from a doctoral thesis or a masters' dissertation. The latter generally being more constraining than the former. When we are writing as a student we submit what we write to a set of abstracted academic criteria and our writing is assessed and may be graded, and so we are constrained to write with those criteria in mind. The student writer is a neophyte whose voice is to be judged by those who are higher in the hierarchy of research. The prospect of public examination may well, for example, inhibit a writer from attempting to develop or stretch a genre, to risk an only partially supported generalization or to over-write the methodology section. Student status may have a conservative impact on the conduct and writing of the research. When we write to communicate we need to have an image of the reader in mind. How we write is tempered by how we construct potential readers. We are writing now principally for public service professionals who use their research capacity in the development of their professional practice. However, many of the issues we tackle in this book will be of interest to social researchers of all sorts. Writing for a peer and student audience gives us freedom to use a much wider connotative field both in the topics that we choose to write about and also in the ways that we construct the discourse. The constraining and ultimately judging audience is not in this case an examiner but peers and publishers who will scrutinize the text according to their own particular concerns.

Reading

What our audience will do and what you, the reader, are doing now is the act of reading. In general our understanding of ourselves as readers is constructed largely by schooling. In the West literacy is the vital meta-skill of becoming an educated person. It is framed within a neutral psychology. Reading is understood as the cognitive skill to decode text and writing as the skill to encode text. Reading is about passively accessing the text and writing is about actively creating the text. Insofar as any model of the reader is assumed it is a vaguely hermeneutical one. The task of the reader is to discover the intention of the writer. Thus, the best reading is that which most precisely coincides or corresponds with the author's intention. This assumes that authors have an unambiguous project in their writing, that text can reflect this in encoded language, and that this is fairly readily communicable through reading. The text itself is understood as stable and enduring through time. What the reader thinks about the decoded message is understood as separate from the decoding itself. However, what Stronach and MacLure (1997: 86) suggest is that we should strive for 'a heteronomic reading that "exceeds" the text (Clark, 1992) and goes beyond hermeneutic exegesis'. The reader moves from consumer to producer of text. That is to say that reading moves from a passive encounter with text to an active construction of a new synthetic text, that is only one amongst many possible texts. (An example would be the deconstructive reading made in Chapter 8.) A useful way of understanding this is through Barthes' (1974) distinction between the readerly and the writerly text. For Barthes (Allen, 2003: 76) text is a protean concept and does not consist of words with a single 'theological' meaning but consists of 'a multi-dimensional space in which are married and contested several writings, none of which is original: the text is a fabric of quotations resulting from a thousand sources of culture'. This is what Barthes means by the writerly text, it is *ourselves writing* before the infinite play of the world . . . the opening of networks, the infinity of languages' (Barthes, 1974: 5, in Lucy, 1997: 75). The readerly text is unidimensional and is one that does not offer the possibility of a plurality of negotiated meanings. For Barthes the readerly texts 'are products (and not productions)' (Barthes, 1974: 5, in Lucy, 1997: 75). The text the reader now confronts makes the point. What we have aimed for in this book is not a manual of research which would invite only a passive readerly response, what Lucy (1997: 75) refers to as 'missionary positionality', but the presentation of a set of possibilities that requires active participation on the part of the reader without foreclosing on the outcome of the encounter.

Intertextuality

We do not write simply out of our individual understanding but as a part of a community. Indeed the very conception of research itself is drawn from our knowledge of other texts. Our texts do not stand alone but are inevitably imbued with the presence of those absent texts that have been part of our experience and have influenced us one way or another as researchers. There is an obvious way in which this is the case and that is through citation. However, we use other texts in the construction of our own in a variety of ways. Other texts inform the research process at every stage from finding a focus, potential theoretical frames and modes of analysis to the final writing up. Some texts will be simply technical and others may affect the way we think in more philosophical and fundamental ways. It is worth noting that texts that appear to be simply technical do nonetheless implicitly contain a theoretical position. Research manuals that present the research process as a series of technical problems are likely to be realist and empirical or positivistic in orientation and thus project a naturalistic and pragmatic view of social research. Intertextuality, the dependence of any text on a range of others for its form and even its existence, affects our understanding of the process of writing and brings up some interesting questions about our agency and identity as research writers that we will consider later.

Form and genre

How we construct ourselves as researchers and writers; what texts and ideas we admit to our own canon determine the devices that we feel allowed to employ in our writing. This is a matter of representation in the sense that according to the methodological and theoretical orientation that we employ then some and not other forms of textual representation will be deemed appropriate. An obvious determinant is whether we are writing a qualitative or quantitative account. There is a range of devices that are employed to present quantitative accounts such as figures, graphs, bar and pie charts and statistical accounts. This is a form of translation. Human experience or language events are relocated within a semiotic system that substitutes number for that experience and allows forms of presentation and modes of manipulation and analysis that are dependent on this translation. The assigning of numerical values to social events and situations also appears to offer an objective account, one that removes both the writer and the subjectivity of the research population from the representation. The representation of national educational performance presented in the language of number allows a whole range of manipulations of the data to be made in creating an image of the state of pupils' cognitive performances. What it does not present is the emotion that surrounds the process, the anxiety experienced by pupils in the face of the tasks/tests, their construction of failure and the anger felt by many of the teachers who reluctantly administer these tests. Thus, we can see that form and genre have not only implicit theoretical dimensions but can also serve to mask political and personal aspects of the realities they represent.

But, of course, all accounts are partial and there is always the possibility of another representation. One strategy that emerged from the Clifford and Marcus critique of ethnography was the attempt to secure a certain authenticity by relying on the verbatim presentation of the voice of the Other. This was achieved by maximizing the use of transcript material. This does, of course, suggest a sort of objectivity in minimizing the distance between the field event and its representation. However, as we have seen both in this chapter and in Chapter 5, the movement from event to transcription to analytic account is itself problematic. This can sometimes feel like being presented with large chunks of raw data with little indication of how they might be approached (see also Chapter 7).

Here we have on the one hand the desire to privilege the Other by reducing the transformations of real events to a minimum. On the other, one might argue that the real work of research is precisely within these representations; otherwise we are left with an edited version of the data, but with no means of understanding (or evaluating) the editing.

Knowledge

The origins of research as a social practice are in philosophy and in particular the natural philosophy of the seventeenth and eighteenth centuries, which still underpins the scientific method. The point of the activity was to enlighten us as to how the universe was made and this included us. It is not at all easy to come to any general definition of knowledge. However, to complete this enquiry into writing it seems pertinent to ask the question, are we producing knowledge and if we think we are then how can we both explain and justify this claim? This fundamental epistemological question is a central concern of the research writer and is answerable in different ways. As we have seen, we can claim to be directly representing the real, to be writing our selves, to be denying our selves or to be the ciphers of larger impersonal discursive realities. In all of these positions what knowledge is and how it is constructed or discovered can be radically different. In some ways the simplest is the positivist empirical belief that language corresponds with what is real. But it would seem that this is increasingly difficult to sustain in a globalized world without drawing tight historical and cultural boundaries around our conceptual universe. This is exemplified by the way in which fundamentalist religion, when faced with a plural global environment, finds a plausible response in the retreat to a non-negotiable certainty (James, 1995; Beyer, 1996). Qualitative research has looked for validity in its writing in many different ways largely occasioned by the continuing spectre of positivist claims to relate uniquely to the real. The hybrid methodology of grounded theory attempts to write the qualitative as real science and its baroque systems of indexes and audits and the distillation of concepts aims at a realist account based on actors' understandings.

Most qualitative research writing works within some variation of a coherence theory of truth, where variations depend upon the degree of commitment to empiricism and the idea of a wholly independent reality. At one extreme the denial of this independent realm can lead to the solipsistic position that the only thing we can have knowledge of is our own experience and thus we write our selves. While in a sense it can be argued that our experience is all we have, this tends to centre the individual and minimizes the role of our social nature and that of real contexts in shaping who we are. It also implies a sort of essentialism in relation to identity that we shall discuss later. Reflexivity, which is variably constructed, is also seen as a hallmark of qualitative writing. At its most basic, it is the idea that what we write is the product not simply of the transcription of our experience but of some form of systematic dialogue with that experience.

Validity through coherence is perhaps best exemplified in the notion of constructing a narrative, something that has form, shape, movement, a beginning and closure. The aim of the narrative writer is often that of the traditional anthropologist working within a phenomenological frame. It is an attempt to empathetically enter into the discursive world of meaning that operates for those in the field and uses narrative to provide both coherence and also a sort of verisimilitude in that our sociality can appear to us as a narrative or dramatic construction. Narrative of itself implies the use of metaphor. The story is not a natural object but a seemingly universal form we impose on social reality and on imagined cosmologies that help us create both order and meaning out of what might otherwise be the random or chaotic flow of experience.

We hope to have demonstrated that writing is not a simple technical matter but lies at the heart of the research process. If as researchers we are primarily writers this suggests that we might also want to concern ourselves with the matter of research and identity.

10

The selfish text – research and identity

Research and identity are rarely discussed in those research manuals where the process of research is constructed as a learnt technique; an addition to a technical and professional repertoire. Where this is the case identity is likely to be understood in terms of issues such as role strain brought about by tensions between researcher and professional roles. Also, if working within a positivist or naturalistic framework then the person of the researcher can be seen as a danger to validity and to the truth, a source of bias or subjectivity. However, throughout this book we have begun to develop a more complex view of the complicity of identity in research processes. What we want to do here is broaden the scope of thinking about research and identity and, while the researcher as an individual is central to this, researching the social means we must consider both its nature and our own as a part of it.

Methodologies that are seen as a technical apparatus for knowledge production may not see the social as problematic. The social can be constructed as simply the boundaried field of the research site. In particular, we want to look at the debates around how we might model the individual and the social in the twenty-first century, as this would seem in some ways prior to our aim of providing accounts of social realities that include us in some way. Following this we look at the implications for some of these different constructions of identity, self and the subject for understanding the research process and our place as researchers in it.

The dominant language of identity in the twentieth century was the scientific discourse of psychology. This discourse, in the guise of cognitive psychology, has come back on the tide of neo-liberalism to dominate our understanding of the knowing subject especially in schooling (Yates, 2001). The person was seen as a psychological entity and science provided a solid epistemological base for understanding the truth of the person both normal and pathological. The vernacular understanding of identity drew obliquely on this discourse and was of a subject that was individual and unique; more or less stable and having an essential and enduring core, a sort of secular soul. This picture of identity has been challenged by new ways of thinking that question all of the settled assumptions of the normal psychological self and also the common sense idea of the subject as the author and the locus of social action. This is important for social researchers, because how we understand ourselves and ourselves in relation to others in the research field will largely determine how we understand our capacity to reconstruct that experience in our writing.

A significant shift has been in the discussion of issues of agency, of how we determine the dynamic or the animus of social action of both ourselves and others. This is a variation of the ancient debate on free will and determinism and asks the question, what is the nature and what are the limits of individual action? Is our subjective experience of having the freedom to act at will illusory? This issue has been variously addressed. The problem of the relationship between the individual and the social has been a key debate in social and political thought. On the one hand, there are varieties of structuralism that privilege social structure over individual autonomy, and on the other, explanations that build the social through the vehicle of the individual. In the former category we would find Marxism, structural functionalism and continental structuralism. In the latter category we might include psychology, hermeneutics and phenomenology, symbolic interactionism and ethnomethodology. Giddens's (1984) structuration theory is an attempt to synthesize the individual and the social by positing the dual nature of a model of social action that combines both the structural and the individual. The second half of the twentieth century saw the development of the ongoing critique of modernity and the emergence of post-structuralism and postmodernism, feminist and postcolonial theory and, more latterly, theories of globalization.

The late modern self

Du Gay *et al.* (2000) divide the field into three domains. First, issues around identity as the 'subject-of-language' an 'approach (that is) far from uniform, drawing on an overlapping body of mainly French theory' (Du Gay *et al.*, 2000: 9); second, the more scientifically grounded approach from clinically-based psychoanalytic literature. The third domain is that of more synthetic and broadly sociological writing 'focused upon the social relations, techniques and forms of training and practice through which human beings have acquired definite capacities and attributes for social existence as particular sorts of person' (Du Gay *et al.*, 2000: 4).

The problem with discussing identity is not that the concept and the reality have changed, which would attract broad agreement, but that the nature and the significance of change are contested. Identity might be conceived as a typical site of incredulity in that what was once thought to be almost a natural scientific object has become a contested site (Lyotard, 1984). Du Gay *et al.*, (2000: 2) suggest that although the term

'identity' takes on different connotations depending upon the context within which it is deployed . . . 'identity' has achieved its contemporary centrality both theoretically and substantively because that to which it is held to refer – whether the 'it' in question is, for example, the category 'man', 'black', 'work', 'nation' or 'community' – is regarded in some sense as being more contingent, fragile and incomplete and thus more amenable to reconstitution than was previously thought possible.

For Hall (2000: 15) the term 'identity' should be put 'under erasure'. This is a Derridean term where a word is employed because there are currently no good alternatives, but in the knowledge that its metaphysical implications are rejected 'the usefulness of the term is, *for us*, that it brings with it, *as part of the role it can play*, a story (*trace*) of permanence and stability' (Parker, 1997: 89).

One critical aspect of the move away from scientifically legitimated models of the person that allowed identity to be seen as an almost neutral attribute is that in the last half century identity has become politicized. Ethnicity, race, gender and sexuality, as well as locality, region and community are not only elements in the shifting tectonic plates of late modern identity, but they also tend to be collective as well as individual identities, with a concern for rights of expression and legal recognition and more local forms of empowerment. The discourse of the individual, however, will inevitably predominate, for while it may be the case that new types of collective identity are being formed by larger numbers of people, individualism in its old liberal and new postmodern forms remains a basic aspect of the social although, as with identity, what it represents may be increasingly unclear.

We will look at a traditional modernist version of identity from Bruner (1999), at Giddens' attempts to find a model that can simultaneously combine macro and micro features and at the postmodern critique of identity and the context of globalization that have critical implications for social research.

Narrating the self

Bruner (1999: 175) suggests we use story to generate self-understanding: 'our immediate experience, what happened yesterday or the day before, is framed in the same storied way. Even more striking we represent our lives (to ourselves as well as to others) in the form of narrative.' However, in terms of our professional lives this may not be a credible strategy. Very often the organizations we find ourselves a part of as adults are themselves driven by instrumental rationality, with an intense focus on ends. Thus, they are unable to recognize the expression of the narrative self because to do so would transgress the boundaries of the bureaucratic self, the subject of controlled production. This can have an important effect on the ways in which we can plausibly construct ourselves as researchers.

Reference to the use of the concept of narrative is commonplace in current texts on qualitative styles of research, where it is often advocated as a mode of representation for interview data (Hitchcock and Hughes, 1995; Coffey and Atkinson, 1996; Denzin and Lincoln, 1998a, 1998b, 1998c; Silverman, 2000, 2004; Cohen, Manion and Morison, 2000; Arksey and Knight, 1999). Key assumptions are often that narrative preserves the integrity of the person and presents their experience as a centred and coherent flow of events. Bruner (1999) uses a narrative model and draws firmly on modernist sources in his critique of schooling and identity. He argues from a liberal humanist position, where the experience of the individual is understood as a universal human essential. For Bruner (1999: 172) 'perhaps the single most universal thing about human experience is the phenomenon of "Self" '. Bruner also argues for autonomous agency against both radical constructivists and behaviourists in order to link the self to esteem that is derived from our reflective evaluation of our performances in the light of our goals. While this is not seen as part of the essential self it is nonetheless 'a ubiquitous feature of selfhood . . . this mix of agentive efficacy and self-evaluation' (Bruner, 1999: 173). Giddens (1991: 68) similarly suggests that self-referential shame now characterizes moral evaluation in late modern society where 'shame derives from a failure to live up to expectations built into the ego-ideal'. Within postmodern understandings of the self the notion of a universal or essential self is challenged by new models that stress plasticity and flux. While the concept of structure itself may be universally applied, how individuals construct themselves locally may be determined by the cultural contexts they define themselves within; and the plurality of narratives they draw upon and are drawn into.

Bruner (1999: 174) also makes a distinction between 'logical-scientific thinking' and 'narrative thinking' which he again confidently asserts are universal: 'no culture is without both of them though different cultures privilege them differently'. Both Bruner and Giddens point to the role of narrative in relation to self-construction and the maintenance of identity. Narrative may also have been negatively constructed for us in our own socialization, where the vernacular positivism of schooling equates story with the unreal and the untrue. Bruner rather gently makes the point that 'it has been the convention of most schools to treat the arts of narrative – song, drama, fiction, theatre, whatever – as more "decoration" than necessity, something to grace leisure' (Bruner, 1999: 175).

A generalized model of the traditional Western sense of self would be of an essential, inherent and relatively stable identity authenticated by the 'grand narratives' of the human sciences especially psychology. This contrasts with the model of self that Giddens suggests typifies late modernity. Giddens (1991) draws on the therapeutic uses of narrative to construct his notion of the self as a reflexive project on a trajectory from the past to an anticipated, but essentially uncontrollable, future for which the individual feels responsible. This level of responsibility for self construction is contrasted with a 'traditional' society where the nature of the person was determined by fixed points of kinship and gender identity, locality and inherited social status, none of which have the power to sustain self-identity in late modernity and all of which are impermanent in themselves to some degree. For much of the nineteenth and twentieth centuries, the life trajectory of people in a settled industrial state was to an extent foreseeable and reliable and involved limited choice.

Postmodern selves: agency and determinism

It is perhaps in the notion of narrative that we can dissolve the distinction between actual and invented selves, that a bridge can be seen between a modern conception of self and the postmodern critique. McGuigan (1999: 80) talks of 'fractured identities' that is to say the story of self may be more complex and multifaceted than a single linear narrative. Haraway's myth of the cyborg, the entity that is both human and machine, is cited by McGuigan (1999) as a model for the dissolution of traditional boundaries of being. In the cyborg the human/animal distinction is blurred and two other traditional boundaries are breached. First, that between the organic entity and the machine, which echoes the way in which 'smart machines have increasingly put the distinctiveness of human mental and physical capacities into question, and, indeed have also extended such capacities' (McGuigan, 1999: 82). Second, in the combination of microtechnology and human person, the virtual and the actual do not separately signify but are indistinguishable. The cyborg is also devoid of essence and it mirrors the fractured identity of postmodernity where 'there are no essential identities of class, ethnicity, gender or sexuality: everything is potentially fluid and transformable into something else' (McGuigan, 1999: 83).

For Baudrillard (1998) the postmodern world is dominated by the systems of capital. It is a place where it is impossible to locate the real and to separate it from the virtually real, from copies of reality or simulacra. Persons are located and locate themselves through the consumption of things and signs. We are entrapped within these systems where 'intersubjective communication is replaced with the interaction of humans, goods and whole systems that surround the manipulation of these goods' (Lane, 2000: 66). Personal identity is no longer forged through life in an affective community of human values and so 'instead of a world of human beings communicating at a one-to-one level (about daily life, political or spiritual beliefs, and so on), human beings become commodities, like consumer goods' (Lane, 2000: 66).

McGuigan (1999: 87) quotes Hall (1996) attempting to come to a synthetic and positive sense of identity that avoids the potential alienation of some postmodern critiques.

> I use 'identity' to refer to the meeting point, the point of *suture*, between on the one hand the discourse and practices which attempt to 'interpellate', speak to us or hail us into place as the social subjects of particular discourses, and on the other hand, the processes which produce subjectivities, which construct us as subjects which can be 'spoken'.

Part of the context of the debates about identity is the issue of agency, that is, how far are we to be considered the authors of our own subjectivities and how far are we the creatures of social and discursive forces? Foucault would have us almost totally determined, Butler (1990, 1993) would have our subjectivities as plastic and under our control, while Giddens finds the third way in his synthesis of structure and agency. Hall's (2000: 17) concept of identity combines elements of agency and determinism; it is 'a strategic and positional one'. We exist at an 'intersection' of a continuous discursive play, 'identities are thus points of temporary attachment to the subject positions that discursive practices construct for us all' (Hall, 2000: 19). For McGuigan (1999: 103), identity can be understood as 'a multi-accentual concept, mediating self and history in many complex ways'. An aspect of the application of postmodern thought to our understanding of our selves as researchers is the challenge to essentialist thinking in constructing the researched and their attributes of class, race, ethnicity, gender and sexuality. The solidity and stability of the social world cannot be assumed where the human subject is 'constantly in process of becoming and increasingly hybrid' (McGuigan, 1999: 103). For example, as a sports enthusiast, one might identify with Englishness for football, but with Indian-ness for cricket. Thus identity might be thought of not as an inherited status, but a complex of choices invoked across a range of social sites that require of us some form of engagement.

One way to understand identity as the subject-of-language is through the idea of *difference* popularized by Saussure (Culler, 1986) and elaborated by Derrida (1978). The common sense view of language is that the world precedes it and that it is a collection of terms that have some direct correspondence with an enduring external reality that it truly represents to us. This is extended to include our selves in the modern understanding of what it is to be a person. Thus, our identity is constituted positively. That is to say we construct the world from the inside of our identity and similarly reflexively construct our selves. Thus, our model of our selves is the essential point of reference from which the world is constructed. Saussure argued against common sense that language had no positive terms and although it clearly referred to things that were outside us and independently existing, it did this through a system of differences. The idea of the timetable was the perfect illustration. The eleven o'clock Paris–Geneva Express did not take its identity from its overt characteristics, the number of coaches or the colours of the livery, nor was it absolutely necessary for it to leave at eleven o'clock. Its identity was achieved negatively by the fact of it not being any other train in the system of trains and times that makes up the timetable. If we transpose this model of language to the making of identity, as arguably Hall does, then our selves are constituted by the networks of relations that we find ourselves moving within. These can be both personal and also constructed through the ways in which we locate ourselves in the increasingly mobile cultural codes of our social worlds. This could include our politics, our sexuality and religion and also our aesthetics in bodily presentation, styles of living and matters of taste. This way of thinking about identity 'accepts that identities are never unified and, in late modern times, increasingly fragmented and fractured; never singular but multiply constructed across different, often intersecting and antagonistic, discourses, practices and positions' (Hall, 2000: 17).

It would seem there is little support for the existence of a transcendentally guaranteed essential subject; indeed, in order to avoid even the hint of a metaphysical validation of our identity Foucault denies the theological, the Cartesian and the essentialist view of our selves. Barker (1998: 76) succinctly renders his position thus: 'it is as material beings in the world that we interrogate our relation between the world and our existence in it, and this interrogation can only be undertaken from where we find ourselves located at a specific historical and cultural juncture'.

This is unexceptional in itself; however, for Foucault the relationship we have with the world provides no sure ground of truth of being: what we achieve is a series of coherences 'on which relations with ourselves and others are elaborated and which emerge from the encounters with the cultural milieu in which we find ourselves' (Barker, 1998: 78). It is in this way that our subjectivity is constructed within the discourses of the human sciences.

'It is the elaboration of oneself in relation to a series of new master/experts – psychiatrists, psychologists, psychoanalysts, social workers – that constitutes who we are today, a subject that is completely subjected not in a negative sense but in terms of a multiplicity of positivities' (Barker, 1998: 81). This model of self compares with Giddens's (1991) late modern person, who constructs their own life trajectory partly through recourse to expert knowledges that constitute a set of constraining contexts and discourses. However, in contrast to Foucault, within Giddens's (1984) general model of structuration it is knowledgeable creative agency that characterizes the subject, who self-creates within the recursive interplay between individual and social structure. In short, for Foucault we seem to be in thrall to the discursive practices that represent our selves to our selves, whereas for Giddens we actively and reflexively participate in our own self-construction.

Identity and social theory

In a piece of empirical research conducted with British Asian adolescents, I used a simple technique that I found in a research manual to give me some insight into their self-perception. I asked each participant to complete ten sentences beginning 'I am . . .'. It was on the whole fairly unenlightening as after declaring their age, sex and ethnicity responses became largely unreflective and impersonal with a few references to popular culture. The instrument itself is interesting because it had built in to it assumptions about the boundaried nature of the individual and their capacity for self-reflection and self-knowledge. It could be understood as an invitation to disclose a sort of personal topography describing the public persona as in 'I am a priest' or 'I am a father'. It could also be radically interpreted ontologically as in 'I am suffering from weltschmerz' or 'I am a cultural artefact' or 'I am my social performances' or even 'I am not'. The point is that the instrument assumes that there is a something called identity that pre-exists any enquiry, is sufficiently stable and commonly shared and that it can be readily tapped into. Identity is understood as unproblematic and, as we have seen, this is no longer the case.

Different research frameworks differentially construct the person and identity. By the middle of the twentieth century within classical Marxism the individual was understood as decentred and had become epiphenomenal to the forces of historical materialism. The bourgeois subject was understood as a refraction of the material relations, which underpinned the real social truth, the final analysis. Other forms of structuralism were arguably equally deterministic with the subject more acted upon than acting. Determinism survives also in much later models of the social. Within Foucault's discourses of the social, the individual is an embodied point of confluence of the flow and flux of normalizing discourses. Paradoxically, this may include the discourse of the subject, which makes our own sense of a naturally occurring and enduring self become an abstracted social construct. In much of Foucault's writing, agency is barely present except in his idea that in the combination of power and knowledge, which is the motor of the life of discourse, there is also present an element of resistance. The sense of agency is far stronger in Giddens' writing. However, Giddens (1991) denies the idea of the essential self and while his theory of structuration includes some autonomous agency through reflexivity and discursive consciousness, the person is a set of social performances with no enduring core identity. Some postmodern writers, as we have seen, emphasize the plasticity of identity and our sense of agency in relation to it. Butler (1990, 1993) argues that our gender identity is not attached to some immutable biological binary of male/female. It is something that we create and sustain through performance and it is the iterative nature of these performances that creates the illusion of the indelible self. Thus, gender can be seen as malleable and we can choose to change it by altering our performance. For the intensely radical Deleuze (Deleuze and Guattari, 2002) 'the human subject and its stable outside world was a *fiction* produced within the flow of experience' (Colebrook, 2002: 3). Life for Deleuze is a matrix of connections without boundaries, it is simply endless becoming and he suggested 'that there was a creative tendency in life itself: the tendency for human life to form images of itself, such as the image of the rational mind or "subject" ' (Colebrook, 2002: 3).

As we can see the settled understandings of modernity that allowed for the development of a stable and psychological/scientific understanding of human identity has given way to a proliferation of discursive planes. For the researcher this means that both self-understanding and the identity of those who populate the research field can no longer be taken for granted but invite careful reflection.

Culture and the global perspective

Within postcolonial thought the increasingly plural nature of the metropolitan social milieu has both deconstructed and politicized identity. What is the identity of a British-Indian visiting the Taj Mahal as a tourist as opposed to working as a maths teacher in Manchester? The notion of hybridity (Bhabha, 1990; Browning *et al.*, 2000) implies that one person may compose themselves of, for example, two national identities such as British-Indian or Chinese-American where one or the other may be more or less pertinent through time and space. With increasing population flow the connection of identity with a particular historic site is less normal than once it was. The concept of the 'plastic paddy' is applied to the diasporic Irish by those living in Eire. The implication is that diasporic identity is in some sense ersatz, with plastic connoting a cheap copy of an authentic original. There is another issue that the concept of the plastic paddy exemplifies and that is the ontological insecurity that can accompany social being in late modernity where 'feelings of restlessness, foreboding and desperation may mingle in individual experience with faith in the reliability of certain forms of social and technical framework' (Giddens, 1991: 181). Identity, and perhaps particularly hybridity, can itself be problematic. Giddens (1991: 181) suggests that 'radical doubt filters into most aspects of day-to-day life' and that the experience of security in our identity intersects 'sometimes in subtle, sometimes in nakedly disturbing ways, with generalized sources of unease'.

Within anthropology this issue is being worked out by researchers and writers who have themselves hybrid identities, what Abhu-Lughod calls 'halfies'. These hybrid researchers are working within a Western epistemological frame of which they are highly critical (Abhu-Lughod, 1991; Ong, 1996; Yang, 1996). One question that arises from the combination of non-Western and Western sources of identity coexisting in the one person's experience of being a social researcher, is the whole question of the validity of the hegemony of universalizing Western concepts such as modernity or culture. For example, is modernity something that began in Europe and spread to the rest of the world? If this is the case, should we construct Chinese modernity as a variegated form of the original Western stem or should we begin to think less Eurocentrically about the modern period and reconceive recent world history in terms of multiple and intersecting modernities?

Part of this critique is to do with the way in which the concept of culture has been used to impose boundaries and homogeneity on discrete populations and to confirm the identity of the researcher. As Abhu-Lughod (1991: 143) suggests in her critique of Western anthropology, 'culture is important to anthropology, because the anthropological distinction between self and other rests on it'. I think it is arguable that it is not only anthropologists but many social researchers, who maintain their identity against that of those they study through employing the concept of culture. The notion of the discrete nature of cultures, that they are consensual and boundaried entities, imposes on the field of study an unchallenged theoretical frame that predisposes us to see consensus and boundaries in our classrooms, our wards and our organizations. To an extent, this can act to suppress both the connectedness of social groups to other times and spaces and most particularly it can devalue and deny the presence and the importance of the concept and the reality of difference.

While we may continue to use the language and the ideas of a settled modernity in our thinking about ourselves and our researches, the world does not give back the steady reflection of a reliable and predictable reality. The growth of interest in globalization is a good example of postmodern knowledge. It fits the shape of a discourse in that a lot of people are talking about it and writing on it, but it has no clearly agreed object of study and no associated methodology and thus cannot be confined to any particular traditional discipline. Indeed, it is perhaps the more dynamic and hybrid configurations of knowledge such as media studies that have the capacity to embrace areas of knowledge that are not readily definable and to make sense of what is a complex and fugitive phenomenon. Lewellen (2002) provides a vignette of the effects of globalization on our settled concept of coherent culture with the example of aboriginal tribesmen videotaping their negotiations with government agents in order to secure an accurate record of the event.

The process of globalization is relevant to understanding the nature of the research process and the research site. The idea of a research process not only connotes a connection between the phases of research, but also implies change. For early anthropologists, in a world of much slower communications than we now have, years could elapse between fieldwork and writing up such that the world depicted in the monograph had effectively ceased to exist. Writing represented what was called the 'ethnographic present'. As we have seen with the issue of writing, there are many factors that influence our accounts of our research. The relationships between objects and subjects and the constraints of history and culture and change bear both on ourselves and on what we might be able to construct as representations. It is useful to recognize that in our research (even in longitudinal research) we are intervening in the flux and flow of what are actually seamless events. In trying to arrest the real, we are taking, as it were, a transverse section of social time and this is an important element in our understanding of the nature of the enterprise.

Long (1996: 50) suggests that 'we should view global ordering in terms of a complex pattern of homogenization and diversity. Moreover, the autonomy and boundedness of social and cultural units is better conceptualized as a matter of degree rather than as a set of sharply delineated forms.' Long also suggests the term 'glocalization' to refer to the local embeddedness of global features, the ways in which local populations domesticate images, technologies and social practices drawn from a global repertoire. In white English urban youth culture, there is a category 'wigga' which denotes a white youth who identifies with black youth culture, thereby transgressing racial and ethnic boundaries. Lifshitz (2004) reports the ways in which Jewish Ethiopian male adolescents, understanding themselves as rejected by Jewish Israeli society, draw an identity from American black youth culture. This identity is sustained through their access to global media which provide images, narratives, identifications with music, body styles and fashionable clothes from which they can create a local version of a set of social practices drawn from a very different cultural and historical setting. The cult of the Goth is not gendered in the same way as the previous examples and combines a distinctive self-presentation with all the accoutrements of a subculture. However, like the previous examples it is largely confined to young people. This suggests another aspect of identity in late modernity, the idea that it is not an indelible condition but temporary identities can be opted into and out of. It would seem that who we are no longer necessarily grows out of rooted social contexts. The idea of community with its implications of consensus and commonality is disrupted. This is partly because, in understanding current social forms, the idea of difference can be seen as having the more positive value than consensus in modelling real life. This can create problems for the researcher about how to interpret their own experience and in determining what frameworks can be legitimately employed to understand social phenomena.

This can lead us to rethink conventional understanding. For example, we might say that what is significant about the English is not that they embrace national values and a national culture but on the contrary that they are highly differentiated and use difference as the more significant concept in the construction of their identity (Yates, 2000b).

The democratization of research

A traditional model of the researcher is that of a member of an intellectual elite. Such people would be seen to be licensed by virtue of their social location, perhaps in a university or a private laboratory, to produce legitimate and valid knowledge. Critically, the knowledge produced by social researchers of all sorts is not private knowledge. To be a researcher is to be someone who is systematically engaged in the production of knowledge that will be in some way, however limited, in the public sphere. Levi-Strauss (1966) examined needs theories of human society, where human activity was seen to be motivated by the satisfaction of some fundamental material need. The application of biological and evolutionary models to explain human society would be a current example. However, Levi-Strauss argued that humans innately find satisfaction in turning the world into an object of intellectual scrutiny. We are perhaps predisposed to enjoy making structures of understanding, patterning existence and creating social realities.

Thus we might ask, is social research and the identity, researcher, synonymous with historical notions of an intellectual elite or is it more simply one way of expressing our humanity? Elitism is still very much there in the social structures of knowledge production and the cultures of academe. Election to the venerable and honourable Royal Society in England or the College de France mythologizes and legitimizes both the person and their knowledge production. The College de France, founded in the sixteenth century, does, however, have a democratic element in that members are bound to give free public lectures.

As sources of knowledge multiply and diversify what it means to be a knowledge producer becomes less clear, and with it the identity and status of social researchers. Boggs (2000) identifies a tension between critical and technocratic intellectuals that partly echoes the distinction between positivist and constructivist models of research. The world is characterized by social ferment and a fragmentation that in itself brings a degree of freedom from the hegemony of technocracy and helps create the conditions for the democratization of knowledge production. For Boggs (2000: 303) 'critical intellectual activity is no longer the domain of elite strata'. This broadening of intellectual activity, part of which can be located in the wide range of persons who are currently likely to be engaged in some form of research, suggests to Boggs (2000: 303) that 'modern intellectuals can best be understood as the locus of many conflicting pressures and identities rather than as a single cohesive social formation'.

As a student I read a lot of fashionable contemporary French philosophy and entered a very small world of people who seemed to be writing letters to one another. It was as something of a shock that I realized that the authors were not trying to be accessible but rather were in the business of creating and sustaining a small and exclusive elite discourse (see Bourdieu, 1988). Said (1978, 1993) writing from a postcolonial perspective advocates a 'secular criticism' and suggests that the intellectual as critic needs to rediscover a language that can be more generally understood than the jargon of academic enclaves. This is because criticism for Said is 'personal, active, entwined with the world, implicated in its processes of representation and committed to the almost disappearing notion that the intellectual . . . can reveal hypocrisy, uncover the false, prepare the ground for change' (Ashcroft and Ahluwalia, 2001: 32). Identity for Said, himself a Palestinian American, is a critical and political term in the postcolonial world, particularly in relation to hybridity.

Scott and Usher (1999: 160) elaborate the concept of 'transgressive research' as a counter to the closed research paradigm of performativity, where 'performativity appears to be the most contemporary form taken by foundationalism, the latest version of the desire for closure and presence, for the "given" of an authorizing centre, in this case that of optimal efficiency'. This is not research, as it might be understood by the sort of communitarian democracy that underpins much practitioner research, where the point is to guide the improvement of some set of social practices. For example, much school-based action research would fit this mould. Following Lather (1991), Scott and Usher advocate a form of hybrid research where 'negotiation was not simply *post hoc* or a preliminary to fieldwork but at the heart of the research process where knowledge was being produced'. The resultant text is not simply authored by the researcher but can be seen as a provisional and negotiable statement. Scott and Usher (1999: 159) cite Stronach and MacLure's interest in postmodern research, where there is 'interaction between the respondents' and the researchers' texts, and the informal re-writing of the researchers' texts'. This makes problematic both the nature of textual production and also the identity of the researcher.

Against this notion of democratization and the collapsing of researcher as an elite identity, there is the countervailing proliferation of the professional and their exclusive expertise. This expertise may itself be partially validated by a research base. Many of our readers will, as we do, understand themselves as professionals and this in itself calls to mind discourses that may in some sense be antithetical to a critical awareness of a post- or late modern world. Boggs (2000: 301) sees the exponential growth of the professional in the last century as providing a defining stratum in society: 'professions evolved into vast empires of institutional and economic control in virtually every sphere: medicine, law, academia, mass media, business and of course science'. Science is understood as a critical category in the legitimation of professional status and identity maintenance. As Boggs (2000: 301) suggests 'like the scientific rationality that underpins it, modern professionalism flows from an Enlightenment optimism which upholds a dynamic role and elevated status for intellectuals'. For Boggs (2000: 302) that critical intellectualism, implicit in the world being 'good to think', has been eroded and displaced by a 'technocratic intelligentsia'. In late modernity, Boggs (2000: 300) argues, bureaucratization and the growth of a professional stratum 'were all part of the same historical dynamic, one that was shaped and controlled by "corporate rationalizers" '. In becoming a researcher, we are impelled through the research process to become a part of a community, and in writing, we join the vast world of intertextual knowledge. However, that world is also highly specialized and is full of expert and inaccessible discourses, 'the esoteric codes of specialists' that operate at one level to create enclaves of knowledge, subworlds of thinking to which only insiders have access and so a genuinely public discursive arena ceases to exist. As Boggs (2000: 301) suggests, in relation to the universities, 'the technocratic, yet fragmented world of academic life militates against development of a common public discourse within which intellectuals could address the larger philosophical and social concerns which have preoccupied human beings throughout history'. This unprecedented fragmentation of knowledges is a part of our postmodern landscape. However, for many who are adopting a researcher identity as part of a professional repertoire, the freedom that this suggests may be circumscribed.

Most researchers, and particularly researchers in the public service and practitioner researchers, will have in mind an official version of the reality that they are to study and an image of how they are expected to construct themselves as researchers. There may be key words such as accountability, practical application, transparency and ethics, that begin to construct the world for researchers themselves and their social practices within it; which prompts the question, just how transgressive can we be as social researchers? The committed nature of much small-scale research makes the exercise of a critical reconstruction potentially difficult. The researcher is likely to be constrained by their organizational identity and allegiances and by the boundaries of organizational reality. According to legend, in Margaret Thatcher's administrations, whatever the question, the answer was the market. In schools today whatever the problem, the answer is leadership. Action research presents an interesting case. It can be ethically grounded, saturated with the students' or the clients' voice, fully collaborative and collegial, but insofar as axiomatically the exercise is geared to improved practice or increased efficiency, can it simultaneously be properly critical?

The answer to this is found in the way we have been understanding research – not as a technical operation where the researcher as person is subordinated to technical mastery of methods or methodology, but something that engages the person in relation to others in the construction of text. Through selection and interpretation we can write ourselves in different moods. Our formal curriculum vitae is likely to be a very different sort of narrative from that of our emotional lives. In much the same way our account of the field often ignores our emotion or negativity, even though part of that experience might be dislike of the people we have to deal with and occasional boredom. The social researcher engages with others and, as we have seen, how we construct otherness and relatedness are fundamentals of the research process. If the other is objectified, then the researcher remains the omniscient constructor of the real. If the other is constructed in relation to the researcher, then both parties are subjects in a mutual and potentially reciprocal process. There is also the issue of whether as researchers we identify with intellectuals or technicians, and of how we construct ourselves within the research process. Also, we can distinguish between what we feel as subjects – which may be a continuous and essential sense of self and what we assent to as real, which may be a more fluid, and less permanent model of self. We are all likely to have a notion of the biographical self and this gives a sense of narrative continuity to both our selves and our research, but we also know that we can construct alternative stories. Finally, we can say that the identity of the researcher cannot in the late modern world be adequately understood as the acquisition of a set of externally generated skills. In researching the social our selves are inevitably propelled to the frontiers of a dynamic social and political world that invites us to engage with the fugitive complexity of the real.

Methods and methodology

What is methodology?

In writing this book we have attempted to produce a text that is different from the many how-to-do-it guides that are available, but which provides a series of arguments that engage with the concerns of people who are becoming researchers. The chapters are arranged more or less around the different methods that researchers in education and the social sciences are liable to use, but our concern has been with methodology rather than method. If you are reading the book in conventional order, by the time you get to this chapter we hope you will have formed some ideas about what methodology means to you. More than this, we hope that, in the context of your research these ideas will have gone through a number of changes so that, when asked about the methodology of your research, you may feel both more confident and possibly less definitive about your response.

The word 'methodology' is problematic. It is frequently used in everyday life and sometimes even in academic circles interchangeably with 'methods'. This elision is understandable and is compounded by the linguistic forms. If we want to use an adjective meaning appertaining to methods, we have to use 'methodological' since 'methodical' means something rather different. Thus, the two nouns share adjectival forms. However, as we have already seen in this book, for a researcher distinguishing between them is more than an exercise in pedantry.

The definition of methods is relatively straightforward. It is derived from the Greek *meta* meaning after, beyond – usually used in English words to mean beyond in the sense of more developed or higher order – and *hodos* meaning way or means. Methods then are the systematic means by which something is accomplished. In research, therefore, methods denote the ways in which data are produced, interpreted and reported.

They consist of procedures and techniques exemplified by particular research instruments so questionnaires, semi-structured interviews, participant observation and role playing are all examples of research methods and although in themselves different methods may be difficult to operationalize and may be highly problematic in different situations, what is meant by 'a method' is actually quite straightforward.

Methodology, however, has an extended and more problematic meaning and is quite complex as an idea. The Greek *logos*, the final element, means word or reason and is used in a number of ways in English but as the suffix -logy generally denotes study or theory. Thus, methodology in essence can be seen as the study of, or a theory of, the way that methods are used. Thus, a discussion of methodology in a well-known research methods book contains this fairly traditional but comprehensive enumeration of its aims (Kaplan, 1973, quoted by Cohen and Manion, 1994: 39).

> to describe and analyse . . . methods, throwing light on their limitations and resources, clarifying their presuppositions and consequences, relating their potentialities to the twilight zone at the frontiers of knowledge. It is to venture generalizations from the success of particular techniques, suggesting new applications, and to unfold the specific bearings of logical and metaphysical principles on concrete problems, suggesting new formulations.

Cohen and Manion (Cohen *et al.*, 2000: 6) continue their discussion by referring to Burrell and Morgan's (1979) dichotomous images of human beings, 'the one portrays them as responding mechanically to their environment; the other, as initiators of their own actions'. They then suggest that the assumptions of most social researchers are pitched somewhere in the range between. There are seen to be four kinds of assumptions, which are represented schematically in Figure 11.1 (we have added the words in italics as explanation).

There are elements of this scheme that are consonant with arguments that we have made in this book. However, there are parts that we find problematic. For example, the term anti-positivism might be better replaced with constructivism and it would not be hard to see further positions more extreme than those represented in the right-hand column. Nevertheless, the particular point that we wish to engage with most strongly is the fourth dimension. This would seem to be another aspect of epistemology, in that the assumptions are about knowledge. However, by labelling only this dimension as methodology the scheme seems to be suggesting that the other assumptions are somehow outside methodology. We would argue that ontology, epistemology and human nature (perhaps better put as one's understanding of the nature of the social) are very much *within* methodology, since it involves the consideration of and

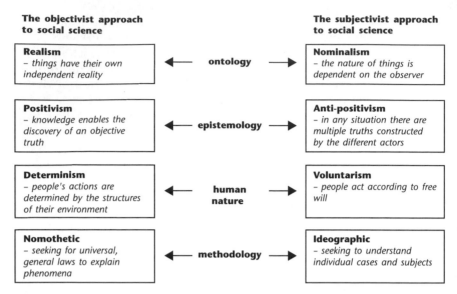

The objectivist approach
to social science

The subjectivist approach
to social science

Realism
– things have their own
independent reality

◀—— **ontology** ——▶

Nominalism
– the nature of things is
dependent on the observer

Positivism
– knowledge enables the
discovery of an objective
truth

◀—— **epistemology** ——▶

Anti-positivism
– in any situation there are
multiple truths constructed
by the different actors

Determinism
– people's actions are
determined by the structures
of their environment

◀—— **human
nature** ——▶

Voluntarism
– people act according to free
will

Nomothetic
– seeking for universal,
general laws to explain
phenomena

◀—— **methodology** ——▶

Ideographic
– seeking to understand
individual cases and subjects

Figure 11.1   Scheme for analysing assumptions about the nature of social science (adapted from Burrell and Morgan, 1979 reproduced from Cohen *et al.* 2000: 7)

reflection on what is at stake in the processes of research, including the orientation of the researcher towards the research and all that is implicated by that.

Reflecting on research in a postcolonial situation, we might identify six different sets of issues: ontological, epistemological, ethical, macropolitical, micropolitical and practical (Pryor and Ampiah, 2004). Since these are all implicated in considering research we might consider methodology as a space where six different issues intersect as represented in Figure 11.2. The pairing of the sets of issues owes something to the practicalities of drawing a Venn diagram but nevertheless carries some logic. Within research it is difficult to speak of epistemology without invoking ontology. So, one can state an epistemological position, for example, that it is possible to discover knowledge of the world, which can be substantiated or disproved with accuracy and reliability. However, in order to make these assertions particular ontological premises are needed, in this case that there is an objective reality separate from the knower. Similarly, as we saw in Chapter 8, it is very difficult to talk of one's political views without reference to ethical issues. Individuals often have recourse to the one to justify the other, and both tend to relate to generalized positions outside the particular situation in which one is operating. Finally, both practical issues and micropolitics depend upon local conditions. Moreover, they are strongly connected since which method or instrument is suitable to use

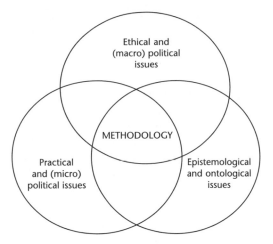

Figure 11.2   Methodology as intersecting sets (source: Pryor and Ampiah, 2004: 162)

and how will be strongly affected by the micropolitics of the situation. For example, a busy, powerful headteacher as respondent will call for different techniques from working with a 'captive' group of students; enquiring about institutional strength may need to be approached in a different way from asking about perceived weakness.

So, this model contends that what the researcher counts as reality and truth, the choice of methods and the constraints on these provided by the social context, as well as the ideological or ethical beliefs and motivations of the researcher are all strongly implicated in the methodological stance. This diagram can act, therefore, as a heuristic for a researcher in describing and explaining their approach, because, ultimately, although they may be analytically separate all these sets of issues are linked and have the power to affect each other.

Methodology, the research process and identity

The Venn diagram image seems a convenient heuristic for conceptualizing methodology in the abstract – methodology in general. However, it may be less useful procedurally when talking more specifically and especially when we are seeking to describe our methodology in a particular situation – the methodology of a particular project. In talking about the research process Hitchcock and Hughes (1995: 21) suggest that there is a logical procedural sequence:

ontological assumptions → epistemological assumptions → methodological considerations → instrumentation and data collection.

If one allows that the adjective 'methodological' is here referring to methods rather that methodology, then there is some attraction to this. However, as we have repeatedly seen in this book, the research process is not as linear as this would suggest. An interest in contributing to a particular debate, or a necessity to report the research to a particular audience will reflexively influence what may be seen as the previous stages of the research (*cf.* especially the argument about the triple mimesis in Chapter 5). Thus, one process can give rise to another, which appears to precede it; so this sequential model seems to represent a rather static and one-dimensional view of the relationships between its different elements.

However, in doing social research, very little is actually static. On a substantive level, what starts as an emerging theme often assumes much greater importance as the research progresses. Thus, research questions produced so laboriously and with so much thought at the start of a piece of doctoral research, often seem slightly off-centre or even tangential when the thesis finally comes to be written. This is because the focus of a piece of a research is not just a question of what is considered, but how it is done. As the research happens there are often new theoretical insights and different theoretical resources that shift the gaze. Good research is not just a question of the application of theory to data, but is an act of theorization. Thus, at some level, no matter how open the researcher is beforehand about their research focus, they cannot fully describe what it will be by the time the research is reported. Indeed, by communicating a very narrow, sharp focus, they may, in fact, be misleading their collaborators. The interaction between substantive and methodological issues means, therefore, that both the content and the methodology are dynamic, involving constant shifting.

An image which may be useful in conceptualizing methodology is borrowed from topology ('rubber sheet geometry') (see Figure 11.3). The shape of the methodology is produced by 'pulls' from the six different dimensions identified in the Venn diagram. However, social research does not take place in an idealized environment, but takes place in and investigates specific and changing contexts. In seeking for coherence, one may attempt to be consistent and to hold methodology still. However, contextual flux at all stages of the research process means that it is subject to pulling from different directions. The methodology of a piece of research is therefore always liable to change its shape subtly or sometimes quite markedly. Often, as with the writing of the word methodology in Figure 11.3, what was intended at the outset becomes distorted. This image suggests that methodology is dynamic, contingent, dialogic and context specific. The more complex the research project, the greater the number of researchers, respondents, trips to the field, the more this will be so as the pulls, though coming from similar sets of issues, may well be of different strengths and from different directions.

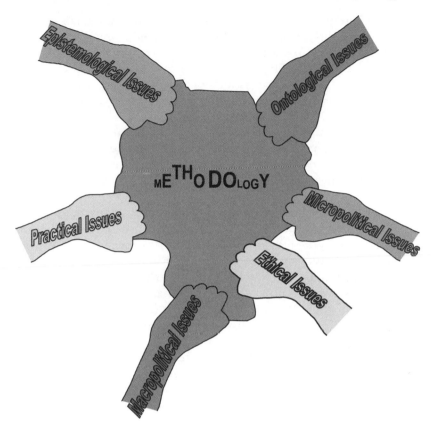

Figure 11.3   Methodology as an elastic plane (adapted from Pryor and Ampiah (2004: 162)

Similarly, this image of methodology suggests how different research ers doing ostensibly similar research may end up with something that looks very different. At this point, it is worth returning to the argument about incommensurability, which has emerged in several chapters. Here the distinction between methods and methodology was fundamental to understanding continuities and discontinuities between research positions. We suggested that the practical elements of method were places where researchers of different persuasions might 'meet' and be seen to be doing the same sort of thing. Within the diagram, methods are part of the practical issues. However, a convergence of pulls on this one dimension still leaves the potential for other elements to produce something of a very different shape.

In the argument above 'context' was what we saw as producing pulls from the different sets of issues. Once more though, this scheme may oversimplify matters, for there are contextual elements that seem to cut across the different six sets of issues that we have identified. For example, when we were discussing the difference between linguists and post-structural sociologists in Chapter 7 we found that questions of ontology, epistemology and the politics (both micro and macro) of the academy might be at stake. Several other aspects of the context of a research project both sit across these different sets of issues and are closely linked with each other. For example, the idea of the 'interests' of the researcher, which is often given great prominence in books about research methods for postgraduate researchers, is clearly linked to academic subject areas. It will then also be connected to the idea of the purpose of the research, to its focus and then to the research questions that are seen to guide the project.

There are obvious parallels to be drawn between the dynamic view of methodology advanced in this chapter and the notion of researcher identity as it emerged in the previous one. Indeed, if we see identity as 'something that is continuously made and remade in activity; it is a being in continuous becoming . . . [which] arises from the dialectic of how we experience ourselves and how others experience us', the parallels become very close (Roth, 2003: 19). In looking again at the diagram in Figure 11.3 it might be possible to substitute for 'Methodology' the words 'Researcher Identity'.

Behind this lies the suggestion that our research identity, like our other identities, is not something that we ever 'have', but rather something that we bring into being through performing it (Butler, 1990; Sarup, 1996). We import into it many influences from our past but these are constantly pulled and pushed by the methodological context factors. For example, we may see a general ethical commitment towards openness as an essential part of our identity as a researcher. However, engagement with a research context where disclosing our purpose may close our access to it, is likely to change the way we position ourselves in this particular instance (see, for example, Punch, 1989). This kind of 'pull' may also provoke a shift in our view of ourselves as researchers, in the way that we present ourselves and in the way that we are seen.

Sarup (1996: 25) speaks of identity in textual terms of as 'a multi-dimensional space in which a variety of writings blend and clash'. He might also have added readings to the writings. The discrepancies or differences within writings and between them and our current circumstances create a discursive space in which we can have some measure of freedom. Within this space the individual, who is never a unified member of a single unified group, can, as Sarup (1996: 25) says, 'work' on the different writings and readings. We are thus always in a state of becoming and are shifting our position to deal with the contingencies of the different pulls. A good example of the play of these pulls on my research identity comes from my own doctoral work. I was working as a teacher in the school I was researching so my identity as a teacher was important. This had a big impact on the way that I saw myself within the school, was seen by the children and teachers I was working with, and chose to present the research in the thesis and in articles. My identity as a man and the hetero-sexual father of a boy was important in a project that was looking at gender. I was a research student working on an ethnographic study within a department that had produced one of the classic school ethnographies and headed by a professor who had written another. I was a development education activist who was both running and commissioning courses on gender and race awareness. I could no doubt find other identities to list. However, each of these was influenced by and gave rise to pulls from the different sets of issues, some obviously more salient than others – for example, the ethnographic researcher identity and epistemological issues. The play of the writings and readings produced me as researcher and produced the research itself in a reciprocal cycle of relations.

Methodology and legitimacy – identity and narrative

The issue of my identity as a researcher became a central concern when I had to write my methodology chapter. For a researcher, the idea that one may be expected to justify one's methodology is important. Similar to our notion of the abstract and particular uses of the word methodology, Daly (2003) sees it in what she describes as a 'two fold way'. On the one hand, it is a set of rules and logical structures, which allow the researcher to pro-ceed in a reasoned and systematic way; on the other hand, it is a form of communication, where conventions allow the researcher to organize ideas and provide a language for communicating ideas with peers. In this sense it provides the means for establishing legitimacy. The methodology of a text is both individual, particular to the actual project, and general, in that one is writing within a tradition, a discourse, and is invoking rules that are normative. This leaves us as researchers with some space in which to work. Above all, it means that by positioning ourselves methodologic-ally within a tradition or discourse, we can to a certain extent choose our set of rules.

As we have seen in this book there is no dominant methodology in the social sciences today. What appears to hold sway in one arena may be treated with suspicion or contempt in others. Yvonna Lincoln's (Denzin and Lincoln, 1998b) idea of overlapping 'moments' seems to be an apt description of the methodological fragmentation of current prac-tice. Therefore, within a research text the author will invoke a particular discourse and indicate their allegiance to a set of rules. Compare, for example, these two brief extracts from the abstracts of two articles in the same recent edition of a prominent education journal:

The emphasis on 'problem solving', collaboration and 'communities of learning' sanctify science and scientists as possessing authoritative knowledge over increasing realms of human phenomena, thus narrowing the boundaries of possible action and critical thought.

Popkewitz, 2004: 3

Children with low initial performance benefited less from integrated language arts instruction as measured by direct measures of achievement; such differential effects of instruction were not observed for teacher ratings of children's achievement and learning style.

Xue and Meisels, 2004: 191

The writers of both of these articles are communicating their findings. In doing so they do not explicitly state that they subscribe to a specific approach, but the terms they use nonetheless position themselves within a particular methodological discourse. Even at this stage, the text is announcing their identity as researchers and thus beginning to indicate what the reader might expect. In some contexts, this shorthand may be seen as enough to show their awareness of the normative rules and to suggest how they are playing by them. The rules for 'scientific' research aligned with positivism are fixed since its aims are universal and it pursues generalization, which holds independent of context. Thus, it rarely states or discusses the rules as such, though it will usually seek to establish methodological legitimacy through devices such as statistical tests. However, for constructivist research, where context is seen as so much more important, and approaches are much less fixed and pluralistic, it becomes important to state more explicitly what rules you are playing by so that a position can be established. As a supervisor of research students I often encounter student writing which is criticized on grounds of poor methodology. However, engagement with the problem shows it to be a purely textual error rather than a methodological one. The writing of the report has suggested to the reader a methodological position different from that actually held. As Stronach and MacLure (1997: 56) point out:

> for *the reader*, texts can only be authenticated in themselves: the reader has no other resource than the persuasiveness of the text. But for *the researcher*, the problem of the interrelationship of methodology and text remains important . . . We do not seek to dismiss methodology, but rather to bring its textual properties to light.

Throughout this book, we have explored the methodological minefield of social research. Our task has been to suggest that there are paths through, but that in negotiating a passage, it would be rash to ignore the complications of the field. We talked about the idea that in becoming a researcher we adopt an identity, part of which enables us to choose which set of rules we wish to adhere to. However, to extend the analogy of the minefield, this should be seen more as a question of having an idea of where the mines are rather than of having disarmed them. This is all the more so since, as we have discussed on several occasions, although it may be possible to choose those whom we would like as a reference group, the social, political and professional context for many researchers means that the room for choice is often constrained. In practice, the dominant discourse may be very different from what we would wish to adhere to. Within education, there is a strong pull towards realism and positivism. This causes a problem for many researchers in that it appears intellectually impossible to address the social within postmodernity using the tools of modernity. Paradoxically though, the structures of globalism and neo-liberalism, which are their economic and political manifestations, seem to require the technologies that modernist research delivers. This means that our research identities are liable to be multiple and pragmatic.

As we have seen, the sets of issues identified in Figure 11.3 act together to produce the methodology of projects in a shifting and dynamic way. We have suggested elsewhere that rather than these factors being confined to a particular part of the research process they may be at work throughout and indeed they interact both retrospectively and prospectively (see Chapter 6). This means that although it may be possible in some cases to justify your approach by listing the set of rules you are working to, this is liable to be a great simplification, this will probably not do justice to the complexity of your methodology and crucially will lack the element of persuasiveness that is needed. Moreover, saying what rules you wish to play by does not necessarily mean that you will be able to stick to them. The possibility of transgression is always there. However, in the very act of transgression, you will want to establish your own legitimacy.

A way through these problems of coherence and time is offered by the connection between methodology and research identity. To explain yourself you need to tell a good story, to construct a narrative, so the evolution of the methodology can receive coherence through being linked to narrative of the identity of the researcher. Sometimes this can be explicit. In my thesis I hit upon the method of discussing different types of researcher in turn – qualitative researcher, ethnographic researcher, gender researcher, action researcher – discussing how I had worked within and against the rules of each (Pryor, 1993). For Máiréad her methodology chapter was all about the transformation of her stance through the research (Dunne, 1998). In a more recent jointly written article my collaborator and I dialogued with our joint voice to tell the story of the way that we were attempting to negotiate the issues of joint postcolonial research (Pryor and Ampiah, 2004). However, methodological narratives are not always so personally explicit. They always contain various forms of intertextuality, ranging from the overt, such as quotation of other researchers' experiences or citation or academic authorities, to the kind of subtle textual flagging that we saw in the two abstracts quoted above and, of course, those that become internalized and unflagged.

However, telling a narrative is not an easy solution to the problems of legitimizing methodology. In writing our own narratives and identities we are seeking what Ricoeur (1984) calls 'narrative hospitality' in the reader which may then be reconfigured by an alien logic (Rapport and Overing, 2000). Moreover, as we suggested in Chapters 6 and 9, methodology is there not to help guarantee true representations of the world, but because research is a 'discursive practice of "languaging" ' (Usher, 1996b: 39), the nature of representations and their relation to the reality they point to is always problematic. Nevertheless the more complex the issues and the more protean the nature of both methodology and identity, the greater our need to find some form of structure to make sense of it and give it meaning. Arranging issues as events in a narrative provides a way of 'hemming them in' (Barthes, 1982). Polkinghorne (1988: 149) suggests that 'we come to know ourselves by discerning a plot that unifies the actions and events or our past with future actions . . . [which] . . . involves the cognitive operation of narrative structuring'. Narrative affords us the possibility of fluidity within coherence, which other ways of asserting our identity do not. It seems to offer a path, though often a tortuous one, through the double crisis of representation and legitimation.

Thus, narratives of methodology/research identity are a way of owning up to our problems and the tensions in our position, and 'working' on the spaces between them. This is what we have referred to elsewhere as reflexivity. It is the idea that what we write is not just an account of experience, but a systematic dialogue with that experience, exploring the u-turns and s-bends and detailing what has been suppressed and omitted, as well as what has been presented and brought forward. We can seek to legitimize our approach to ourselves through reflection on the play of our identities as researchers; for our readers we can inscribe it in the story of our becoming a researcher.

In putting together this book we have attempted to engage with the dilemmas of our readers, who as we said in the introduction we have conceptualized as the people we work with as postgraduate students and colleagues. We experience the central drama of their intellectual lives as similar to our own, namely the tensions and frustrations of the incommensurable discourses within which we have to operate. At different times in this book we have characterized this in different ways. One dichotomy has been between North American and European Continental approaches to social science. While science can point to the way it has transformed the world through the technologies it has produced, social science is hard put to show similar achievements. Scientific knowledge is what Aristotle called episteme, it is 'universal, invariable, context-independent' and is 'based on general analytical rationality' (Flyvbjerg,

2001: 57). In their model of professional expertise Dreyfus and Dreyfus (1986) argue that proficiency in professional situations does not depend on rule-following, but instead is highly contextualized. Indeed their analysis places the kind of the generalizable, context-free knowledge that is prized within scientistic approaches as characteristic of the novice or advanced beginner. As Flyvbjerg (2001: 3) maintains:

> ... the social sciences are strongest where the natural sciences are weakest: just as the social sciences have not contributed much to explanatory and predictive theory, neither have the natural sciences contributed to the reflexive analysis and discussion of values and interests, which is the prerequisite for an enlightened political, economic, and cultural development in any society.

However, within social research, power remains fundamental to understanding practice and process. Closely allied to the methodological discussion in this book has been a discursive understanding of power as distributed and non-possessive. While possessive notions of power emphasize the coercive, Foucault's version of discursive power uses the image of the capillary whereby power is pervasive and flows in all directions through every social interaction. Power then produces regimes of truth that present an appearance of stability and in which social researchers are both located and tasked with describing. Regimes of truth are often legitimated through systems of values, but we need to connect these large abstract models with concrete social practices. Foucault's (1977: 89) idea of *Wirkliche Historie* (real history) that 'shortens its vision to those things nearest to it' makes this connection. This can be exemplified in case study where the immediacy of local contexts can also be related to the global and theoretical.

Epilogue

So, at the end of this book we ask the question, what does it mean to become a researcher? Whatever else it may mean, it involves a great deal of effort, usually both physical and intellectual. Moreover, we have tried to emphasize that the process of becoming implies a continually receding horizon and so there is no point at which our research identity solidifies. We have attempted to present research as a complex process, which not only transforms social reality into text, but also transforms the researcher. Indeed we might go so far as to say that, if you do not feel transformed at the end of a substantial piece of research, you might want to question whether it was worth all the effort. We hope that reading this book is enabling (or if you are starting your reading at this point, will enable) you to become a different researcher. However, as we have often repeated, meaning derives from reading rather than writing and readings may be unpredictable, multiple and certainly outside our control. What kind of researcher you become depends on your reading. If the book has interested, worried, pleased or enraged you, then it has done its job.

We have tried throughout the book to disrupt the notion of research as method, to question the distinction between the subjects and objects of research, and to place both research in the social and the social in research. The idea of becoming a researcher is about how we activate selectively different texts and inscribe ourselves in our research. We have conceptualized the book as a companion to the research process. As a companion, we hope that by turns it reassures you, asks you difficult questions and stimulates you to theorize your position. We want you to feel reassured but not too comfortable; to be able to identify the tensions, but be brave enough to embrace them as part and parcel of what *Becoming a researcher* is.

References

Abhu-Lughod, L. (1991) Writing Against Culture, in Fox, R. (ed.) *Recapturing Anthropology; Working in the Present*. Santa Fe: School of American Research Press.

Ainley, P. (1999) *Learning Policy, Towards the Certified Society*. Basingstoke: Macmillan.

Allen, G. (2003) *Roland Barthes*. London: Routledge.

Altheide, D.L. and Johnson, J.M. (1998) Criteria for Assessing Interpretive Validity in Qualitative Research, in Denzin, N.K. and Lincoln, Y.S. (eds) (1998) *Collecting and Interpreting Qualitative Materials*. London: Sage, 283–312.

Altrichter, H. Posch, P. and Somekh, B. (1993) *Teachers Investigate Their Work, an introduction to the methods of action research*. London: Routledge.

Antaki, C., Billig, M., Edwards, D. and Potter, J. (2003) Discourse Analysis Means Doing Analysis: A Critique Of Six Analytic Shortcomings, *Discourse Analysis Online* 1. http://www.lboro.ac.uk/departments/ss/centres/dargindex.htm (accessed 3 May 2004).

Arber, S. and Gilbert, N. (1992) *Women and Working Lives – Divisions and Change*. Basingstoke: Macmillan.

Arksey, H. and Knight, P. (1999) *Interviewing for Social Scientists: an introductory resource with examples*. London: Sage.

Ashcroft, B. and Ahluwalia, P. (2001) *Edward Said*. London: Routledge.

Atkinson, P. (1990) *The Ethnographic Imagination: textual constructions of reality*. London: Routledge.

Atkinson, P. (1992) *Understanding Ethnographic Texts*. Newbury Park, CA: Sage.

Atkinson, P. and Hammersley, M. (1998) Ethnography and Participant Observation in Denzin, N. and Lincoln, Y. *Strategies of Qualitative Inquiry*. Thousand Oaks, CA: Sage.

Atkinson, R. (2002) The life story interview, in Gubrium, J.E. and Holstein, J.A. (eds) *Handbook of Interview Research. Context and Method*. Thousand Oaks, Sage.

Back, L. (1998) Reading and Writing Research. In Seale, C. (ed.) *Researching Society and Culture*. London: Sage.

Bal, M. (1999) *Quoting Caravaggio: Contemporary Art, preposterous History*. Chicago, IL: University of Chicago Press.

Ball, S.J. (1992) *Politics and Policy Making in Education: Explorations in Policy Sociology.* London: Routledge.

Ball, S.J. (1994) *Education Reform: A critical and post-structural approach.* Buckingham: Open University Press.

Ball, S.J. (1995) Culture, Crisis and Morality: The Struggle Over the National Curriculum, in Atkinson, P., Davies, B., Delamont, S. and Bernstein, B. (eds) *Discourse and Reproduction, Essays in Honor of Basil Bernstein.* Cresskill, New Jersey: Hampton Press.

Barker, P. (1998) *Michel Foucault: an introduction.* Edinburgh: Edinburgh University Press.

Barnes, B. and Bloor, D. (1982) Relativism, Rationalism and the Sociology of Knowledge, in Hollis, M. and Lukes, S. (eds) *Rationality and Relativism*, 21–47. Oxford: Blackwell.

Barthes, R. (1974) *S/Z* (trans. Miller, R.). New York: Hill and Wang.

Barthes, R. (1975) *The Pleasure of the Text* (trans. Miller, R.). New York: Hill and Wang.

Barthes, R. (1981) The Discourse of History (trans. Bann, S.) *Comparative Criticism*, 3: 7–20.

Barthes, R. (1982) *A Barthes Reader* (edited by Sontag, S.). London: Jonathan Cape.

Bartlett, S., Burton, D. and Peim, N. (2001) *Introduction to Education Studies.* London: Paul Chapman/Sage.

Baudrillard, J. (1988) *The Consumer Society: Myths and Structures.* London: Sage.

Baudrillard, J. (1998) Simulacra and Simulations, in Poster, M. (ed.) *Jean Baudrillard, Selected Writings*, p. 167. London: Falmer Press.

Bell, J. (1993) *Doing Your Research Project: a guide for first-time researchers in education and social science.* Buckingham: Open University Press.

Bell, J. (1999) *Doing your Research Project*, 3rd edn. Buckingham: Open University Press.

Best, R. (ed.) (1996) *Education, Spirituality and the Whole Child.* London: Cassell.

Best, R. (ed.) (2000) *Education for Spiritual, Moral, Social and Cultural Development.* London: Cassell.

Beyer, P. (1996) *Religion and Globalization.* London: Sage.

Bhabha, H.K. (ed.) (1990) *Nation and Narration.* London: Routledge.

Bhaskar, R. (1979) *Possibility of Naturalism.* London: Harvester Wheatsheaf.

Billig, M. (1998) Dialogic repression and the Oedipus complex: Reinterpreting the little Hans case, *Culture & Psychology*, 4(1): 11–47.

Billig, M. (nd) The Dialogic Unconscious: psycho-analysis, discursive psychology and the nature of repression, http://www.massey.ac.nz/~alock/virtual/p-a4.htm (accessed 22 July 2004).

Bliss, J., Monk, M, and Ogborn, J. (1983) *Qualitative data analysis for educational research: a guide to uses of systemic networks.* London: Croom Helm.

Boggs, C. (2000) Intellectuals, in Browning, G., Halcli, A. and Webster, F. (eds) *Understanding Contemporary Society: theories of the present.* London: Sage.

Bourdieu, P. (1987) What Makes a Social Class? On the Theoretical and Practical Existence of Groups, *Berkeley Journal of Sociology*, 32: 1–17.

Bourdieu, P. (1988) *Homo Academicus.* Cambridge: Polity Press.

Bourdieu, P., Accardo, A., Balazs, G., Beaud, S., Bonvin, F., Bourdieu, E., Bougois,

P., Broccolichi, S., Champagne, P., Christin, R., Fauguer, J-P., Garcia, S., Lenoir, R., Œuvrard, F., Pialoux, M., Pinto, L., Podalydès, D., Dayad, A., Soulié, C. and Wacquant, L. (1999) *The Weight of the World: Social Suffering in Contemporary Society*, (trans. Ferguson, P., Emmanuel, S., Johnson, J. and Waryn, S.). Cambridge: Polity.

Bourdieu, P. and Wacquant, L. (1992) *An Invitation to Reflexive Sociology*. Chicago: Chicago University Press.

Bowie, M. (1991) *Lacan*. London: Fontana.

Brew, A. (2001) *The Nature of Research: inquiry in academic contexts*. London: Falmer Press.

Briggs, C.L. (2002) Interviewing, power/knowledge, and social inequality, in Gubrium, J.E. and Holstein, J.A. (eds) (2002) *Handbook of Interview Research. Context and Method*. Thousand Oaks: Sage.

Brown, A. and Dowling, P. (1998) *Doing Research/Reading Research*. London: Falmer.

Brown, P. and Lauder, H. (1992) *Education for Economic Survival: from fordism to post-fordism*. London: Routledge.

Brown, T. and Jones, L. (2001) *Action Research and Postmodernism: congruence and critique*. Buckingham: Open University Press.

Browning, G., Halcli, A. and Webster, F. (eds) (2000) *Understanding Contemporary Society: theories of the present*. London: Sage.

Bruner, J. (1999) Culture, Mind and Education, in Moon, B. and Murphy, P. (eds) *Curriculum in Context*. London: Paul Chapman/The Open University.

Bryman, A. (1988) *Quantity and Quality in Social Research*. London: Unwin Hyman.

Bulmer, M. (1982) The research ethics of pseudo-patient studies: A new look at the merits of covert ethnographic methods. *Sociological Review*, 30(4): 627–46.

Burman, E. (2003) Discourse analysis means analysing discourse: some comments on Antaki, Billig, Edwards and Potter 'Discourse analysis means doing analysis: A critique of six analytic shortcomings', *Discourse Analysis Online* 1. http://www.lboro.ac.uk/departments/ss/centres/dargindex.htm (accessed 5 May 2004).

Burrell, G. and Morgan, G. (1979) *Sociological Paradigms and Organisational Analysis*. London: Heinemann.

Butler, J. (1990) *Gender Trouble . . . Feminism and the Subversion of Identity*. London: Routledge.

Butler, J. (1993) *Bodies That Matter*. London: Routledge.

Byrne, D. (2002) *Interpreting Quantitative Data*. London: Sage.

Carr, D. (1986) *Time, Narrative, and History*. Bloomington, Indiana University Press.

Chandler, D. (2004) *Semiotics: The Basics*. London: Routledge.

Clark, T. (1992) *Derrida, Heidegger, Blanchot. Sources of Derrida's Notion and Practice of Literature*. Cambridge: Cambridge University Press.

Clifford, J. and Marcus, G.E. (1986) *Writing Culture: The Poetics and Politics of Ethnography*. Berkeley: University of California Press.

Coffey, A. and Atkinson, P. (1996) *Making Sense of Qualitative Data: complementary research strategies*. Thousand Oaks: Sage.

Coffin, C., Swann, J., Hewings, A., Curry, M.J., Goodman, S. and Lillis, T. (2003) *Teaching Academic Writing: a toolkit for Higher Education*. London: Routledge.

Cohen, L. and Manion, L. (1994) *Research Methods in Education*, 4th edn. London: Routledge Falmer.

Cohen, L., Manion, L. and Morison, K. (2000) *Research Methods in Education*, 5th edn. London: Routledge Falmer.

Colebrook, C. (2002) *Gilles Deleuze*. London: Routledge.

Cresswell, J.W. (1998) *Qualitative Enquiry and Research Design: choosing among five traditions*. Thousand Oaks: Sage.

Culler, J.D. (1976) *Saussure*, London: Harvester Press.

Culler, J. (1986) *Saussure*. Ithaca: Cornell University Press.

Czarniawska, C. (2004) *Narratives in Social Science Research*. London: Sage.

Daly, M. (2003) Methodology, in Miller, R. and Brewer, J. (eds) *A–Z of Social Research*. London: Sage.

Darlington, Y. and Scott, D. (2002) *Qualitative Research in Practice: Stories from the Field*. Buckingham: Open University Press.

Davies, A. (1999) *An Introduction to Applied Linguistics*. Edinburgh: Edinburgh University Press.

Davies, B. (1982) *Life in the Classroom and Playground: the Accounts of Primary School Children*. London: Routledge and Kegan Paul.

Davies, B. and Harré, R. (1990) Positioning: the discursive production of selves, *Journal of the Theory of Social Behaviour*, 20: 43–65.

Deleuze, G. and Guattari, F. (2002) *A Thousand Plateaus: Capitalism and Schizophrenia*. London: Continuum.

Denzin, N.K. (1998) The Art and Politics of Interpretation, in Denzin, N.K. and Lincoln, Y.S. (eds) (1998) *Collecting and Interpreting Qualitative Materials*. London: Sage, 313–344.

Denzin, N.K. and Lincoln, Y.S. (eds) (1998a) *Strategies of Qualitative Inquiry*. London: Sage.

Denzin, N.K. and Lincoln Y.S. (eds) (1998b) *Collecting and Interpreting Qualitative Materials*. London: Sage.

Denzin, N.K. and Lincoln, Y.S. (eds) (1998c) *The Landscape of Qualitative Inquiry*. London: Sage.

Denzin, N.K. and Lincoln, Y.S. (1998d) Entering the Field of Qualitative Research, in Denzin, N.K. and Lincoln, Y.S. (eds) (1998) *Collecting and Interpreting Qualitative Materials*. London: Sage.

Derrida, J. (1973) (trans. Allison, D.) *Speech and Phenomena and Other Essays on Husserl's Theory of Signs*. Evanston Illinois: Northwestern University Press.

Derrida, J. (1976) [1967a] (trans. Spivak, G.C.) *Of Grammatology*. Baltimore: Johns Hopkins University Press.

Derrida, J. (1978) (trans. Bass, A.) *Writing and Difference*. London: Routledge and Kegan Paul.

Derrida, J. (1990) Some statements and truisms about neologisms, newisms, postisms, parasitisms and other small seisisms, in Carroll, D. (ed.) *The States of 'Theory': History, Art and Culture*. New York: Columbia Press.

Dowling, P. (1998) *The Sociology of Mathematics Education*. London: Falmer Press.

Drake, R.F. (2001) *The Principles of Social Policy*. Basingstoke: Palgrave.

Dreyfus, H. and Dreyfus, S. (1986) *Mind over machine: the power of human intuition and expertise in the age of the computer*. New York: Free Press.

Du Gay, P., Evans, J. and Redman, P. (eds) (2000) *Identity: a reader*. London: Sage/Open University Press.

Dunne, M. (1996) The Power of Numbers: Quantitative Data and Equal

Opportunities Research, in Walsh, V. and Morley, L. (eds) *Breaking Boundaries: Women and Higher Education*. London: Taylor Francis.

Dunne, M. (1998) Getting pissed off with teachers: the methodological implications of positioned annoyance. *International Journal of Cynical Studies*, 78(3): 234–271.

Dunne, M. and Johnston, J. (1994) Gender Research In Mathematics Education: The Production of Difference, in Ernest, P. (ed.) *Mathematics, Philosophy and Education: An International Perspective*. London: Falmer Press: 221–230.

Dunne, M. and King, R. (2003) Outside Theory: an explanation of the links between education and work for Ghanaiain Market traders, *Journal of Education and Work*, 16(1): 27–44.

Dunne, M., Leach, F., Chilisa, B., Maundeni, T., Tabulawa, R., Kutor, N., Asamoah, A. and Forde, L.D. (2005) *Gendered School Experiences: impacts on retention and achievement in Botswana and Ghana*. London: DFID.

Dweck, C. (1989) Motivation, in Lesgold, A. and Glaser, R. (eds) *Foundations for a Psychology of Education*. Hillsdale NJ: Erlbaum.

Edley, N. (2001) Analysing Masculinity: Interpretative Repertoires, Ideological Dilemmas and Subject Positions, in Wetherell, M., Taylor, S. and Yates, S.J. (2001) *Discourse as data. A Guide for Analysis*. Buckingham: Open University Press.

Edwards, A. (1992) Teacher Talk and Pupil Competence, in Norman, K. *Thinking Voices*. London: Hodder & Stoughton.

Edwards, D. and Mercer, N. (1987) *Common Knowledge: the development of understanding in the classroom*. London: Methuen.

Edwards, A. and Westgate, D. (1987) *Investigating Classroom Talk*. Lewes: Falmer Press.

Eisner, E. (1993) Objectivity in Educational Research, in Hammersley, M. (ed.) *Educational Research: Current Issues. Volume I*. London: Paul Chapman.

Elliott, J. (1991) *Action Research for Educational Change*. Buckingham: Open University Press.

Elliott, J. (1998) *The Curriculum Experiment, Meeting the Challenge of Social Change*. Buckingham: Open University Press.

Elsworth, E. (1989) Why doesn't this feel empowering? Working through the repressive myths of Critical Pedagogy, *Harvard Educational Review*, 59(3): 297–324.

Fairclough, N. (1989) *Language and Power*. London: Longman.

Fairclough, N. (1995) *Critical Discourse Analysis: The Critical Study of Language*. London: Longman.

Fairclough, N. (2003) *Analysing Discourse: Textual Analysis for Social*. London: Routledge.

Filmer, P., Jenks, C., Seale, C. and Walsh, D. (1998) Developments in Social Theory, in Seale, C. (ed.) *Researching Society and Culture*. London: Sage.

Fine, G. and Glassner, B. (1979) Participant observation with children: Promise and Problems, *Urban Life*, 8: 153–174.

Fine, M. (1994) Dis-stance and Other Stances: Negotiations of Power Inside Feminist Research, in Gitlin, A. (ed.) *Power and Method. Political Activisms and Educational Research*. London: Routledge.

Fine, M. (1998) Working the Hyphens. Reinventing Self and Other in Qualitative

Research, in Denzin, N.K. and Lincoln, Y.S. (eds) *The Landscape of Qualitative Inquiry*. London: Sage.

Flick, U. (2002) *An Introduction to Qualitative Research*. London: Sage.

Flyvbjerg, B. (2001) *Making Social Science Matter: Why social inquiry fails and how it can succeed again*. Cambridge University Press.

Flyvbjerg, B. (2004) Five Misunderstandings about case study research, in Gobo, G. Gubrium, J. and Silverman, D. (eds) *Qualitative Research Practice*. London: Sage.

Foster, P. (1996) *Observing Schools: A Methodological Guide*. London: Paul Chapman.

Foucault, M. (1972) *The Archaeology of Knowledge* (trans. Sheridan Smith, A.). London: Tavistock.

Foucault, M. (1977) Truth and power, in Rabinow, P. (ed.) (1991) *The Foucault Reader*. Harmondsworth: Penguin.

Foucault, M. (1980) Truth and Power, in Gordon, C. (ed.) *Power/Knowledge*. Brighton: Harvester.

Foucault, M. (1984) What is an author? in Rabinow, P. (ed.) (1991) *The Foucault Reader*. London: Penguin.

Foucault, M. (1988) *Technologies of the Self* (edited by Martin, L.H., Gutman, H. and Hutton, P.H.). London: Tavistock.

Foucault, M. (1990) [1976] *The Will to Knowledge: The History of Sexuality: 1*. London: Penguin.

Gage, N. (1989) The Paradigm Wars and their Aftermath. *Teachers College Record*, 91 (2): 135–150.

Gans, H. (1982) The participant observer as a human being: observations on the personal aspects of fieldwork, in Burgess R. (ed.) *Field Research: A source book and Field Manual*. London: Allen and Unwin, 53–61.

Garfinkel, H. (1967) *Studies in Ethnomethodology*. Englewood Cliffs, NJ: Prentice-Hall.

Geertz, C. (1988) *Works and Lives: The Anthropologist as Author*. Stanford, CA: Stanford University Press.

Gewirtz, S., Ball, S. and Bowe, R. (1995) *Markets, Choice and Equity in Education*. Buckingham: Open University Press.

Giddens, A. (1984) *The Constitution of Society*. Cambridge: Polity Press/Basil Blackwell.

Giddens, A. (1991) *Modernity and Self-Identity, Self and Society in the Late Modern Age*. Cambridge: Polity Press/Basil Blackwell.

Giddens, A. (1993) *New Rules of Sociological Method*. Cambridge: Polity Press.

Gilligan, C. (1982) *In a Different Voice: Psychological Theory and Women's Development*. Cambridge, MA: Harvard University Press.

Glaser, B. and Strauss, A. (1967) *The Discovery of Grounded Theory*. Chicago: Aldine.

Goffman, E. (1981) *Forms of Talk*. Oxford: Blackwell.

Gold, R. (1958) Roles in Sociological Field Observations, *Social Forces* 36: 217–223.

Gray, J. (1995) *Enlightenment's Wake: politics and culture at the close of the modern age*. London: Routledge.

Guba, E.G. and Lincoln, Y. (1994) Competing Paradigms in Qualitiative Research, in Denzin, N. and Lincoln, Y. (eds) *Handbook of Qualitative Research*. London: Sage.

Guba, E.G. and Lincoln, Y.S. (1998) Competing Paradigms in Qualitative Research, in Denzin, N.K. and Lincoln, Y.S. (eds) (1998) *The Landscape of Qualitative Inquiry*. London: Sage, 195–220.

Gubrium, J.E. and Holstein, J.A. (2002) From the Individual Interview to the Interview Society, in Gubrium, J.E. and Holstein, J.A. (cds) (2002) *Handbook of Interview Research. Context and Method*. Thousand Oaks: Sage, pp. 3–32.

Hall, S. (1996) Who needs 'identity'? in Hall, S. and du Gay, P. (eds) *Questions of Cultural Identity*. London: Sage.

Hall, S. (2000) Who needs 'identity'? in Du Gay, P., Evans, J. and Redman, P. (eds) *Identity: a reader*. London: Sage/Open University.

Halstead, J.M. (1996) Values and Values Education in Schools, in Halstead, J.M. and Taylor, M.J. *Values in Education and Education in Values*. London: Falmer Press.

Halstead, J.M. and Taylor, M.J. (1996) *Values in Education and Education in Values*. London: Falmer Press.

Hammersley, M. (1990) *Reading Ethnographic Research: A Critical Guide*. London: Longman.

Hammersley, M. (1992) *What's Wrong with Ethnography?* London: Routledge.

Hammersley, M. (1997) On the foundations of critical discourse analysis, *Language & Communication*, 17(3): 237–248.

Hammersley, M. (1999) Taking Sides, in Scott, D. (ed.) (1999) *Values and Educational Research*. London: Institute of Education.

Hammersley, M. (2002) *Eductional Research: Policymaking and Practice*. London: Paul Chapman Publishing.

Harding, S. (1986) *The Science Question and Feminism*. Bloomington: Indiana University Press.

Harding, S. (1991) *Whose Science? Whose Knowledge? Thinking from Women's Lives*. London: Open University Press.

Hassan, I. (1985) The Culture of Postmodernism. *Theory, Culture and Society*, 2(3): 119–32.

Herrera, C. (2003) A Clash of Methodology and Ethics in 'Undercover' Social Science, *Philosophy of the Social Sciences*, 33(3): 351–362.

Hitchcock, G. and Hughes, D. (1995) *Research and the Teacher: A Qualitative Introduction to School-based Research*, 2nd edn. London: Routledge.

Hodder, I. (1998) The interpretation of Documents and Material Culture, in Denzin, N.K. and Lincoln, Y.S. (eds) *Collecting and Interpreting Qualitative Materials*. London: Sage.

Hodkinson, P. (2004) Research as a form of work: expertise, community and methodological objectivity, *British Educational Research Journal*, 30(1): 9–26.

Hollis, M. and Lukes, S. (eds) *Rationality and Relativism*. Oxford: Basil Blackwell.

Holstein, J.A. and Gubrium, J.F. (1998) Phenomenology, Ethnomethodology, and Interpretive Practice, in Denzin, N.K. and Lincoln Y.S. (eds) (1998b) *Collecting and Interpreting Qualitative Materials*. London: Sage.

Huberman, A.M. and Miles, M.B. (1998) Data Management and Analysis Methods, in Denzin, N.K. and Lincoln, Y.S. (eds) *Collecting and Interpreting Qualitative Materials*. London: Sage.

James, W. (ed.) (1995) *The Pursuit of Certainty: Religious and Cultural Formulations*. London: Routledge.

Janesick, V.J. (1998) The Dance of Qualitative Research Design, in Denzin, N.K. and Lincoln, Y.S. (eds) *Strategies of Qualitative Inquiry*. London: Sage.

Jayaratne, T.E. and Stewart, A. (1991) Quantitative and Qualitative Methods in the Social Sciences: Current Feminist Issues and Practical Strategies, in Fonow, M.M. and Cook, J.A. (eds) *Beyond Methodology: Feminist Scholarship as Lived Research*. Bloomington: Indiana University Press.

Kaplan, A. (1973) *The Conduct of Inquiry*. Aylesbury: Intertext Books.

Kincheloe, J.L. and McLaren, P.L. (1998) Rethinking Critical Theory and Qualitative Research, in Denzin, N.K. and Lincoln, Y.S. (eds) (1998) *The Landscape of Qualitative Inquiry*. London: Sage, 260–299.

King, R. (1978) *All things bright and beautiful? – a sociological study of infants' classrooms*. London: Wiley.

Kolokowski, L. (1972) *Positivist Philosophy*. Harmondsworth: Penguin.

Kress, G. (1996) Representational resources and the production of subjectivity: questions for the theoretical development of critical discourse analysis in a multicultural society, in Caldas-Coulthard, C. and Coulthard, M. (eds) *Text and Practice: readings in critical discourse analysis*. London: Routledge.

Krieger, S. (1991) *Social Science and the Self: personal essays as an art form*. New Brunswick, NJ: Rutgers University Press.

Kuhn, T. (1970) *The Structure of Scientific Revolutions*. Chicago: The University of Chicago Press.

Kvale, S. (1996) *InterViews: an introduction to qualitative research interviewing*. London: Sage.

Labov, W. (1987) How I got into linguistics, and what I got out of it. Essay reprinted on Labov's personal website. http://www.ling.upenn.edu/~wlabov/papers.html (accessed 4 May 2004).

Lacey, C. (1970) *Hightown Grammar: the school as a social system*. Manchester: Manchester University Press.

Lane, R. (2000) *Jean Baudrillard*. London: Routledge.

Lather, P. (1986a) Research as Praxis, *Harvard Educational Review*, 56(3): 257–277.

Lather, P. (1986b) Issues of validity in openly ideological research: Between a rock and a soft place, *Interchange*, 17(4): 63–84.

Lather, P. (1991) *Getting Smart: Feminist Research and Pedagogy with/in the Postmodern*. London: Routledge.

Lather, P. (1994) Fertile Obsession: Validity After Poststructuralism, in Gitlin, A. (ed.) *Power and Method: Political Activisms and Educational Research*. London: Routledge.

Latour, B. and Woolgar, S. (1979) *Laboratory Life: The Social Construction of Scientific Facts*. Beverley Hills: Sage.

Levi-Strauss, C. (1964) *Totemism*. (trans. Needham, R.). London: Merlin Press.

Levi-Strauss, C. (1966) *The Savage Mind*. London: Weidenfeld and Nicolson.

Lewellen, T.C. (2002) *The Anthropology of Globalization*. Westport: Bergin and Garvey.

Lifshitz, C. (2004) Aspects of the Integration of Ethiopian Immigrant Youth and their Parents into Israel. University Of Sussex: unpublished PhD thesis.

Lincoln, Y.S. and Denzin, N.K. (1998) The Fifth Moment, in Denzin, N.K. and Lincoln, Y.S. (eds) (1998) *Collecting and Interpreting Qualitative Materials*. London: Sage, 407–430.

Long, N. (1996) Globalization and Localization: new challenges to rural research, in Moore, H.L. (ed.) *The Future of Anthropological Knowledge*. London: Routledge.

Lucy, N. (1997) *Postmodern Literary Theory: an introduction*. Oxford: Blackwell.
Luke, A. (1995) Text and discourse in education: an introduction to critical discourse analysis, *Review of Research in Education*, 21: 3–47.
Lukes, S. (ed.) (1986) *Power*. Oxford: Blackwell.
Lyotard, J-F. (1984) (trans. Bennington, G. and Massumi, B.) *The Postmodern Condition: A Report on Knowledge*. Manchester: Manchester University Press.
MacIntyre, A. (1984) *After Virtue: A study in moral theory*. Notre Dame, IN: University of Notre Dame Press.
MacIntyre, A. (1985) *After Virtue: A study in moral theory*. London: Duckworth.
MacLure, M. (2003) *Discourse in Educational and Social Research*. Buckingham: Open University Press.
Mandell, N. (1988) The Least Adult Role in Studying Children, *Journal of Contemporary Ethnography*, 16: 433–467.
Manning, P.K. and Culum-Swan, B. (1998) Narrative, Content and Semiotic Analysis. In Denzin, N.K. and Lincoln, Y.S. (eds) (1998) *Collecting and Interpreting Qualitative Materials*. London: Sage, 246–273.
Marcus, G.E. (1998) What Comes (Just) After 'Post'? The Case of Ethnography, in Denzin, N.K. and Lincoln, Y.S. (eds), *The Landscape of Qualitative Inquiry*. London: Sage.
Mattingly, C. (1991) Narrative Reflections on Practical Actions: Two learning experiments in reflective storytelling, in Schön, D. (ed.) *The Reflective Turn: Case Studies in and on Educational Practice*. New York: Teachers College Press.
May, T. (2001) *Social research: Issues, Methods and Process*. Buckingham: Open University Press.
Maybin, J. (1993) Dialogic Relationships and the Construction of Knowledge in Children's Informal Talk, in Graddol, D., Thompson, L. and Byram, M. (eds) *Language and Culture*. Philadelphia, PA: Multilingual Matters.
McGuigan, J. (1999) *Modernity and Postmodern Culture*. Buckingham: Open University Press.
McNiff, J. (1988) *Action Research: Principles and Practice*. London: Macmillan.
Mehan, H. (1979) *Learning Lessons: social organisation in the classroom*. Cambridge, MA: Harvard University Press.
Miles, M.B. and Huberman, A.M. (1994) *Qualitative data analysis: An expanded sourcebook*. Thousand Oaks, CA: Sage.
Mills, C. Wright, (1959) *The Sociological Imagination*. London: Oxford University Press.
Mills, S. (2003) *Michel Foucault*. London: Routledge.
Mink, L.O. (1978) Narrative form as a cognitive instrument, in: Canary, R.H. and Kozicki, H. (eds) *The Writing of History: Literary form and historical understanding*. Madison, WI: University of Wisconsin Press.
Modood, T. (1992) *Not Easy Being British: Colour, Culture and Citizenship*. Stoke on Trent: Runnymede Trust and Trentham Books.
Mohanty, C.T. (1991) Under Western Eyes: Feminist Schoalrship and Colonial Discourses, in Mohanty, C.T., Russo, A. and Torres, L. (eds) *Third World Women and the Politics of Feminism*. Bloomington and Indiana: Indiana University Press.
Moser, C.A. and Kalton, G. (1971) *Survey Methods in Social Investigation*, 2nd edn. London: Heinemann.

Mullard, M. and Spicker, P. (1998) *Social Policy in a Changing Society*. London: Routledge.

Munn, P. and Drever, E. (1990) *Using Questionnaires in Small-Scale Research*. Midlothian: SCRE.

National Curriculum Council (1993) *Spiritual and Moral Development – a discussion Paper*. York: National Curriculum Council.

Norris, C. (1982) *Uncritical Theory: Postmodernism, Intellectuals and the Gulf War*. London: Lawrence and Wishart.

Oakley, A. (1981) Interviewing Women: a Contradiction in Terms, in Roberts, H. (ed.) *Doing feminist research*. London: Routledge, 30–61.

O'Connell Davidson, J. and Layder, D. (1994) *Methods, Sex and Madness*. London: Routledge.

Ong, A. (1996) Anthropology, China and Modernities: the geopolitics of cultural knowledge, in Moore, H.L. (ed.) *The Future of Anthropological Knowledge*. London: Routledge.

Oppenheim, A.N. (1992) *Questionnaire Design, Interviewing and Attitude Measurement*. London: Continuum.

Parker, S. (1997) *Reflective Teaching in the Postmodern World: a manifesto for education in postmodernity*. Buckingham: Open University Press.

Pattai, D. (1994) When Method Becomes Power (Response), in Gitlin, A. (ed.) *Power and Method. Political Activisms and Educational Research*. London: Routledge.

Pennycook, A. (1994) Incommensuarble Disourses? *Applied Linguistics*, 15(2): 115–37.

Polkinghorne, D. (1988) *Narrative Knowing and The Human Sciences*. Albany, NY: State University of New York Press.

Popkewitz, T. (2004) The Alchemy of the Mathematics Curriculum: Inscriptions and the Fabrication of the Child, *American Educational Research Journal*, 41(1): 3–34.

Popper, K.R. (1963) *Conjectures and Refutations: the Growth of Scientific Knowledge*. London: Routledge and Kegan Paul.

Pryor, J. (1993) He, She and IT: A case Study of Groupwork in a Gender-Sensitive Area. Unpublished doctoral thesis, University of Sussex.

Pryor, J. (2004) Formative assessment, the Internet and Academic Identity. Paper presented to the Fifth International Conference of the Association of Internet Researchers, Brighton, September 2004.

Pryor, J. and Ampiah, J.G. (2003) *Understandings of Education in an African Village: the Role of Information and Communication Technologies*. London: Department for International Development.

Pryor, J. and Ampiah, J.G. (2004) Listening to voices in the village: collaborating through data chains, in Swadener, E. and Mutua, K. (eds) *Decolonizing Research in Cross-Cultural Contexts: Critical Personal Narratives*. Albany, NY: State University of New York Press.

Pryor, J. and Torrance, H. (1998) The Interaction of Teachers and Pupils in Formative Assessment: where psychological theory meets social practice, *Social Psychology of Education*, 2(2): 151–176.

Pryor, J. and Torrance, H. (2000) Questioning the Three Bears: The Social Construction of Classroom Assessment, in Filer, A. (ed.) *Assessment: Social Practice and Social Product*. London: Falmer Press.

Punch, M. (1996) Observation and the Police: The Research Experience, in Hammersley, M. (ed.) *Social Research Philosophy, Politics and Practice*. London: Sage Publications.

Qualifications and Curriculum Authority (1997) *Draft Guidance for Pilot Work*. London: Qualifications and Curriculum Authority.

Ragin, C. (1994) *Constructing Social Research*. Thousand Oaks: Pine Forge Press.

Rapport, N. and Overing, J. (2000) *Social and Cultural Anthropology: The Key concepts*. London: Routledge.

Ricoeur, P. (1981a) *Hermeneutics and the Human Sciences*. New York: Cambridge University Press.

Ricoeur, P. (1981b) Mimesis and Representation, *Annals of Scholarship*, 2: 15–32.

Ricoeur, P. (1984) *Time and Narrative, Volume 2*. Chicago: University of Chicago Press.

Robson, C. (1993) *Real World Research*. Oxford: Blackwell.

Rosaldo, R. (1989) *Culture and Truth: The remaking of social analysis*. Boston: Beacon.

Roth, W-M. (2003) Culture and Identity, Review Essay of *Sicher in Kreuzberg, Constructing Diasporas: Turkish Hip-Hop Youth in Berlin* by Ayan Kaya and *Cultural Psychology: Theory and Method* by Carl Ratner, *Forum Qualitative Sozialforschung/ Forum: Qualitative Social Research (Online Journal)*, 4(1). www.qualitative-research.net/fqs-texte/1-03/1-03review-roth-e.htm (accessed 12 July 2004).

Royle, N. (2003) *Jacques Derrida*. London: Routledge.

Ryen, A. (2002) Cross-cultural interviewing, in Gubrium, J.E. and Holstein, J.A. (eds) *Handbook of Interview Research. Context and Method*. Thousand Oaks: Sage.

Said, E. (1978) *Orientalism*, New York: Vintage.

Said, E. (1993) *Culture and Imperialism*. London: Chatto and Windus.

Sardar, Z. and Van Loon, B. (2004) *Introducing Cultural Studies*. Royston: Icon Books.

Sarup, M. (1996) *Identity, Culture and the Postmodern World*. Edinburgh University Press.

School Curriculum and Assessment Authority (1996a) *Education for Adult Life: the spiritual and moral development of young people*. London: SCAA.

School Curriculum and Assessment Authority (1996b) *Consultation on Values in Education and the Community*, Com/96/608. London: SCAA.

Schwandt, T.A. (1998) Constructivist, Interpretivist Approaches to Human Inquiry, in Denzin, N.K. and Lincoln, Y.S. (eds) (1998) *The Landscape of Qualitative Inquiry*. London: Sage, 221–259.

Scott, D. (1996a) Ethnography and Education, in: Scott, D. and Usher, R. (eds) *Understanding Educational Research*. London: Routledge.

Scott, D. (1996b) Methods and Data in Educational Research, in Scott, D. and Usher, R. (eds) *Understanding Educational Research*. London: Routledge.

Scott, D. (ed.) (1999) *Values and Educational Research*. London: Institute of Education.

Scott, D. (2000) *Realism and Educational Research: New Perspectives and Possibilities*. London: RoutledgeFalmer.

Scott, D. and Usher, R. (eds) (1996) *Understanding Educational Research*. London: Routledge.

Scott, D. and Usher, R. (1999) *Researching Education: data, methods and theory in educational enquiry*. London: Cassell.

Seale, C. (1998) Qualitative Interviewing, in Seale, C. (ed.) *Researching Society and Culture*. London: Sage.

Seale, C. and Filmer, P. (1998) Doing Social Surveys, in Seale, C. (ed.) *Researching Society and Culture*. London: Sage.

Seale, C. and Kelly, M. (1998) Coding and Analysing Data, in Seale, C. (ed.) *Researching Society and Culture*. London: Sage.

Seidman, I. (1998) *Interviewing as Qualitative Research*, 2nd edn. New York: Teachers College Press.

Shacklock, G. and Smyth, J. (eds) (1998) *Being Reflexive in Critical Educational and Social Research*. London: Falmer Press.

Silverman, D. (1993) *Interpreting Qualitative Data*. London: Sage.

Silverman, D. (1998) Research and Social Policy, in Seale, C. (ed.) *Researching Society and Culture*. London: Sage.

Silverman, D. (2000) *Doing Qualitative Research: a practical handbook*. London: Sage.

Silverman, D. (2004) *Qualitative Research; theory, method and practice*. London: Sage.

Simpson, M. and Tuson, J. (1995) *Using Observations in Small-scale research: A beginner's guide*. Edinburgh: Scottish Council for Research in Education.

Sinclair, J. (1990) *The structure of teacher talk*. Birmingham: English Language Research, University of Birmingham.

Sinclair, J. and Coulthard, R. (1975) *Towards an analysis of discourse*. London: Oxford University Press.

Siraj-Blatchford, I. and Siraj-Blatchford, J. (1999) Reflexivity, social justice and educational research in Scott, D. (ed.) *Values and Educational Research*. London: Institute of Education.

Slater, D. (1998a) Using Official Statistics, in Seale, C. (ed.) *Researching Society and Culture*. London: Sage.

Slater, D. (1998b) Analysing Cultural Objects: Content Analysis and Semiotics, in Seale, C. (ed.) *Researching Society and Culture*. London: Sage.

Slee, R., Weiner, G. and Tomlinson, S. (eds) (1998) *School Effectiveness for Whom? Challenges to the school effectiveness and school improvement movements*. London: Falmer Press.

Smith, D.E. (1990) *Texts, Facts and Feminity. Exploring the Relations of Ruling*. London: Routledge.

Smith, L.T. (1999) *Decolonizing Methodologies: Research and Indigenous Peoples*. Dunedin: University of New Zealand Press.

Spindler, G. and Spindler, L. (1982) The Ethnographic World View, in Spindler, G. (ed.) (1982) *Doing the Ethnography of Schooling: Educational Anthropology in Action*, New York: Holt, Rinehart and Winston.

Spradley, J.P. (ed.) (1980) *Participant Observation*. New York: Rinehart and Winston.

Stanley, L. and Wise, S. (1990) Method, methodology and epistemology in feminist research processes, in Stanley, L. (ed.) *Feminist Praxis*. London: Routledge.

Stenhouse, L. (1975) *An Introduction to Curriculum Research and Development*. London: Heinemann.

Strauss, A. and Corbin, J. (1998) Grounded Theory Methodology, in Denzin, N.K. and Lincoln, Y.S. (eds) *Strategies of Qualitative Inquiry*. London: Sage.

Street, B.V. (ed.) (2001) *Literacy and Development: ethnographic perspectives*. London: Routledge.

Stronach, I. and MacLure, M. (1997) *Educational Research Undone: The Postmoaern Embrace*. Buckingham: Open University Press.

Stubbs, M. (1997) Whorf's Children: critical comments on critical discourse analysis (CDA), in Ryan, A. and Wray, A. (eds) *Evolving Models of Language*. Clevedon: Multilingual Matters.

Swingewood, A. (2000) *A Short History of Sociological Thought*. Basingstoke: Palgrave.

Tanesini, A. (1999) *An Introduction to Feminist Epistemologies*. Oxford: Blackwell.

Tonkiss, F. (1998a) The History of the Social Survey, in Seale, C. (ed.) *Researching Society and Culture*. London: Sage.

Tonkiss, F. (1998b) Analysing Discourse, in Seale, C. (ed.) *Researching Society and Culture*. London: Sage.

Tooley, J. and Darby, D. (1998) *Educational Research: A Critique*. London: Ofsted.

Torrance, H. and Pryor, J. (1998) *Investigating Formative Assessment: Teaching, Learning and Assessment in the Classroom*. Buckingham: Open University Press.

Tripp, D. (1998) Critical incidents in action enquiry, in Shacklock, G. and Smyth, J. (eds) *Being Reflexive in Critical Educational and Social Research*, 36–49. London: Falmer Press.

Usher, R. (1996a) A critique of the neglected epistemological assumptions of educational research, in Scott, D. and Usher, R. (eds) *Understanding Educational Research*. London: Routledge.

Usher, R. (1996b) Textuality and Reflexivity in Educational Research, in Scott, D. and Usher, R. (eds) *Understanding Educational Research*. London: Routledge.

Usher, R. and Scott, D. (1994) *Postmodernism and Education*. London: Routledge.

Usher, R. and Scott, D. (1996) Afterword. The politics of educational research, in Scott, D. and Usher, R. (eds) *Understanding Educational Research*. London: Routledge.

Van Dijk, T. (1993) Principles of critical discourse analysis, *Discourse and Society*, 4: 249–283 reprinted in Wetherell, M., Taylor, S. and Yates, S. (2001) *Discourse Theory and Practice: A reader*. London: Sage.

Verhesschen, P. (2003) 'The Poem's Invitation': Ricoeur's Concept of Mimesis and its Consequences for Narrative Educational Research, *Journal of Philosophy of Education*, 37(3): 449–465.

Vygotsky, L. (1978) *Mind in Society*. Cambridge, MA: Harvard University Press.

Walkerdine, V. (1988) *The Mastery of Reason. Cognitive Development and the Production of Rationality*. London: Routledge.

Walsh, P. (1999) Values and Objectivity in Educational Research: the need for nuance, in Scott, D. (ed.) *Values and Educational Research*. London: Institute of Education.

Wetherell, M., Taylor, S. and Yates, S.J. (2001) *Discourse as Data. A Guide for Analysis*. London: Sage/Open University Press.

Widdicombe, S. (1995) Identity, politics and talk: a case for the mundane and the everyday, in Wilkinson, S. and Kitzinger, C. (eds) *Feminism and Discourse*. London: Sage.

Widdowson, H. (2000) On the Limitations of Linguistics Applied, *Applied Linguistics*, 21(1): 3–25.

Willis, P.E. (1977) *Learning to Labour: how working class kids get working class jobs*. Farnborough: Saxon House.

Wilson, B.R. (ed.) (1979) *Rationality*. Oxford: Basil Blackwell.

Wiseman, J.P. and Aron, M.S. (1972) *Field Reports in Sociology*. London: Transworld Publishers.

Wong, E.D. (1995) Challenges Confronting the Researcher/Teacher: Conflicts of Purpose and Conduct. *Educational Researcher*, 24(4): 22–8.

Wood, D. (1992) Teaching talk: How Modes of Teacher Talk Affect Pupil Participation, in Norman, K. *Thinking Voices*. London: Hodder & Stoughton.

Xue, Y. and Meisels, S. (2004) Early Literacy Instruction and in Kindergarten: Evidence from the Early Childhood Longitudinal Study – Kindergarten Class of 1998–1999, *American Educational Research Journal*, 41(1): 191–229.

Yang, M. (1996) Tradition, travelling theory, Anthropology and the discourse of modernity in China, in Moore, H.L. (ed.) *The Future of Anthropological Knowledge*. London: Routledge.

Yates, P. (1999) The Bureaucratization of Spirituality, *International Journal of Children's Spirituality*, 4(2): 179–193.

Yates, P. (2000a) Legitimating the Moral Curriculum, in Gardner, R., Cairns, J. and Lawton, D. (eds) *Education for Values: Morals, Ethics and Citizenship in Contemporary Teaching*. London: Kogan Page.

Yates, P. (2000b) The Spirit and the Empty Matrix: The construction of spiritual, moral, social and cultural education, in Best, R. (ed.) *Education for Spiritual, Moral, Social and Cultural Development*. London: Continuum.

Yates, P. (2001) Postmodernism, Spirituality and Education in Late Modernity, in Erricker, J., Ota, C. and Erricker, C. (eds) *Spiritual Education: cultural, religious and social differences*. Brighton: Sussex Academic Press.

Yin, R.K. (1984) *Case Study Research: Design and Methods*. London: Sage.

Index

Related books from Open University Press
Purchase from www.openup.co.uk or order through your local bookseller

---

A HANDBOOK FOR TEACHER RESEARCH
FROM DESIGN TO IMPLEMENTATION

Colin Lankshear and Michele Knobel

A Handbook for Teacher Research provides a comprehensive and detailed approach to teacher research as systematic, methodical and informed practice. It identifies five requirements for all kinds of research, and provides clear and accessible guidelines for teachers to use in conducting their own classroom-based studies.

- A clear definition of teacher research which insists on more than 'stories' and anecdotal 'retrospectives'
- Innovative organizational structure based on the collection and analysis of spoken, written and observed data, with strong emphasis on the design of research projects
- Easy-to-use and widely applicable tools and techniques for collecting and analysing data in qualitative research

Informed by the authors' own wide-ranging experiences, *A Handbook for Teacher Research* provides everything the teacher researcher needs in order to conduct good quality practitioner research. It is ideal for upper level undergraduate Education programmes and for postgraduate research, as well as for teacher researchers who conceive and drive their own independent studies.

Contents

An introduction to teacher research – Teacher research as systematic inquiry – Three kinds of teacher research – Problems, purposes, and design in teacher research – Producing clear and manageable research questions – Informing and framing teacher research projects – Quantitative inquiry and teacher research – Teacher research as 'scholarly' inquiry – Collecting spoken data in qualitative research – Collecting observed data in qualitative research – Collecting written data in qualitative research – Analysing spoken data in qualitative research – Analysing observed data in qualitative research – Analysing written data in qualitative research – Interpretation, representation and validity in teacher research – Ethics in teacher research – Glossary – Bibliography – Index.

320pp   0 335 21064 3 (Paperback)   0 335 21065 1 (Hardback)

THE MORAL FOUNDATIONS OF EDUCATIONAL RESEARCH
Knowledge, Inquiry and Values

Pat Sikes, Jon Nixon and Wilfred Carr (eds)
University of Sheffield, UK

"This is a book for everyone doing educational research. It is not simply a routine provocation directed at positivists by a group of researchers advocating qualitative methods. The book makes a valuable contribution to the literature on the ethics of educational research by offering something more than opposition to the narrow utilitarian research agenda."

British Journal of Educational Studies

The Moral Foundations of Educational Research considers what is distinctive about educational research in comparison with other research in the social sciences.

As the contributors all agree that education is always an essentially moral enterprise, discussion about methodology starts, not with the widely endorsed claim that educational research should be 'useful' and 'relevant', but with the attempt to justify and elaborate that claim with reference to its moral foundations. Determining the nature of 'usefulness' and 'relevance' is not simply a matter of focusing on impact and influence but involves a radical re-conceptualization of the moral and educational significance of what is deemed to be 'useful' and 'relevant'. There is no argument with this emphasis on the generation of 'useful' and 'relevant' knowledge, but the contributors suggest that educational research requires a fuller and more rounded understanding that takes account of the moral values of those who conduct it. Educational research is grounded, epistemologically, in the moral foundations of educational practice. It is the epistemological and moral purposes underlying the 'usefulness' and 'relevance' of educational research that matter.

This book is important reading for Educational students, as well as academics and professionals undertaking educational research,

Contributors: *Pierre Bourdieu, Peter Clough, Ivor Goodson, Fred Inglis, Gary McCulloch, Jon Nixon, Carrie Paechter, Richard Pring, Pat Sikes, Melanie Walker.*

192pp 0 335 21046 5 Paperback